FAITH,
FAMILY,
AND FLAG

FAITH, FAMILY, AND FLAG

Branson Entertainment and the Idea of America

Joanna Dee Das

THE UNIVERSITY OF CHICAGO PRESS || CHICAGO AND LONDON

The University of Chicago Press, Chicago 60637
The University of Chicago Press, Ltd., London
© 2025 by Joanna Dee Das

Published 2025
Printed in the United States of America

34 33 32 31 30 29 28 27 26 25   1 2 3 4 5

ISBN-13: 978-0-226-82840-4 (cloth)
ISBN-13: 978-0-226-82841-1 (ebook)
DOI: https://doi.org/10.7208/chicago/9780226828411.001.0001

Library of Congress Cataloging-in-Publication Data

Names: Das, Joanna Dee, author.
Title: Faith, family, and flag : Branson entertainment and the idea of America / Joanna
    Dee Das.
Other titles: Branson entertainment and the idea of America
Description: Chicago : The University of Chicago Press, 2025. | Includes bibliographical
    references and index.
Identifiers: LCCN 2025022965 | ISBN 9780226828404 (cloth) | ISBN 9780226828411 (ebook)
Subjects: LCSH: Entertainment events — Missouri — Branson. | Entertainment events —
    Political aspects — Missouri — Branson. | Conservatism — United States. | American
    Dream.
Classification: LCC GV54.M8 D37 2025 | DDC 791.09778/797 — dc23/eng/20250615
LC record available at https://lccn.loc.gov/2025022965

♾ This paper meets the requirements of ANSI/NISO Z39.48-1992 (Permanence of
Paper).

Authorized Representative for EU General Product Safety Regulation (GPSR) queries:
Easy Access System Europe — Mustamäe tee 50, 10621 Tallinn, Estonia, gpsr.requests
@easproject.com
Any other queries: https://press.uchicago.edu/press/contact.html

CONTENTS

INTRODUCTION

Branson as Real America

Branson is a God-blessed area.
Randy Plummer, Branson performer

Branson is as close to Hell as anything I
have seen in my life.
Joe Queenan, journalist

If you want to understand the tourist mecca of Branson, Missouri, you have to understand the Shoji Tabuchi Theatre. Shut your eyes and imagine this faded, abandoned building as it was in its 1990s heyday, when a full mile of purple, pink, and blue neon lined the Art Deco exterior, and the giant letters S-H-O-J-I glittered above the entrance. Twice a day, six days a week, forty weeks a year, thousands of people from across the United States packed in to see *The Shoji Tabuchi Show*, a fast-paced cornucopia of Broadway song-and-dance numbers, country music hits, pop medleys, jokes about Japanese people eating bait, performers in cow costumes, a girl flying atop a magic carpet, a gospel choir, and a rousing rendition of "America the Beautiful."

And then there were the restrooms: million-dollar oases where photography was encouraged. (If you forgot your camera, you could buy a postcard of them in the gift shop.) Over on the men's side, patrons could play billiards while waiting to sit on black porcelain toilets imported from Italy. On the women's side, fresh orchids adorned granite and onyx pedestal sinks below gilded mirrors. Purple crystals in the chandelier cast violet hues upon the red and green wallpaper featuring cherubs. Visitors called the bathrooms "amazing," "stunning," "unbelievable," and "a destination in their own right." But East Coast culture critics recoiled in horror. They saw Tabuchi's toilets as they saw the city's entertainment industry overall: tacky, gaudy glitz trying to cover up crap.[1]

Branson functions as a litmus test for where you stand in America's long culture wars. It has done so since its beginnings as a tourist destination more than a century ago. In 1907, author Harold Bell Wright published *The Shepherd of the Hills*, a novel he set in rural Taney County, Missouri, in the area that would become Branson. Literary critics mocked Wright for his sentimentality and overt moralism, but *The Shepherd* became a runaway bestseller. Avid readers flocked to Branson (officially incorporated as a city in 1912) to see the real-life inspirations for Wright's characters. Residents obliged. They led curious tourists through caves and drove them down bumpy roads while regaling them with Ozarks humor and tall tales. They eventually began to monetize their depictions of hillbilly folk through performances in an outdoor amphitheater, at a theme park called Silver Dollar City, and on stage. In 1959, the Mabe family started a variety show called the *Baldknobbers Hillbilly Jamboree*, and in 1967, the Presley family built a theater three miles outside town to house their own variety show called the *Mountain Music Jubilee*. Variety has long represented "lowbrow" performance in America, the opposite of so-called "legitimate" theater. Local families turned lowbrow on its head, claiming a mantle of just-folks realness that could connect authentically with audiences. One theater grew to two and then to twenty in the 1980s as country music stars arrived to perform along Branson's Highway 76. These Nashville transplants "Bransonized" their shows, transforming concerts into variety fare. Tourism exploded in the 1990s after the television program *60 Minutes* shone a national spotlight on the city. Las Vegas entertainers came for a piece of the pie, as did journalists who competed to boost their tastemaker credentials by writing witty takedowns of what they considered culturally retrograde performances.

Their scathing remarks did not stem the tide. By the dawn of the twenty-first century, Branson boasted more theater seats (57,180) than Broadway, despite a local population of less than 10,000 in comparison to New York City's eight million.[2] Across forty-five different venues, audiences could see over one hundred shows: variety shows, magic shows, acrobat shows, gospel shows, celebrity impersonation (or "tribute") shows, musicals, and outdoor religious dramas. In the 2010s, attractions such as the Aquarium began to replace some of the theaters, but live performance endures. Today, you can find both Elvis Presley and Baby Jesus on a Branson stage. You can laugh at a hillbilly comedian in goofy, oversized clothing or admire a singer in a glittering ball gown. You can eat a four-course dinner at some shows and breakfast at others. You can sit in a strip-mall theater that seats 200 people or in a grand auditorium that seats 2,000. Everywhere, you can participate. You can shout "Amen" as a performer testifies to the miracle of Christ, play toilet-seat horseshoe in a dirt arena, or rise to sing the National Anthem. You can join approximately 10.3 million annual visitors who contribute to a $2 billion tourist economy. The national discourse about small-town America is that it is in perpetual crisis. In contrast, Branson has survived.[3]

Branson persists because its tourism industry offers more than just lighthearted entertainment. Instead, it presents a vision of the American dream. Live theater is a place where performers build worlds onstage and invite audiences to imagine with them what the past, present, and future could be. In Branson, a Japanese immigrant like Tabuchi, who arrived on US shores with a couple hundred dollars in his shoe, can succeed in building a business while proclaiming the values of Christian faith, dedication to family, and patriotic zeal. He and other entertainers have treated visitors to memorable experiences at affordable prices. Branson is more than a kitschy tourist town; it is a cultural and economic project with political consequences.

While local boosters tout that the city's American dream is for everyone, that dream has had particular resonance for self-identified conservatives. Over the past several decades, Branson's entertainment industry has provided cultural scaffolding for the development of the modern conservative movement. As elements of that movement have shifted, Branson performances have shifted with them, making changes seem like part of an unbroken tradition. As someone who has spent her life in the world of dance and theater, I was intrigued. Most people I know associate live performance with the political left. I have read countless books about dance as an act of resistance to racial oppression, or theater as a place to rehearse revolution. Commentators on conservative media outlets routinely disparage "Hollywood liberals." How, then, did Branson, a place boosters call the "live show capital of the world," become so important to the political right?

This book answers that question. It traces how Branson's entertainment industry developed an adherence to a set of ideals that begin with the letter F: Folk, Frontier, Family, Faith, Flag, and Free Enterprise. These ideas, woven together onstage in performance, present Branson as the tangible manifestation of a mythic place conservatives like to call Real America. Of course, the nation is too diverse and complex for any one place to exemplify what it "really" is. Nonetheless, Branson's claim to represent real America has been a powerful part of its draw for over a hundred years.

The foundation of this claim is geographic. In the far southwest corner of Missouri, near Arkansas, Oklahoma, and Kansas, Branson geographically code-switches, sometimes Southern, sometimes Midwestern, sometimes Western, but always rural (despite technically being a city). This fluidity stems back to the Civil War, when Missouri was a slave state that never seceded and residents fought on both sides. Since then, Branson has grown to represent that broad expanse imagined as the "Heartland" or "Middle America." The Ozarks have remained sparsely populated even as much of the country has urbanized. Branson embraces with zeal the myth, dating back to the time of Thomas Jefferson, that rural America is real America.

The second claim is racial. In the 1930s and 1940s, folklorists such as Otto Rayburn and Vance Randolph wrote that the Missouri Ozarks contained the country's last vestiges of undiluted Anglo-Saxonism, making its residents "genuine American[s]." Randolph sounded a mournful note in his book *The Ozarks: An American Survival of Primitive Society*: "The American people are making their last stand in the wilderness, and it is here."[4] In the earliest phases of Branson entertainment, performers emphasized two concepts — the folk and the frontier — to reiterate the idea that white pioneers in the Ozarks were real Americans.

The idea that real Americans are native-born, rural, from the middle of the continent, and white continues in Branson entertainment to this day, albeit more submerged. In the late twentieth century, boosters switched to a third, colorblind argument: Branson is the heart of real America because it lives by the code of faith, family, and flag. Everyone from the mayor to museum volunteers espouses the three F's. If performers want to succeed in Branson, they have to follow the three F's. The city's marketing team insists that these are universal values that welcome all people. Who would denounce religious faith in a country based on religious freedom? Who would have disregard for family? And who would refuse to support the American flag?[5]

It is true that the words *faith*, *family*, and *flag* can be widely interpreted. Over the past several decades, however, the conservative political movement has successfully narrowed the commonsense understanding. Faith means Christian; family means a heterosexual, married couple with children; flag means declaring that the United States is the greatest country in the world and offering unequivocal support for its military. Often the word *freedom* replaces *flag* in the trifecta. To declare allegiance to faith, family, and flag signals one's conservative *bona fides* — not one's desire to create unity among America's diverse constituents. The catchphrase became prevalent starting in 1988, when Gary Bauer invoked "Faith, Family, and Freedom" as president of the Family Research Council, an evangelical Christian lobbying group. The Council later trademarked the phrase. Republican candidates for office and conservative activists spread it throughout the 1990s. Faith, family, and flag (or freedom) proliferated as a political slogan alongside the Tea Party Movement in 2009 and exploded among right-wing populist candidates after 2016.[6] But ideology needs more than political slogans to turn it into common sense. People have to *feel* what the three F's are in order to believe in them as natural. In the Show-Me State of Missouri, Branson performers make faith, family, and flag come alive, imbuing the words with specific meaning.

They also market that vision expertly. In Branson, there is another F: free enterprise. The city may have no legitimate claim to being real America, but its performers sell the idea of real America better than almost anywhere else. In many ways, entertainment is the engine of the United States. Our politics, our religion, our commerce, and even our art funnel through a show-biz filter. The popularity of places like Hollywood, Disney World, and Las Vegas shows how we gleefully embrace the fake, the surreal, and the spectacle. Branson is all that and something more — earnest. Americans believe, and they believe hard. After visiting Branson in 1994, *GQ* writer Jeanne Laskas averred, "Disneyland is a fantasy, a place you know is fake and enter with the understanding that it will be a respite from the real world. Branson, on the other hand, is the real world."[7] It is Branson's simultaneous embrace of spectacle and sincerity that has made it so compelling.

Branson entertainers excel at reconciling other contradictions to make modern conservatism cohere as common sense. Through the power of performance, they suture together glamour and affordability, familiarity and novelty, authenticity and theatricality, spirituality and pursuit of profit, celebrity and "just-folks" humility. The experience of a Branson show creates a feeling of utopia, a respite from partisan politics rather than a reinforcement of it. Unlike vitriolic commentators who lurk in dark corners of the internet, performers share their vision with hope and joy. Branson offers you fun. Branson makes you happy. And Branson brings you into a warm community. Performers talk with you, shake your hand, give you a hug, and pray for you. You, too, can be a part of that American dream on the stage.

Which is all fine and good unless you think the mantra of faith, family, and flag is a cynical marketing scheme or dangerous political slogan that dog-whistles Christian nationalism. For many people, Branson is at best an unimportant tourist trap, or at worst, an American nightmare that threatens to undo the promise of a pluralistic, democratic society. Perhaps even more to the point of our deepening polarization, many coastal residents have never heard of Branson at all. Academics tend to ignore it altogether. To put it bluntly, it is not the kind of place scholars like to write about.[8] The five-mile Strip, lined with glittering theater marquees, a giant King Kong, and signs declaring GET 2-FOR-1 TICKETS HERE, could make you wonder: Is this carnival midway, full of schtick, schlock, and kitsch, simply trying to part people from their money? Are faith, family, and flag simply Branson's clever brand differentiation in a crowded tourism market, just as hollow as some megacorporation with an all-white executive team suddenly proclaiming Black Lives Matter?

Branson does face challenges. While it has survived, it has not always thrived. Tourism is an industry that involves both psychological and financial risks. As social media influencers understand only too well, selling yourself as a commodity is hazardous, because you constantly have to live up to the image you promote. Imperfection is entirely normal and forgivable, except when you brand yourself as exceptional and divinely blessed. It can be hard to hold on to a strong sense of self when constantly performing a version of that self for others. On an economic level, the tourism economy in Branson, as elsewhere, is not year-round. Seasonal service workers earn low wages and struggle to afford housing. Outside investment firms have muscled in to the local ecosystem, degrading the dream of independent business ownership. Visitation numbers break records year after year, but entertainers voice fears that their livelihoods will disappear.

The power of Branson's story lies in such tensions. It is home to the grifter, the Christian nationalist, and the true believer alike; it is simultaneously successful and struggling. Trying to pin the city down is like walking a tightrope, wavering between romanticization and demonization. It's too easy to call Branson either God's country or Hell on earth, the American dream or the American nightmare. Instead, I approach the city with a deep appreciation for entertainment and take seriously what its performers offer. As a former professional dancer with a PhD in history, I have dedicated my scholarly career to understanding how the stories we tell ourselves through live performance shape our social and political worlds. For the past seven years, I have driven from my home in St. Louis to Branson to comb through archives, attend performances, and conduct oral histories. I also amassed a personal archive of Branson show recordings from the past sixty years. In this book, I place Branson in the broad matrix of America's long culture wars in order to understand its impact on our nation's political development.

There are many people who are important to the story of Branson, many points of origin. We could start with the Osage and Delaware Indians, who hunted in the Ozarks for centuries. We could start with Spanish and French explorers and traders. We could start with the white settlers, some holding slaves, some not, who forced Indigenous peoples off the land. But much of that narrative is not unique to Branson. Communities across the United States share that history. To understand Branson's distinction, the best place to begin is with the humble preacher and author Harold Bell Wright, who inspired a US president. With the power of his pen, Wright unwittingly set in motion the city's future as a place where the battle to define America could take place night after night on the stage.

1 FOUNDATION

God's Country

On Monday, March 5, 1984, President Ronald Reagan found himself with "no breathing room." Dealing with the USSR occupied tremendous time and energy. He was facing criticism for ordering an invasion of Grenada. There was also fallout from the recent terrorist bombing of a US military barracks in Beirut, in which 220 marines died; Democrats questioned why Reagan was involving America in the Lebanese Civil War in the first place. He had recently announced his bid for reelection and added campaign stops to his already-full schedule. He started Tuesday, March 6, with meetings at the White House about national security and Soviet arms treaties, then flew to Ohio to address 2,000 delegates of the National Association of Evangelicals (who gave him four standing ovations), then flew to New York for a $1,000-a-ticket Republican fundraiser, then flew back to Washington to retire at 11:25 p.m. Reagan also had domestic policy matters to handle. The economy, which had struggled for the first few years of his presidency, was finally turning a corner, and he needed to make crucial decisions to ensure that the positive direction lasted. In several meetings that week, he tussled with congressional leaders in his own party about spending cuts to balance the budget. "With some of our friends, we don't need enemies," he wrote in frustration on March 8.[1]

At the end of the trying week, Reagan and his wife Nancy retreated to Camp David for a much-needed reprieve. The room to breathe gave him the opportunity to reflect on the course of his remarkable journey from a working-class childhood in a small town to the most powerful office on the planet. He shared these reflections in a letter he wrote that evening, perhaps while sitting by a crackling fire, to a constituent named Jean Wright. Mrs. Wright had heard in an interview that her father-in-law, the author Harold Bell Wright, had profoundly influenced Reagan. She and her husband Norman were opening a museum dedicated to the author and had written to the White House asking for the president's endorsement.[2]

That evening, Reagan obliged. In scrawling cursive, he recounted that around age ten, he picked up Wright's book *That Printer of Udell's*, which his highly religious mother had been reading, and devoured it "cover to cover." The novel's main character, Dick, had an alcoholic father like Reagan and also lived in a Midwestern small town. In the local churches, Dick seeks Christ but finds only coldness and hypocrisy. He then meets printer George Udell, who offers the impoverished lad a job. Together, through hard work and faith, Dick and George find Jesus Christ. Dick becomes a leader of the town and eventually moves to Washington, DC, to pursue a successful political career. A few days after finishing *That Printer of Udell's*, Reagan told his mother that he wanted to be baptized at her Disciples of Christ church.

Sixty-something years later, Reagan wrote to Jean Wright that her father-in-law "set me on a course I've tried to follow even unto this day. I shall always be grateful." That course: faith based on a personal relationship with Jesus Christ; a belief in the triumph of good over evil; a determination that individual hard work mattered more than institutions or structures.[3] A few months later, with his "Morning in America" campaign, Reagan would win reelection in a landslide. Conservatism, a political philosophy considered dead in the water twenty years earlier, now dominated.

Why is Reagan's letter to Jean Wright in Branson?

While Harold Bell Wright inspired Reagan, Branson inspired the author. *That Printer of Udell's* did not receive much notice upon its publication in 1902. It was Wright's second book, *The Shepherd of the Hills*, that made him a sensation. Wright sketched out *The Shepherd* in the summer of 1906 while living in the Branson area. He drew upon the people, the stories, and the majestic natural landscape of the Missouri Ozarks to weave a morality tale of rural, Christian virtue triumphing over urban decadence. While the vision of the United States as an agrarian "republic of virtue" had been in circulation since the days of Thomas Jefferson, Wright popularized it in the decade when the country went from being majority-rural to majority-urban. He was celebrating something that was beginning to vanish, and thus the book came with a note of warning: if Americans wanted to keep their country, they needed to turn to places like Branson. *The Shepherd* became an immediate hit upon publication in 1907 and turned Wright into the first literary millionaire in US history. It also catalyzed the Branson tourism industry by putting it on the radar as "God's country."[4] In 1984, Jean and Norman opened the Harold Bell Wright Museum not in one of the places he lived as a wealthy author (Tucson, Arizona, and Escondido, California) but in the Ozark mountain city that started it all, with Reagan's letter prominently displayed.[5]

To understand the broader significance of the relationship between Wright's fiction, Branson's reality, and the modern conservative movement, we have to start with the author himself. Branson was the pivot point in Wright's rags-to-riches story — the place that made his American dream come true. He was born in 1872 in upstate New York to an alcoholic Civil War veteran who preferred to reminisce about the battlefield over a pint rather than work a steady job. Today we might consider that William Wright suffered post-traumatic stress disorder from joining the army at age eighteen and spending four years in a brutal, bloody war against his fellow countrymen, but Harold viewed his father as a "pitiful failure" who "dragged" his wife and children from place to place, "sinking deeper and deeper, as the years passed, into the slough of wretched poverty."[6] The family lived in decrepit, cramped row houses, where Wright and his brother played in piles of trash while his frail mother struggled under the weight of endless household chores. One day, when he was eleven, his mother started coughing up blood uncontrollably while bending over a tub of laundry. He dropped out of school to manage the house while she spent the last months of her life in bed. Once she died, his father split up the family. Wright worked as an unpaid child laborer in exchange for housing and food, bouncing around from family to family. At one farm, the owners woke him at 3 a.m. in order to lug buckets of potatoes that were heavy even for grown men. His biographer attributes Wright's chronic respiratory ailments in adulthood to his childhood years of undernourishment and overwork.[7] Wright also observed hypocrisy during these years. One employer who prayed piously on Sundays at church made him sell "sour rain water" as apple cider vinegar. Another took him in to make a positive impression on the neighbors for extending Christian charity but would not even let her children talk to him because of his low status. The experiences sowed Wright's deep distrust of organized religion and antipathy toward class distinctions.[8]

In his teens, Wright decided to learn the painter's trade so he could live independently. One day, an evangelist arrived in town for a tent meeting and asked him to paint advertisements. Wright listened with fascination to the preacher offer "a view of the Christian religion which was entirely new to me" — in which one did not have to join one of the "warring denominations," but instead could focus on living in service to God. The evangelist called himself a member of the Disciples of Christ (the eventual church of Ronald Reagan's mother and Reagan himself). While these new ideas about Christianity swirled in Wright's head, he saw a theatrical production of *Faust*, in which Dr. Faust sells his soul to the demon Mephistopheles in exchange for worldly knowledge and pleasure. In the version by Goethe, Faust is ultimately saved by God and goes to Heaven. Wright later wrote that the performance "made an impression upon me, so deep and lasting that to a large degree it shaped my future and determined the character of my life work." Viewing the play "remained one of the most powerful influences in my life. Is it strange, then, that I should look upon the theater with something of the feeling that one looks upon a temple?"[9]

It was Wright's first experience with what he would call "applied Christianity" — the idea that God is experienced most powerfully in everyday life, rather than in the pews of a church.[10] Theater, with its melodrama, spectacle, and emotional connection, conveyed God's grace and spiritual messages as well as if not better than any sermon. This embrace of theater put him at odds with many Christians in the United States, who looked upon the stage with suspicion. But for Wright, and for many of Branson's founding entertainers many years later, any activity that aimed to serve God was ministry.[11]

Wright did try standard preaching first, after some unaccredited theological training at Hiram College. Two years in, he suffered a bout of pneumonia and an affliction that left him unable to read. Then he made a fateful decision that would alter the course of his life: he took up a longstanding invitation to visit an uncle's farm near the White River in the Missouri Ozarks.

There, in rural Taney County, Wright found his ideal America. He camped, fished, painted, and attended church in a one-room log schoolhouse. He gave his first sermon on Thanksgiving Day when the local preacher failed to show. The residents, whom he found honest and direct, enjoyed Wright's unscripted sermon so much that he preached every Sunday that winter. The sojourn left its mark, but he still had not given up the idea of leading his own church full-time. He spent a decade preaching in Kansas, with occasional summer trips back to Branson. Meanwhile, his health continued to deteriorate. After a case of pneumonia that left doctors warning him he would die if he continued, he abandoned formal ministry in the summer of 1906 and relocated to the Taney County property of John and Anna Ross. In his tent along the ridgeline, looking out at Mutton Hollow, he drafted *The Shepherd of the Hills*.[12]

Wright's idealization of the Missouri Ozarks smoothed over several harsh truths. The population was sparse not by choice but because inhospitable terrain and brutal violence triggered people to leave. In the early nineteenth century, the US government removed Indigenous tribes from the newly purchased Louisiana Territory, which included Missouri, to make way for white settlers. In the 1820s,

Harold Bell Wright in his tent on the Ross property, ca. 1906. Author's personal collection.

William Clark and others made treaties that pushed Kickapoo, Shawnee, and Osage peoples from the Ozarks into Kansas and Oklahoma; in 1837, the Missouri state militia (with the assistance of local vigilantes) forced out the remaining Osage.[13] As elsewhere in North America in the mid-1800s, white settlers began to see the Ozarks as a blank slate of wilderness upon which they could write their destiny, instead of a place where humans had lived for several centuries.

The Ozarks then endured the violence of the Civil War "with a ferocity and relentlessness witnessed in few other places in North America."[14] Right on the border of the Mason–Dixon line, Missouri was a slave state that simultaneously had strong allegiances to the North and the dream of free enterprise. Few Ozarkers were slaveholders, but many had Southern roots. In the Civil War, the population split between the Union and the Confederacy. Neighbors, even brothers, killed each other. Worse than the official armies were the "bushwhackers," many of them deserters hiding out in the woods or caves, who claimed allegiance to neither side. The bushwhackers terrorized the region, ostensibly for financial gain but also, it seems, out of mere cruelty and demonstration of power. Alf Bolin and his gang bragged of killing dozens of Union and Confederate soldiers. They also robbed, raped, and murdered civilians throughout Taney County. Finally, a Union soldier bludgeoned and stabbed Bolin to death in 1863. Soldiers severed Bolin's head from his rotting body, put it on a pike, and displayed it in the public square of the town of Ozark. Legend has it that families danced around the pole to rejoice. In the midst of such violence, Taney County's population dropped from 3,500 in 1861 to 1,000 by 1865, or only 1.5 people per square mile.[15]

After the Civil War, bushwhacking became a way of life in the Ozarks. Absent law enforcement or social norms, locals were subjected to violent raids. Over thirty murders were committed in Taney County between 1860 and 1886, and not one resulted in a conviction. The county government was in shambles. Into this plagued region came the railroad, which brought new industries like timber but also new threats to the social order like saloons and gambling dens.[16]

In 1884 a group of Taney County men assembled on Dewey's Bald (a type of Ozark hill with trees on the sides and prairie on the top) and formed a vigilante group to end the chaos. But the Bald Knobbers, as they called themselves, soon enacted their own reign of terror. Founder Nathaniel Kinney railed against perceived violations of social norms, such as men and women cohabiting before marriage. Beatings, whippings, and campaigns of intimidation became regular occurrences. The night riders would leave a bundle of hickory sticks on transgressors' doorsteps, with the number of sticks representing the number of days the owner had to vacate their property before the Bald Knobbers would return to violently enforce eviction.[17] In 1886, Bald Knobber groups formed in neighboring Christian and Douglas counties. Upset about the new vice economy and resentful of the wealth newcomers had started to amass, these Bald Knobbers donned black masks with twisted horns and started their own intimidation campaigns. Anti–Bald Knobber groups arose as well, the violence begetting violence. The St. Louis press complained that southwest Missouri gave the entire state a bad name and inhibited progress.[18]

Bald Knobber vigilantes. Artist unknown, cover illustration from *Bald Knobbers* by Lucile Morris (Caxton Publishing, 1939). Courtesy Lebanon-Laclede County Library, Lebanon, Missouri.

Federal officials began to arrest Bald Knobbers for intimidating homesteaders, but they did not get much help from fearful locals. Public opinion finally turned when Bald Knobbers murdered William Edens and Charles Greene for speaking out against the vigilante group. The violence had finally gone too far. In March 1887, the Christian County sheriff arrested twenty-six Bald Knobbers for conspiracy to murder. Eventually, a grand jury handed out 250 separate indictments, including for raids, whippings, and unlawful assembly, against eighty people. Most were convicted, but in spectacular news that made headlines across the country, two of the men sentenced to death for the Edens-Greene murders escaped from jail. In Taney County, the Bald Knobbers movement dissipated after Billy Miles murdered leader Nat Kinney in 1888. Miles and his co-conspirator were acquitted, taking the wind out of the sails of the Bald Knobbers movement. The years of vigilante violence finally ended.[19]

In *The Shepherd of the Hills*, Wright submerged the uglier history of the area under a morality tale of rural goodness versus urban rot.

The novel starts with a thinly veiled version of Wright himself: Dan ("Dad") Howitt, a disillusioned preacher from Chicago, wanders onto the property of mill owners Grant and Mollie Matthews, modeled on Wright's hosts John and Anna Ross. The Matthewses welcome him. Howitt becomes the titular shepherd literally, by watching over the Matthewses' sheep, and also figuratively, as he becomes a moral guide for the community. Several convoluted plotlines overlap, but the heart of the story lies in the love triangle that develops between the beautiful Sammy Lane, her effete fiancé Ollie, and the Matthewses' virile son, Young Matt.

Through these three characters, Wright explicitly asserted that rural America was better than urban America. The moral distinctions were first physical and racial. Wright was a follower of his era's widely popular eugenics movement, which claimed that selective breeding improved the human population (eugenics has since been debunked as a form of pseudoscientific racism). Sammy was a woman "keenly alive to the life that throbbed and surged about her," a result of "good breeding" between her father's "Southern blood" and her Native American mother's "warm red life." Sammy's mother passed away young, tying neatly into the eugenicist idea that Indigenous peoples were noble but weak, destined to die out in the face of the superior white race. Sammy's father "counted a good bit" on "the old stock" of "proud southerners" in order to raise her as a single parent, and "it sure showed up right." The "women of the cities" were "pale, sickly, colourless, hot-house posies" by comparison.[20] Similarly, Ollie's unsuitability for the erotically charged mountain beauty was right there in his body: his "shoulders were too narrow and he stooped; his limbs were thin; his hair black and straight; and his eyes dull."[21] Ollie goes to Kansas City, which becomes another mark against him. Wright blamed industrial urbanism for creating class distinctions where men gained "advantage of rank, regardless of worth."[22] In the backwoods, natural ability rather than rank was what mattered: Could you build a house? Could you run a mill? And most importantly, could you use your physical strength to protect women?

Young Matt, "the finest specimen of manhood . . . ever seen," certainly could. His masculinity comes on display when facing Wash Gibbs, leader of a gang of former Bald Knobbers. Wright's Bald Knobbers were not the righteous vigilantes of historical record but a band of ne'er-do-wells. Gibbs was often drunk, instigating violence for no good reason. He robbed men and attempted to sexually assault women. When Gibbs and his gang turn their leering eyes to Sammy, Young Matt steps in and throws one thug into the bushes, causing Sammy to give "a low cry, 'Oh, *what a man!*'"[23] Her orgasmic rapture stems from admiration of more than just his physical prowess. Wright wrote, "Was there not that which lay deeper? Something of which the brute strength, after all, was only an expression?"[24] Wright implied that Young Matt displayed something *essential* about manhood in coming to Sammy's rescue. Unlike Ollie, he will never lord over other men in a managerial role. He will, however, win the girl: Young Matt and Sammy marry, while Ollie departs for Kansas City. The villain Wash Gibbs dies, the shepherd Howitt finds redemption, and the community enjoys serenity and prosperity.

Despite the happy resolution for the characters, Wright ended the book with a note of pessimism. The newlyweds hear a booming sound in the distance as workers build train tracks. Howitt observes, "Before many years a railroad will find its way yonder. Then many will come, and the beautiful hills that have been my strength and peace will become the haunt of careless idlers and a place of revelry."[25]

As it turns out, the railroad was not the cause of Branson's turn to revelry; The Shepherd of the Hills was. Wright was both a prophet and a primary cause of the town's transformation into a tourist mecca. The book sold hundreds of thousands of copies within the first year, and The Shepherd was the most-read book in America after the Bible during the 1910s. For over fifty years, it remained in the top five most-sold books of all time. Wright went on to publish several more novels and was one of the nation's most beloved authors of the early twentieth century.[26]

Not everyone loved Wright. Cultural tastemakers railed against his writing, finding it overly simplistic, sentimental, and evangelistic. One contemporary observer stated, "No critic has ever damned Wright with even the faintest of praise."[27] Instead, these critics "developed an entire industry of defaming Wright in witty and erudite ways."[28] They also disparaged his fans in ways that presaged how cultural critics would disparage Branson and its visitors in the coming decades. The *New York Times* averred that Wright catered to the "obviousness of the American yokel." Writer Hildegarde Hawthorne argued that "many of those who read him are not readers at all," a paradox that has endured in depictions of Branson as theater for people who don't go to the theater. Prominent literary critic H. L. Mencken "crusaded" to "evict" Wright from the US literary canon. He wrote in 1920 that Wright's work "touches such depths of banality that it would be difficult to match it in any other country. . . . It is the natural outpouring of a naïve and yet half barbarous people."[29] Barnard College professor Charles Baldwin went even further in 1924: "[Wright] and his kind, in their exalted manhood . . . are the rank and file of the Ku Klux Klan."[30]

Wright's method of distributing *Shepherd of the Hills* also lowered his cultural status. He sold his novel not in bookstores, which tended to exist only in cities, but through mail-order catalogs such as Sears, Roebuck & Company, which catered to small-town and rural populations. Sears began book advertising in 1910 and featured Wright's work prominently. It is most likely that Ronald Reagan's mother bought her copy of *That Printer of Udell's* through a catalog. One bookseller in 1915 explained Wright's success as "no mystery at all, just a matter of sheer advertising, like selling patent medicines or breakfast foods!" That same year, *Atlantic Monthly* writer Owen Wister called Wright's oeuvre "Quack-Novels," the literary equivalent of quack medicines, and described his writing as "a mess of mildewed pap."[31]

The battle lines of the culture war had been drawn, with the one-dimensional stereotypes propped up into place. On one side: rural, white, Christian, racist, backward, tasteless, prone to hucksters, and epitomized by a writer who had never made it past middle school. On the other: urban, racially diverse, educated, artistic, and nominally sophisticated, represented by the sounds of jazz and the poetry of the avant-garde. The authors Mencken celebrated, such as F. Scott Fitzgerald, Eugene O'Neill, Willa Cather, and Langston Hughes, have endured in classrooms as staples of the literary canon. Wright is absent. Yet his ideas have embedded themselves deeply into the nation's DNA, providing fuel for the long culture wars. The large swath of Americans who loved Wright's novels, whom Mencken dismissed as "half barbarous," also did not disappear. Instead, they came to Branson.

People did not buy Wright's books solely because they saw advertisements. Simply put, readers enjoyed his stories and found meaning in them. *The Shepherd of the Hills* fed into many white Americans' longings for a rural yesteryear that had seemingly been lost with the closing of the frontier. The myth of the lost frontier had crystallized in Chicago in 1893 with two major events. The first was Buffalo Bill's Wild West Show, which entertained thousands through the summer. Blurring reality and fiction, actual Sioux veterans of the Battle of the Little Big Horn and the Massacre at Wounded Knee reenacted their victory and ultimate defeat for the pleasure of a paying public. The show depicted the frontier as a place of fierce battle between Native American "savages" and valiant white American scouts. Its vision endured in film, television, and novelistic depictions of the American West for decades to come.[32]

Meanwhile, down the street from Buffalo Bill, historian Frederick Jackson Turner declared his Frontier Thesis: the idea that the history of the United States was one of a continuously westward movement of white settlers conquering the wilderness. According to Turner, the pursuit of the frontier promoted democracy and individualism as well as traits such as pragmatism, materialism, expediency, and optimism. Because the availability of free or very cheap land on the frontier allowed a pioneer to remake himself, America symbolized opportunity. Unfortunately, the Census Bureau had declared in 1890 that the frontier was no more. Thus Turner claimed that Americans had to search for new ways to keep their national traits alive.[33]

Except, maybe they didn't. What if the frontier was not closed?

The Shepherd of the Hills tantalizingly described a place where the frontier myth became truth, filled out by the flesh and bones of real people. People began to call the region "God's country," adding a sense of divine blessing to an area that promised to restore American greatness.[34] Almost immediately after the novel's publication in 1907, tourists began to arrive in the Branson area — coming not only by railroad, but also by car, horseback, and foot — in search of *Shepherd*'s world. Once the trickle of visitors started, it did not stop. Tourism got an additional boost in 1913 when a local company with backing from St. Louis financiers built Powersite Dam on the White River. The dam supplied hydroelectric power and created Lake Taneycomo, a man-made idyll that supported the image of the Ozarks as a place of bucolic respite from urban life.[35]

During the decade when *The Shepherd* started to transform Branson, popular theater was also transforming to disseminate the myth of rural virtue more fully. Variety, a type of live entertainment made up of short acts featuring musicians, singers, jugglers, contortionists, dancers, sword-swallowers, hypnotists, trick rope acts, and comedians, had been the national rage since the 1880s. It was called vaudeville when performed on an urban stage, a medicine show when performed on a flatbed truck to sell quack medicines, or a tent show when performed under white canvas on the outskirts of a small town. Up until the early twentieth century, blackface was ubiquitous, as variety descended in part from minstrel shows. Comedians played other stock ethnic characters as well — Chinese, Irish, German, Yankee, and the rube.

In 1909, a new variety genre emerged: the Toby Show. Toby, a red-haired, freckle-faced country bumpkin character, was so popular that "tent show" and "Toby Show" became synonymous in the Midwest and Upper South. The use of blackface, previously ubiquitous, plummeted on the rural tent show circuit. While some theatrical entertainment is based on laughing at or exoticizing others,[36] people also attend the theater to see themselves and affirm that their way of life has meaning. Many rural white Americans felt this need in the early twentieth century. Industrial-scale farms were swallowing

Toby Show by the Sun Players in Holden, Missouri, 1959. Courtesy State Historical Society of Missouri.

up small family-run operations; friends and relatives were leaving in droves for Northern cities; the dominance of urban culture was reaching a new height with the ragtime dance craze, Tin Pan Alley songs, and amusement parks like Coney Island. Modern technologies like cars, telephones, and electricity widened the gap between the standard of living in the city versus the country. The United States officially became more urban than rural in the decade of the 1910s. In the face of what seemed like an existential threat, Toby Shows reaffirmed the agrarian myth that rural white folks were more virtuous than other Americans.[37]

The Toby Show wove a melodrama into the typical variety fare. When audiences came in, performers were already onstage playing music. Then Toby arrived to describe the action and name the cast members. Then began a three-act play, interspersed with variety entertainment, which usually followed the same basic plot: Toby rescues a lovely young lady from the wiles of an urban villain and

Audience enjoying a Toby Show in Holden, Missouri, 1952. Courtesy State Historical Society of Missouri.

reunites her with her rightful rural mate. He connected with audiences through jokes that established his character as a simple yet clever country boy, such as the one where the city slicker asks Toby, "You know a lot about hogs?" and Toby replies, "Yes, and how's your family?"[38] Throughout, he affirmed allegiance to "mother, home, and heaven," a precursor to family, flag, and faith. Audience members cheered Toby along. After the melodrama was yet more variety entertainment for an additional fee. Making a profit was centrally important. Every moment the performers were not on stage, they found other ways to help fill the till. Before the show, they took tickets and sold concessions. Between acts they sold candy, pointed out sponsoring businesses' advertisements on tent walls, and hawked tickets to other performances. The Toby Show remained vibrant in rural and small-town America for over two decades, even as the rise of the Hollywood film industry sent vaudeville in urban areas into precipitous decline.[39]

In a popular culture primed to enjoy performances of rural virtue, *The Shepherd of the Hills* fit right in. Wright understood the power of theater and eagerly participated in the adaptation of *The Shepherd of the Hills* into scripts and screenplays. In 1912, theatrical stock companies began touring the play across the United States and Canada; in 1919, the first Hollywood film version premiered. Four more films would come out in 1928, 1941 (starring John Wayne), 1960, and 1964. In print, on stage, and on screen, *The Shepherd of the Hills* entranced millions of Americans during the first half of the twentieth century, and many of them came to see if reality could match the fiction.

Locals had various reactions to the newcomers. John and Anna Ross's gracious hospitality was put to the test. At first they invited visitors to stay, as was Ozarks custom, even letting them sleep in their yard. But soon dozens of people were arriving daily. In December 1910, they sold their cabin in frustration.[40] Other locals did not mind as much. They sensed financial opportunity and eagerly claimed to be inspirations for various characters. Competition to be Sammy Lane was particularly strong. One apocryphal story is that when Wright returned to Branson in 1918, area residents (not knowing him by sight) pointed out three different "Sammy Lanes" to him over the course of a few hours.[41] One resident, Susie B. Johnston, was a fervent contender. When she died at thirty-one, her family added "Sammy Lane" to her tombstone — a kind of claim to "Ozark immortality."[42] Even the Rosses are immortalized this way: "Here Lies Old Matt & Aunt Molly of the Shepherd of the Hills."[43]

The Shepherd of the Hills transformed not only various individuals, but also the entire region into a theatricalized version of itself. *The Shepherd of the Hills* was so foundational to the identity of Branson tourism that until the 1970s boosters called the area "Shepherd of the Hills Country."[44] William Lloyd Driver, a physical education instructor from Kansas who purchased the Ross cabin in 1910, renamed it "Old Matt's Cabin," as it is called by the National Register of Historic Places to this day.[45] In 1926 Lizzie McDaniel, the daughter of a Springfield banker, purchased the homestead and operated it as the Shepherd of the Hills Farm. She opened a hotel with a dining

room, gift shop, and art gallery; she also opened a gas station. Entrepreneur Pearl Spurlock dressed in turn-of-the-century hillbilly
garb and called her cab "The Shepherd of the Hills Taxi." She drove
tourists to visit sites on the farm as well as other places mentioned in
the novel, such as Sammy's Lookout and Mutton Hollow. To entertain
her passengers along the unpaved roads, Spurlock delighted them
with the story of Sammy Lane, which she told "so many times she
believed it gospel truth and was indignant if anyone spoke of it as
fiction." She also brought them to a living tourist object, the local
postmaster Levi Morrill, a.k.a. "Uncle Ike." He was the one character
Wright admitted had been based directly on a real person.[46]

Shepherd of the Hills Country got an additional tourism boost
in the 1930s, when folklorists Vance Randolph and Otto Rayburn
designated the Ozarks as an "arrested frontier." They proposed that
the Ozarks had been skipped over in Frederick Jackson Turner's
stages of frontier development. In their characterization, the Ozarks
remained a frontier zone — and therefore also a haven of democratic ideals.[47] Prior to the 1930s, many writers lumped Appalachia
and the Ozarks together as the Southern Mountain region, with a
homogeneous demographic of poor whites, called "hillbillies." In
1904, Marion Hughes's popular travelogue *Three Years in Arkansaw*
crystallized the contradictory hillbilly stereotype: uncivilized but
shrewd, lazy but self-sufficient, violent but humorous, backward but
therefore also keepers of tradition. In one telling illustration from
the book, labeled an "Interior of a Typical Arkansaw Home," barefoot
and disheveled children run around with pigs, dogs, and chickens,
creating chaos and filth. A woman breastfeeds two babies simultaneously as she smokes a cigarette. The husband sits in repose,
his chair tilted back with the front two legs up in the air. He cannot
spring into action. He plays the fiddle, unperturbed by the chaos
around him.[48]

The hillbilly's positive stereotypes came from his supposed connections to nature, God, music, and the American spirit of individualism. That gave the Ozark hillbilly a leg up over his Appalachian
cousin, whose image was being stripped away by strip mining.

Capitalist speculation transformed Appalachia, which in turn led folklorists and reformers to rush to save what they deemed as essential American heritage, such as folk songs, square dances, and crafts of Anglo-Saxon- and Scotch-Irish-descended mountaineers. The Ozarks were similarly understood as a site of pure white racial heritage, but they were not "discovered" until the 1930s, and then without an urgent call for intervention. Farther from Northeastern capitalists and possessing fewer mineral resources, the Ozarks experienced less industrialization and thus less exploitation by outsiders — though that also meant less economic development. With the folklorists' help, the region could geographically code-switch from Southern Mountain to Western, folk or frontier, embracing whichever identity seemed most useful at any given moment.

Turner had described frontier zones as racially and ethnically diverse, but Randolph and Rayburn championed the Ozarks as home to "real Americans," who for them were Anglo-Saxon. Rayburn even proclaimed that the region was "the last survival of Elizabethan culture in the Western world."[49] Heralded as self-sufficient, independent pioneers, Ozark hillbillies became aspirational figures for white Americans who found themselves dependent on government aid to survive the Great Depression.[50] Branson residents embraced the charge. Further tourist attractions developed, such as the Sammy Lane Resort, the Sammy Lane Boat Line, and the Wash Gibbs Museum. Local artist Steve Miller painted a mural in the Security Bank of Branson depicting Young Matt lifting a steam engine off the ground, a scene from the novel used to demonstrate the youth's superior masculinity and the virtues of the rural white working class overall.[51]

In 1946, Bruce and Mary Trimble of Kansas City took over the Shepherd of the Hills Farm and expanded it as a tourist attraction. Bruce was a professor of history and political science who channeled his enthusiasm for the past into the farm. The Trimbles collected materials about Wright, The Shepherd of the Hills, and Ozarks culture. Eventually they had collected so much of what they called "Americana" (a conflation of national culture and specific regional culture that reaffirmed the real Americanness of the place) that they turned the former owner's house into a museum. The Trimbles also commissioned statues based on the novel's characters, which are still on the property where Wright pitched his tent, now called Inspiration Point.[52]

As a complement to these developments, in 1955 Branson's Chamber of Commerce teamed up with Southern Illinois University's theater program to produce a *Shepherd of the Hills* play during the summer months at Lake Taneycomo. The script, by Charlotte McLeod, lifted most of the dialogue directly from the novel (though not Wright's musings on good breeding). After two summers, the Illinois legislature refused to continue funding an out-of-state theatrical endeavor, so the Chamber switched to working with Central Missouri State College. Both productions included locals performing alongside college acting students. By then, residents had been performing in their everyday lives as Wright's characters for almost forty years, so the leap to the stage was not that daunting. Plus, they were eager to wrest back control of their image from Hollywood. They had become particularly incensed after Paramount's 1941 film version of *Shepherd of the Hills* turned beautiful Sammy into a jeans-wearing tomboy and saintly Aunt Mollie into a moonshiner. The film's Young Matt (played by John Wayne) and Wash Gibbs were half brothers, a clear violation of Wright's edict that genetics determined virtue. In the novel, Wash Gibbs's "yeller kind" and Young Matt's "finest specimen of manhood" could never share blood. Over a decade after the film, residents still "seethed" with "ever-fresh anger" about how Hollywood misrepresented characters whom they considered family.[53]

The summer-stock play, however, was not enough to sustain Branson tourism. Love of Wright's novel, now fifty years old, was waning. The production also faced several issues. Flies swarmed the lakefront in warm months, which was "unbearable" for both performers and audience members. Fog rolled in many evenings and settled on the stage to obscure the audience's view. The Chamber of Commerce's support flagged.[54] Then Bruce Trimble died suddenly of a heart attack, leaving his widow Mary and son Mark to figure out what to do next with Shepherd of the Hills Farm. For help, they turned to a vaudevillian-*cum*-Native American impersonator-*cum*-circus clown named Lloyd Heller. The stage was set for a new phase of Branson entertainment.

2 THE FOLK AND THE FRONTIER

Performing America's Past

A t the start of World War II, two paths diverged in an Arizona desert. One man enlisted in the air force, became a US senator, and ran for president in 1964. The other descended into alcoholism, joined the circus, and ended up in Branson. One has secured a place in history; the other is largely unknown. But for five years prior to the fateful bombing of Pearl Harbor, Barry Goldwater and Lloyd Heller forged a friendship based on their shared passion for the peculiar practice of Native American impersonation. And in the end, each contributed to the warp and woof of modern conservatism in America. Goldwater gave the movement some of its core political principles, initially considered too extreme but eventually central. Heller gave life to those principles on stage. In Branson, he popularized glorious pioneer pasts in order to paint powerful visions of the nation's present and future.

Heller's path to Branson was a winding one. He was born in 1913 in Stroudsburg, Pennsylvania. His father, a builder, had constructed the town's Sherman Theater, where Heller loved watching the magicians, dance teams, acrobats, animal acts, and clowns who made up the fascinating world of vaudeville. From it, he learned lesson number one of show business: provide spectacle and variety. At sixteen he got a job as a carnival barker, learning how to "pitch" marks — that is, how to get people to open their wallets. Therein lay lesson number two: sell, sell, sell. Then the Great Depression hit at the same time that Heller's sister developed tuberculosis and was ordered by doctors to move to a drier climate. During his senior year of high school, Heller joined his mother and sister in Prescott, Arizona, while his father stayed back in Pennsylvania to try to save the struggling family business. During this financially and emotionally stressful time, Heller took his first acting classes in Prescott and gained the basic skills of character development, scene work, and staging. Upon graduation, Heller went back east, where he joined a "legitimate" theater and a vaudeville troupe. Lesson number three: know your craft.

Heller also absorbed lessons from the Great Depression during his adolescence. Unlike millions who found relief in government programs, however, he came to believe that such assistance was making the problem worse. One day he and his father witnessed men digging ditches as part of a Works Progress Administration (WPA) federal project. "About every other man was standing there with his hands on his shovel, watching us go by," Heller recalled. "And my father said to me, 'Son, you see that out there? This government is going to rue the day when they started all of this, because all they're making is a bunch of lazy bums out of those men.' I think there may have been some truth to that. That incident has stayed with me all my life."[1]

Heller's sense that the burgeoning welfare state robbed men of their independence and work ethic fed a nostalgic impulse to reach back into the past. In 1934, he returned to Prescott, got married, and took a job at the Phoenix-based Arizona Distributing Company, delivering draft beer to bars in the area. But his love of performance had not abated. In 1936, he joined the Smoki People.

The Smoki (pronounced Smoke-Eye) was a made-up Native American tribe composed of white men who staged massive outdoor pageants. They claimed to be preserving cultural traditions on the brink of disappearance, without acknowledging the reason for those disappearances. Joining the Smoki was a serious business. Members got matching tattoos on their left hands, and in the months leading up to the annual performance, they would rehearse as often as seven nights a week. A 1936 brochure proclaimed that "the privilege of membership in Smoki is held as sacred as that of any fraternal society that is known to the civilized world."[2] While exclusive to white men (and their wives, or "Squaws," as helpers), they claimed to prize equality. Heller experienced "democratic camaraderie" among the Smoki, finding "little distinction within the group between the banker and the carpenter" as long as one "was willing to work when it was time to put together a show."[3]

And that is how Heller, a truck driver, became so close to Arizona royalty: Barry Goldwater, whose uncle had been the mayor of Prescott for twenty years. Goldwater worked for his father's successful department store in Phoenix, which happened to be on the same street as Heller's employer. The two men became fast friends, and Heller sponsored Goldwater's initiation into the Smoki in 1937. For five years, in addition to the group meetings and rehearsals, the duo huddled together to research Hopi rituals in order to improve the Snake Dance. By his own telling, Heller was particularly adept at this dance, in which he writhed and stomped to a drum with a live snake in his mouth. Many white Americans "played Indian" in the early twentieth century, embracing the romanticized notions that Indigenous peoples were more spiritual and more emotionally in sync with the universe.[4] Similarly, Heller saw his performances as an act of cleansing. When he put on brown makeup and danced in his costume, he felt like a purer version of himself, closer to nature, stripped to a "primitive state."[5] Immersing himself in such a character would prove useful when he moved to Branson and encountered a community that outsiders had similarly romanticized as closer to nature and purer in spirit.[6]

When World War II broke out, Goldwater joined the air force. Heller's life took a different turn. Years of delivering beer had meant lots of time socializing in saloons; he descended into alcoholism and lost his job. Leaving his wife and two small children in 1947, he found work with the Ringling Brothers Circus as a roustabout, putting up and taking down the heavy tents. He was intrigued by the clowns and studied their expert use of makeup, pantomime, and precise physical movement to delight an audience. He eventually wrangled a spot in the clown parade.[7] The circus provided yet another layer of on-the-job training in American popular entertainment.

After seven years with Ringling, during which he divorced his wife, Heller turned his life around by joining Alcoholics Anonymous. He then drove a truck for Acme Chemical and married Ruth Soles, a widow in Kansas who dabbled in community theater. On one of his Acme runs down to the Ozarks, he stumbled upon Branson. Heller found it "difficult to separate the real from the unreal" there, where life imitated fiction.[8] Who was being themselves? Who was playing a character from the novel The Shepherd of the Hills? The surreality was a fascinating, even comforting feeling for someone who had spent his life performing. He attended the summer-stock waterfront production of The Shepherd at Lake Taneycomo and was hooked — but also felt he could improve upon it. Heller and his wife joined the cast in 1957 and relocated permanently to Branson in 1959.

Within a year, Heller became intimately involved with the bedrock of Branson entertainment: The Shepherd of the Hills outdoor drama and the theme park Silver Dollar City. Both venues opened in the summer of 1960, and the timing could not have been better for attracting tourists. Leisure travel exploded in the late 1950s, bolstered by a booming economy and the new federally funded interstate highways. Rural Americans had left the South in droves during the first half of the twentieth century, but now they and their new suburban neighbors had discretionary funds, vacation time, cars, and access to highways that allowed them to return temporarily to the lands of their forebears in the form of a vacation. While Branson had long been a destination for outdoorsmen and fans of Wright's novel, the construction of Table Rock Dam in 1958 expanded possibilities.

Table Rock Dam was the brainchild of US Congressman Dewey Short, a Republican who represented Taney County from 1935 to 1957. Short made his name by ardently opposing Roosevelt's New Deal, calling it the "Raw Deal" and voting "no" on every program save Social Security. One such program was the Tennessee Valley Authority, which funded dams and towers to provide electricity to Appalachia.

As Short railed against the TVA as government overreach by "the most supine, supercilious, superfluous, soporific, pusillanimous body of nit-wits ever gathered beneath the dome of the Capitol," he hypocritically lobbied to get federal funds to build a dam in his home district, and he succeeded when Congress passed the Flood Control Act of 1941.[9] After the delays of World War II and the Korean War, the US Army Corps of Engineers began building Table Rock Dam in 1954 and completed it in 1958, along with Table Rock Lake. The dam provided the electricity needed for hotels, restaurants, and theaters. At the same time, it forced numerous small farmers off their land. Residents of Taney County, instead of pursuing agriculture, found employment performing a theatrical representation of that life for tourists.

The Shepherd of the Hills and the Silver Dollar City theme park were perfect vehicles for these performances. At both, Branson residents continued code-switching between South and West. The Southern folk and the Western frontier were both attractive ideals in the early 1960s. A folk music revival was gaining steam nationwide, with Bob Dylan as the most iconic representative of this genre. The folk revival happened predominantly in urban areas and on college campuses among people who considered themselves politically progressive and countercultural, but their investment in the desire to return to a simpler time aligned them with many Americans whom they considered their antagonists.[10]

Television was another important outlet for fulfilling this desire. Starting in the early 1960s, depictions of the rural South seemed to offer an antidote to the corruption of both urban and suburban America: the violence of the former and the soulless conventionality of the latter. Popular programs such as The Andy Griffith Show, which ran from 1960 to 1968, and The Beverly Hillbillies, which ran from 1962 to 1971, portrayed a South in which no white policemen set vicious dogs on Black teenagers. In fact, there were almost no Black characters in idyllic Mayberry, North Carolina, where Sheriff Andy solved his community's problems. This was a vision of the South as "down home" — not modern, consumerist, or living under the long shadow of slavery.[11] *The Andy Griffith Show* and *The Beverly Hillbillies* were consistently among the most popular shows nationwide.

Right up there with them were Westerns. In the postwar period, Western movies and television shows exploded in popularity. The cowboy lived on the frontier, that border between civilization and wilderness, pulled in both directions. He represented the fundamental "ambivalence about the costs associated with progress," especially the perceived loss of autonomy and self-sufficiency that came with corporatization, suburbanization, and technological development.[12] Essayist Joan Didion wrote in 1968, "When John Wayne rode through my childhood, and perhaps through yours, he determined forever the shape of certain of our dreams." His frontier was "a place where a man could move free, could make his own code and live by it . . . he could one day take the girl and go riding through the draw and find himself home free."[13]

Didion's lyrical writing captured the centrality of nostalgia to both the folk and the frontier, concepts that are generally spoken about elegiacally as already lost. Such sentiments were not new in the 1960s, but they were reinvigorated. The 1960 Democratic primary brought attention to the economic distress of Appalachia, which soon became a "cause célèbre."[14] By the mid-1960s, even civil rights activists proclaimed that white poverty in Kentucky, Tennessee, and West Virginia needed federal attention.[15] The Ozarks inspired no such national concern, despite similar impoverishment. Ozarkers' malnutrition and lack of plumbing were spun as the virtue of simple living, a proud choice rather than an exploited condition forced upon them by outsiders. They lived in poverty, but dirt on their faces came from working their own land, not from the carcinogenic dust of a coal mine. Ozarkers also embraced their racial identity. In 1969, local historian Elmo Ingenthron wrote that the Branson area was characterized by "the blood and cultures of a pure teutonic [sic] Anglo Saxon race."[16] He echoed earlier folklorists who had called Ozarkers "nearly all old-timers of English stock" and, simultaneously, "real Americans" who despite their impoverishment and rough living "belonged to an aristocracy of brains and honor with a pedigree that isolation could not weaken."[17] Taking a vacation to the Ozarks to see "our pioneer ancestors in the flesh,"[18] said one writer, was a trip to both the folk and the frontier—at least for white tourists. Of course, massive government infrastructure projects such as highways and dams were what made it possible for tourists to visit this simpler time.

Rather than protest the characterization that they still lived in the nineteenth century, Branson residents did what they had done ever since *The Shepherd of the Hills* novel came out in 1907: they leaned in. The summer of 1960 was a watershed moment because of the new opportunities to get paid for their performances of frontier folk. Both Lloyd Heller and Mark Trimble claim credit for originating the idea of a dramatic presentation of *The Shepherd of the Hills* at the Homestead. Regardless of who thought of it first, the two men agreed that a private business could put on a show better than the public-private partnership that oversaw the struggling waterfront production. Heller and Trimble had met in April 1960 at Plumb Nelly Days, a local festival to reenact the pioneer past. "Plumb Nelly" was a play on the Ozark pronunciation of "plumb nearly," meaning "anything goes." Women strolled downtown Branson in bonnets and calico dresses; activities included square dancing, hog calling, cakewalks, and fishing contests. Heller served as emcee of the festivities, and Trimble was the chairman. Together with investors from the Dixon & Baker advertising agency of Springfield, they formed the Old Mill Theatre Players, Inc. Heller also recruited James Collie, a theater teacher from his wife Ruth's hometown in Kansas, to write a new script. In the span of three months, the production team built the Old Mill Theatre from scratch and rehearsed a new play that opened on August 6, 1960. Modern technology, including five miles of electrical wires placed underground, aided in recreating the past.[19]

The Old Mill *Shepherd of the Hills* was radically innovative in its depiction of a timeless folk. It was a "new concept in the theater," in which the audience was "put in the position of being almost a participant."[20] Avant-garde performers in New York are often credited with developing such immersive practices in the 1960s, but Heller was doing it in the Ozark hills as well. Instead of simply staging the melodramatic story, he wowed the audience with absorption into this world of yore. The experience began the moment people left their cars at dusk. From the parking lot, patrons followed a trail through the woods, lit by kerosene lamps, that descended to the amphitheater. The sound of loudly whirring cicadas, the smell of humid air, the sight of the rust-orange sun setting behind the hills, and the experience of stepping on forest debris got people "in the mood," said Heller. "It was a beautiful walk. They walked into the past."[21]

The amphitheater design obscured theatricality as much as possible. The stage did not look like a stage — it was a large swath of dirt mixed with sawdust. Nor was the set simply painted façades, but rather three-dimensional structures repurposed from actual nineteenth-century buildings: a grist mill, a barn, a cabin, and stables. The steam engine in the mill worked. Thick forest surrounded on all sides, allowing sounds of night creatures and rustling leaves to add to the sense of having been transported. At 8 p.m., with the summer sun setting, the play would begin. Collie's script condensed the action to one day and relocated all scenes to the outdoors.[22] The characters remained the same: Dan (Dad) Howitt as a frustrated preacher from Chicago who becomes the shepherd of the community; Pete (renamed Little or Lil' Pete) as a mysterious boy who lives in the woods; Wash Gibbs as a baddie; Old Matt and Aunt Mollie as a kindly couple who run the mill and worry about the drought; their son Young Matt as a tall and brawny local competing for the love of Sammy Lane; Sammy as a beautiful young woman torn between Young Matt and her fiancé Ollie, a sissified dandy. To further amplify the novel's melodrama and draw audiences, Heller remembered his first lesson of showbiz: spectacle.

And who better to bring spectacle than a gang of thugs? In *The Shepherd of the Hills*, Wright had reimagined the historical Bald Knobbers not as self-proclaimed defenders of moral virtue but as pure bad guys, bent upon violating women, stealing money, and wreaking havoc. Heller directed the gang to gallop onto the stage on horses and carry real rifles. The actors playing Wash and Matt used real axes in their fight, each swinging his weapon with full force into the ground just as his opponent rolled out of harm's way. "How we kept from killing someone during the fight scene I'll never know," Heller said.[23]

The Bald Knobbers also shot those real rifles, the loud *craaack* reverberating in the hills. They carried torches and set a cabin on fire. They wore black masks with twisted horns, an accurate reproduction of the costuming of the Christian County branch of the vigilante group. This terrifying visage heightened the sense of threat. In the early years, the Bald Knobber characters also nearly lynched Howitt, going so far as putting a noose around his neck and throwing the rope over a tree. The sound, smell, and visuals immersed the audience.

Heller raised the stakes by making the audience a part of the spectacle as well. Rather than just sit at a distance from the stage and watch in silence, here the audience was invited onstage during the first intermission to square-dance with the actors. A tourist could touch the back of someone in a long calico dress and inhale the scent of sweat and dirt intermingled. Others could crowd around on the wooden dance platform, a part of the scene even if not actively twirling a partner 'round and 'round. The audience was pulled into the show at the end of the second act, too, when the wood cabin burst into flames. Actors appealed to audience members for help, and ordinary men, women, and children hurried onto the set. They felt the heat and smelled the burning wood; their hearts raced as they poured water from buckets. As a journalist explained in 1963, "You don't just 'see' a production of Harold Bell Wright's *The Shepherd of the Hills*. It happens to you."[24] Heller was heartened by such words. "It was not to be at all like any theatre I had known," he reflected. "I wanted the audience to experience a time out of the past."[25] Heller's outdoor drama let tourists live out a vision of what it meant to be a real American.

In 1966, Trimble dissolved the old corporation and formed the Shepherd of the Hills Historical Society, Inc.[26] A historical society was a curious name for an organization that produced a play based

Square-dance scene, *Shepherd of the Hills*, ca. 1960s. Courtesy White River Valley Historical Society.

on a novel, but it added to the performance of realism. The Society's souvenir programs of *Shepherd* included a "Historical Facts" section that stated, "Grant Matthews and his family homesteaded this quarter-section farm in the summer of 1884," a false claim given that Grant Matthews never existed and that actual homesteader John Ross probably first lived on the property in 1895.[27] Trimble wrote that he hoped "that in this absorbing drama of the Ozark past, every traveler may come to understand the simple ideals and way of life of our forefathers. . . . From the labor and endurance of these people came our western civilization and the greatest democracy in the history of man."[28] The hardscrabble life of the hills, in this telling, made all white settlers equals, leading to both self-sufficiency and strong community bonds. The outdoor drama reinforced that vision of American history night after night.

In 1966, Trimble made an important change to the production that increased attendance: he hired local amateurs. Heller had cast college students, but Trimble cared little if performers had theatrical training. He wanted a "business" approach to "selling a re-enactment of the most significant historical event in this community" and thus emphasized "typecasting." Heller, a Pennsylvanian who convincingly played Native Americans, circus clowns, and Ozark hillbillies, disagreed vehemently. Dispute over this change, as well as financial disputes, led to Trimble firing Heller. The Homestead owner kept almost everything else from Heller's vision: the staging, the spectacularity, the condensed melodramatic action, and the emphasis on bringing audiences into the past.[29] Trimble's casting furthered the "ultra-realism" of Heller's original idea rather than breaking with it. An often-repeated story of the early years is that one season Trimble needed new Bald Knobbers on short notice. Because it was difficult to find performers who could ride horses well, Trimble hastily contacted his friend, the sheriff, to release some prisoners from the county jail who could ride horses and easily slip into the role of "ruffians."[30] Criminals playing criminals added an uncanny (sur)realism to the production. A souvenir program from 1969 stated that "the cast members' own lives best represent the characters they portray."[31] This ethos has endured despite changes in direction and the script. In 2018, when director Keith Thurman was asked whether he instructed his cast to stay in late nineteenth-century character when square dancing with audiences or be their regular twenty-first-century selves, he gave a sideways grin and responded, "Well, a lot of 'em are both all the time."[32]

Despite his use of amateurs, Trimble boasted that he paid his cast better wages than any other outdoor drama in the United States.[33] While true, this work was still seasonal. The outdoor drama originally only ran in the summer, and eventually extended from spring to fall, but was never full-time, year-round employment. It was a problem that would endure in Branson even as the tourism industry grew. Luckily for Trimble, locals did not seem to mind. The 1969 souvenir program notes that many involved in *Shepherd* have made it "A life's work. This accounts for the pride and professionalism that is so evident in a cast and staff who are, by conventional theatrical standards, relatively untrained."[34] That professionalism also meant that Trimble could charge for tickets. Speaking as a shrewd businessman, Trimble said, "the commodity we are selling here is a local show with local people."[35] Amateurism was a marketing tactic to sell authenticity.

Trimble's savvy packaging of The Shepherd as a profitable commodity did not inhibit the development of a joyous communal spirit around the show. Performing in The Shepherd quickly became a local tradition. Kids who played Little Pete at age eight played Young Matt at twenty and Old Matt at fifty. Thurman, whose great-grandfather had been the Taney County assessor during the Harold Bell Wright years, was with the show for five decades. He first saw Shepherd in 1965 while working on his rock music career. After serving in the Vietnam War, he returned to the area, fell in love with the pretty redhead playing Sammy Lane, Gwen Yeargain, and began hanging out with The Shepherd cast. In 1970 Yeargain broke off their engagement to elope with country music star Hank Williams Jr. Thurman stayed and decided to bulk up to audition for the part of Young Matt. Two seasons in, his manager told him he had to make a choice between rock music and Shepherd. Thurman chose the latter. He played Young Matt for the next eleven years, until he broke his neck during the fight scene, after which he became the director of the show — a position he held for an astonishing thirty-nine years.

The bonds forged through performance proved almost unbreakable. Some would quit the production but come back a few years later, asking for a part. "The actors are like addicts," explained Doug Sullivan, operations manager of The Shepherd of the Hills in the 1990s.[36] Thurman elaborated, "You get so hooked on this story and the atmosphere and the people that are a part of this that literally, you just can't get away from it."[37] Through performing a rural ideal in The Shepherd, actors created that ideal of community in their own lives. Pundits have been proclaiming the alienation of modern life since the 1880s. Whether the culprit is industrialization, immigration, urbanization, automation, railroads, suburbanization, television, consumerism, hippies, secularism, feminism, multinational corporations, the internet, or social media, there is always a technological or sociological force to blame for the fraying of community bonds. That narrative is a little suspicious — community has been said to be dying for 140 years, if not more. Nevertheless, loneliness and alienation have long shaped how many Americans have seen themselves, the dark flip side of the individualism and independence that has defined the American way.[38] Finding authentic community feels rare, and so The Shepherd cast realized it was worth holding on to tightly. Audiences grasped on to this feeling as well. The palpable sense that the community onstage existed in the "real" world offstage dissolved the invisible barrier between performer and audience member and between past and present. The rural utopia existed not only in the long-ago days of the script, but also in the here and now.

Shepherd helped outdoor drama gain prominence in mid-twentieth-century America. This relatively new genre promoted the idea that America's moral and national character lived in the wilderness (rather than in the immoral space of a darkened theater) and depicted characters who purportedly embodied such values: namely, rural white Americans or, to a lesser extent, Native Americans. North Carolina was the initial gravitational center of such productions, with Paul Green's The Lost Colony in 1937 and Kermit Hunter's Unto These Hills in 1950. Hunter also wrote a manifesto in 1953 that laid out the basic principles of the genre. In response to criticisms that outdoor drama was "melodramatic" and too overtly religious, Hunter stated, "if we err in the direction of sentimentality, we are better off than if we err in the direction of abstract fatalism, or unintelligible, super-sophisticated verbiage. . . . In other words, we believe firmly in the existence of God, and we do not feel that saying so makes us sentimental or old-fashioned or unartistic."[39]

Hunter also linked God and country. He claimed that "the real hero is America" in outdoor dramas. The past, he said, was the source of the nation's character, but sadly, that past was "ignored and forgotten." The "very forces which shaped the American dream" — namely, "the devotion to freedom and democracy, the belief in the dignity of man, the sense of fair play, and above all the great American ability to laugh at itself" — had been discarded, he felt, by mainstream culture in the 1950s. It was up to outdoor drama to revive these forces.[40]

The claim that people had forgotten the narrative of white pioneers making their way in the wilderness may seem bewildering, as it is the most dominant trope of American history. It certainly was so in the 1950s, well before textbooks began including perspectives from women, immigrants, Indigenous peoples, or Black Americans. But ideals must be said to be lost before they can be triumphantly resurrected. Resurrection also gives Christian undertones to a political project. Heller's *Shepherd of the Hills* fit perfectly into Hunter's God-and-country schema for outdoor drama. It took on a melancholy tone in bemoaning that urban, modern America had lost its moral compass and suggested that witnessing live performance in a wilderness setting could transport audiences to a better past, where the values of a rural, Christian, (white) nation reigned triumphant.

Cosmopolitan centers woke up to the phenomenon of outdoor drama belatedly and with mild, sporadic interest. In 1970, *New York Times* journalist Frances Shemanski wrote that outdoor dramas were "The Heartland's Answer to Broadway," but elaborated little.[41] Five years later, William Glover in the *Hartford Courant* wrote, "the grassroots array bears little resemblance to professional Broadway formalism. Nobody, however, any longer doubts the public appeal and economic clout of what many now regard as America's most original theatrical innovation."[42] While urban critics acknowledged the popularity of outdoor dramas, they did not value them enough to review or consider their cultural impact in any detail.

Yet that impact was significant. Writers and directors presented a vision of the nation that glorified white, Christian pioneers and claimed to represent the core spiritual and moral values of real America. There was no doubt whom these outdoor dramas were for, either. While technically open to anyone with the means to buy a ticket — and ticket prices were modest or even free — the target audience was assumed to be white. This assumption was made explicit in a 1977 letter from Ted Cramer of the North Carolina Department of Cultural Resources to the director of the Institute for Outdoor Drama. The Institute wanted productions to capture 15 percent of the state population, but Cramer complained about the statistical methods used to determine that. He wrote, "It is not reasonable to use 'total' population because it includes children, the very elderly, and blacks, who make up a large percentage of the southeast population."[43] The 15 percent goal was easier to achieve when the "market" was defined more narrowly — that is, white, middle-aged adults. The director agreed, and presumably the Institute adjusted its methods.[44] Black Americans indeed did not attend these outdoor dramas, and in a vicious cycle, were not considered a potential market for them — thus further excluding them from this genre that boosters claimed was the most original American theatrical innovation and one that preserved the essence of American values.

Among the nation's outdoor dramas, *Shepherd of the Hills* made a durable impression. Five thousand visitors came in that first 1960 season. The next summer, there were 25,000 people. In 1962, the Trimbles had to start turning people away from the 500-seat theater. In 1966, they doubled the seating capacity. The cast size had doubled by then too, with over eighty locals participating. In 1967, *Shepherd* was the fourth-most-attended outdoor theater in the United States and "indisputably" the fastest-growing one, with a 40 percent increase in attendance that year, leading the Trimbles to increase seating capacity again, to 1,500. By 1973, *Shepherd* was the most popular outdoor drama in the country, attracting 151,000 visitors that year, and stayed on top for almost a decade. By the 1980s, *Shepherd* regularly drew almost a quarter of a million people annually.[45]

But an entire tourist industry could not be built upon one show alone, especially not one that started at dusk. Visitors needed something to do in the daytime. The second foundational pillar of Branson entertainment to open that summer was a theme park called Silver Dollar City, just across the county line in Stone County. Once

The Shepherd of the Hills, ca. 1980. Courtesy White River Valley Historical Society.

again, it was a widow named Mary and, in this case, two sons who successfully created performances of frontier folk. And once again, Lloyd Heller helped set the stage.

Silver Dollar City

In 1950, Mary Herschend sobbed throughout the 600-mile car ride from the suburbs of Chicago to rural Stone County, Missouri. She had finally achieved the American dream — she was a happily married housewife — and now it seemed to be receding in her rearview mirror. On a family vacation to the Missouri Ozarks a few years earlier, her husband Hugo had fallen in love with a tourist attraction called Marvel Cave and hatched a plan to operate it as a retirement project. The owners, two elderly sisters, were tired of slithering on their stomachs in the mud to guide tours and eagerly agreed to get the business off their hands. Hugo signed a ninety-nine-year lease, and in 1950, the Herschends left their well-appointed suburban home, surrounded by family, for a cabin that lacked electricity or indoor plumbing, in a place where they knew almost nobody.[46]

Mary quickly dried her tears, rolled up her sleeves, and got busy selling Marvel Cave. For the next five years, she built up the business while Hugo stayed in Chicago to work for the Electrolux Corporation—retirement was still a distant dream. She and her sons Pete and Jack renovated the cave entrance, built a tramway at the exit, hired locals to run the tours, and drummed up publicity. They sponsored square dances in the magnificent underground Cathedral Room, which was the size of a football field. Forty couples danced at one time on a large wooden floor while the caller, the band, and onlookers stood on additional platforms. Electric lights, microphones, and speakers dotted the space, demonstrating the tremendous effort exerted to equip a cave with the latest technology to promote an old-fashioned mode of Ozarks social life. The Herschends also purchased 640 acres surrounding Marvel Cave to keep the bucolic wilderness intact, even as they furiously worked to modernize.[47]

Then, in 1955, Hugo died suddenly of a blood clot to the heart. The tragedy did not deter Mary, who had by then shed her housewife role thoroughly. She, Pete, and Jack kept brainstorming ways to expand the business. Hugo had always envisioned a crafts market at the entrance to the cave, but the plan had never materialized. A more fleshed-out idea came from Russell Pearson, a carnival man. He wandered his way to Marvel Cave in 1958 and pitched an Ozarks version of the "Frontier City" theme park he had recently built in Oklahoma. The Herschends agreed, as they felt that bored tourists needed something to do while they waited for their turn to descend into the cave.[48]

To build the park, the Herschends brought on professional help. The first publicity manager and first designer were Don Richardson and Andy Miller, respectively, both from the hit television show *Ozark Jubilee*, which was recorded in nearby Springfield, Missouri. Richardson came up with the name of Silver Dollar City for the park and the marketing idea to give guests change in silver dollars, which they would then spend at gas stations and convenience stores on their drives home as a form of word-of-mouth advertising. Miller was the "theme conscience," making sure that each new building fit cohesively with the 1880s Ozarks village concept they developed and that this 1880s theme carried through in all marketing materials.[49]

The idea of a theme conscience came from Walt Disney, who revolutionized the amusement park industry when he opened Disneyland in Anaheim, California, in 1955. By the mid-twentieth century, amusement parks had garnered a reputation as seedy sites of urban chaos and crime. Disney introduced the idea of a "theme park," where homogeneity, harmony, and orderliness ruled the day.[50] His primary inspiration? Small-town Missouri. Disney had lived in Marceline, Missouri, as a child in the early 1900s. He would always remember those years as the most magical of his life, when small business owners along the town's main street greeted him with friendly smiles and he spent hours watching trains pull in and out of the town's railroad depot. This idyllic life rudely ended at age nine when his family relocated to Kansas City, a bustling urban metropolis for which Disney felt little love.[51] He never forgot that image of small-town America, frozen in time as he experienced it as a happy child. Disney resurrected Marceline as Main Street, USA, at the entrance to Disneyland. In an ode to free-market entrepreneurship, Main Street was lined with independent businesses, including a pharmacy and a glass shop. Employees called "Citizens" dressed in early twentieth-century garb and chatted with visitors. Train whistles pierced the air from the reduced-scale steam engine that chugged by. Off to the right — namely, West — visitors could travel to Frontierland, where Disney located the American pioneer spirit.[52]

Silver Dollar City went a step further than Disneyland. Instead of a Missouri Main Street transplanted to suburban California, the Herschends built their Missouri Main Street upon the literal ashes of an actual Missouri main street. A man named Henry T. Blow had set the wheels in motion. Blow is most well known for being the son of the original owners of Dred Scott, the slave who sued his subsequent owner, John Emerson, for his family's freedom and lost at the Supreme Court in 1857. Blow himself was an abolitionist who contributed to the Scotts' legal fees and promptly freed the Scotts when Emerson's widow deeded the family to him. In his more minor historical role as an entrepreneur, in 1869 Blow hired a team to search for lead deposits in an Ozarks cave that local Osage Indians had called Devil's Den. The prospectors failed to find lead, but they renamed the cavern Marble Cave after they mistook its limestone white surfaces for marble. In 1884, Union Army veterans from Lamar, Missouri, filed articles of incorporation for the Marble Cave Mining and Manufacturing Company and established Marble City, also known as Marmaros.[53] Finding the cave's mineral deposits worthless, they pivoted to extracting bat guano, used in fertilizer and gunpowder. They shut down the mine in 1889 when the guano ran out. Residents abandoned the town, and most buildings burned down in a forest fire a year later.[54] The Lynch family bought the cave and renamed it Marvel Cave in the early 1900s to attract tourists, but the town was mostly forgotten about until the Herschends' resurrection. Their Main Street included a general store, a blacksmith shop, a gazette print shop that printed a daily town paper, and the Stage Coach Inn. Forking off from the main thoroughfare, they placed two relocated nineteenth-century buildings: the Wilderness Church (formerly a schoolhouse) and the McHaffie Homestead, which dated from 1843.[55]

Because the Herschends built Silver Dollar City (hereafter SDC) on the actual grounds of a Missouri village, they drew inspiration not only from Disneyland, but also from heritage sites like Colonial Williamsburg and Plimoth Plantation, which were gaining popularity in the 1950s as leisure travel increased.[56] The Main Street buildings were not simply façades but fully functional replicas at seven-eighths size. Presumably this scaling down made the town feel quainter and more accessible to children, while also saving money on materials.[57] The Herschends placed horse collars, plows, wagons, dishes, and other late nineteenth-century items around the town to create "atmosphere." Employees, called "Citizens" (most likely borrowed from Disney), wore 1880s-style clothing made from period materials; they spoke in dialect and used old-timey vocabulary. Those hired as blacksmiths, wood carvers, and basket weavers used tools and methods of the late nineteenth century. Mary Herschend, a kind of proto-environmentalist, was "adamant" that no trees be removed unless absolutely necessary.[58] But the Herschends didn't take it too far. They did not hire professional historians or advertise SDC as an educational institution. In fact, they claimed to avoid the "often pretentious historical re-creation of other frontier villages" and the dour atmosphere of "musty museums."[59] It was a middle ground, both geographically and conceptually, between Disneyland's orderly fantasy on the West Coast and the ostensibly educational heritage sites on the East Coast.

What contributed to SDC's success the most was not the architecture, the horseshoes, or the fact of Marmaros's historical existence. It was the visitor's experience of interacting with SDC's Citizen-employees. Therefore, bringing on Lloyd Heller was key. He rang the bell on opening day as mayor of Silver Dollar City. He at one point played the sheriff, too, greeting guests with "Welcome to Silver Dollar City, where the hands of the clock have turned back and people actually relax and enjoy themselves."[60] He played a quack doctor who appeared in medicine man shows. Most enduringly, he played a blacksmith named Shad. Sparks flew from his anvil, but more importantly, he offered a constant stream of storytelling. Tourists were welcome to "visit a spell" in his blacksmith shop and made to feel like they were part of a slower, Ozarkian sociality. They laughed as he bantered daily with Peter Engler, the woodcarver across the way. He melded into his role so deeply that his tombstone reads Lloyd "Shad" Heller.[61]

Publicity emphasized the excitement of the live interactions at SDC. The first press release in April 1960 stated that SDC was "not a ghost town or strictly a museum, but a 'living Ozark Village.'" It also falsely claimed that one of the original settlers of Marmaros was the shepherd from *Shepherd of the Hills*, and that a pioneer family had once minted silver there.[62] Press releases were sent to Missouri newspapers and to the nationwide American Automobile

Association, which featured SDC in its newsletter. SDC also got a big boost from the Ozark Playgrounds Association, an organization that promoted tourism. In statements to the press, the Association's executive director affirmed that the theme park was "entirely different" because the Herschends' creation was "alive with action."[63] That action included not only locals portraying 1880s frontiersmen, but also current celebrities. With Richardson's *Ozark Jubilee* connections, SDC procured two of the television show's beloved characters, Uncle Cyp and Aunt Sap Brasfield, to perform on opening day. Cyp and Sap had gotten their start on the tent show circuit. Cyp was even named "King of Tobys" during the 1920s for his superbly comedic portrayal of the rube character before moving on to the *Grand Ole Opry* radio show and eventually *Ozark Jubilee*.[64]

The promotions worked even beyond the Herschends' expectations. On opening day of May 1, 1960, the line of cars waiting to enter the parking lot stretched for a full mile. Eighteen thousand people from twenty-two states waited patiently for their chance to purchase a pound of coffee ground "grandma's way" and catch a glimpse of the Brasfields engaging in exaggerated, comedic hillbilly antics.[65] Even when the celebrities left the following day, visitors returned. It soon became clear that SDC was the main attraction rather than the side hustle to Marvel Cave. In 1961, the number of visitors climbed to 250,000. In 1965, three-quarters of a million people walked along the expanded Main Street, which now included a miner's shack, candy shop, barbershop, gunsmith, photo gallery, music shop, livery stable, haunted house, sorghum mill, and grist mill with running water.[66] The parking lot was relocated, and the Herschends added green spaces back in over the concrete. Three years later, they opened their first roller-coaster ride, called Flooded Mine, and started charging admission. Thus began Silver Dollar City's slow evolution into an amusement park, as bigger and faster roller coasters were yet to come.

In 1969, Silver Dollar City got a major boost by being featured on *The Beverly Hillbillies*. Publicity director Richardson had a connection to the television show's producer, Paul Henning, who decided to

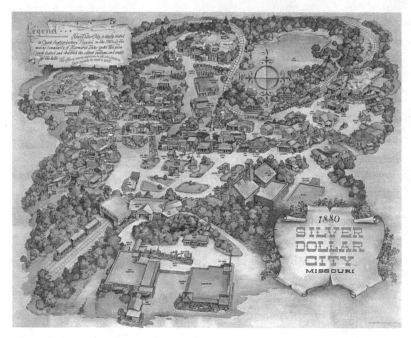

Map of Silver Dollar City, 1973. Courtesy Curtis Wright Maps.

make SDC the hometown of the show's multigenerational fictional family. In the first episode of season eight, Granny Clampett declares that the family must head back to "God's country" to find a suitable husband for Elly May. In episode 2, they arrive in Silver Dollar City, "Population 28," and encounter Shad Heller. They stay at the inn on Main Street and attend the "Silver Dollar City Fair" to secure a suitor. Hijinks ensue during the next three episodes, which double as an extended advertisement for the park. The Clampetts watch square dancers, weave baskets, dip candles, tour the mill, visit the Wilderness Church, and help stage a medicine man show.[67] The tourist season following these episodes saw explosive growth, with visitation up 19 percent. As one out-of-town reporter noted wryly, Silver Dollar City was a place where "the birds and cash registers make sweet music together."[68] The theme park had arrived in the national popular consciousness.

By that time, Heller had spent years training the Citizens in how to perform for tourists. When June Ward began working at the candy shop in 1968, Heller told her, "You're making candy and you're selling candy, but you are in the entertainment business. Don't ever forget that."[69] College student Jae McFerron got a summer job as a street performer in the early 1970s. "My life changed when I met Shad," he said. Street-show bits had to be repeated several times a day, and the elder actor coached McFerron in how to keep such performances fresh by interjecting improvisation. One bit McFerron did was called "rainmaker." Once an hour, he would ride around the park in a mule-pulled wagon bedecked with bells, whistles, and noisemakers to draw a crowd. He eventually gathered the visitors beneath the shot tower — a literal tower where Silver Dollar City made bullets *en masse* by dropping molten lead from forty feet in the air through screens to land in a pan of water — and began his performance. He brought children from the audience up onto the wagon, joked with them, and then, on cue, had a fellow employee press a button to dump water from the tower onto the crowd. "It would catch them flat footed every time; they just couldn't believe [it]," said McFerron, laughing.[70]

Not all bits were planned, especially not in the early years. In spring 1962, Ella Mae Tucker got a job working in the photo studio on Main Street. For eight hours a day, five days a week, she took pictures of park visitors dressed in 1880s costumes and props. Near the end of the summer season, Ruth Heller (also an employee of SDC) swooped into Ella's photo studio dressed as a brothel madam: bright-orange skirt, red fox fur, "lots of rouge and lipstick." The park patrons froze as she "squalled out in a loud dance hall-girl voice, 'Ellie, am I glad to find you . . . Honey, you sure got out of St. Louis just in time! They closed me up!'" Heller's improvised antics continued as she begged Ella Mae for a job, dumped an empty whiskey bottle out of her purse, and claimed that she had "loaded dice" for Ella Mae's husband Byron, who worked in the print shop. The guests stared in shock, uncertain whether Heller was being "real" or not. Byron turned "purple" and "choked with hysterics," but Heller "didn't miss a beat." She pranced out the door and continued to improvise mayhem across the park. That day, Ella wrote, "everybody play[ed] tricks on everybody else . . . a gay, mad place — no one [knew] what to expect, and enjoy[ed] it."[71]

Performance created a feeling of utopia, a sense of possibility not accessible in everyday life. Just putting on a costume "ma[d]e all the difference," said JoDee Remien, who worked at SDC in the early 1960s. "You could talk to people in a different way, tease them, and they would respond in a different way."[72] McFerron recalled that visitors "loved the brash characters that they would run into. I remember thinking, 'Well, I can just about say anything to these people, and they just think it's incredible.'"[73] Reporter Art Gorlick from Chicago wrote about his visit, "Folks for miles around seem to slip back to the late 1800's and revive the friendly atmosphere of what was then an American frontier."[74] Brochures marketed the park as "Our Nation's Reunion with Its Past."[75] As at *Shepherd of the Hills*, visitors could literally touch and interact with people representing that past, making it come to life.

In recreating the 1880s frontier, the Herschends had to figure out how to turn the violence that dominated that decade into family-friendly entertainment. The first strategy was to make violence comedic. The most popular "atmosphere" performance at Silver Dollar City was the Hatfield-McCoy Feud, which happened on Main Street at the top of every hour. The historic Hatfields and McCoys lived on the border between Kentucky and West Virginia and engaged in a multigenerational feud from 1863 to 1891. Members of the families brutally murdered each other, leaving bodies full of bullets and houses burned to the ground. Depicted multiple times in film and on television, the Hatfields and McCoys became the epitome of negative hillbilly stereotypes. The feud thus posed a potential risk to the image of Ozarkers as virtuous rural folk, but it attracted visitors by being familiar.

The SDC sketch focused on the star-crossed lovers aspect of the feud. Zekey Hatfield and Sarey Ellen McCoy's romance set off a chain reaction of shouts, threats, and gunshots. No barricade marked off the space of performance. Instead, park visitors crowded in, standing merely feet away from the dispute. Hearing the deafening shots (albeit from blanks) and smelling the acrid smoke heightened the sense of realism, but other aspects countered it with slapstick comedy. The performers spoke in thick mountain accents to imply backwardness and a lack of education. Physical antics were also key. After her son was shot, Ma Hatfield would squat over his body in an unladylike pose. She would immodestly hitch up her skirt and stick her rear end out farther than necessary. With a corncob pipe in her mouth — a typically masculine prop — she would stare intently as a country doctor got down on his hands and knees to place his ear on Zekey's heart. The doctor, supposedly one of the richest men in town, had a ripped suit jacket and cartoonishly long mustache. He also ended up in an undignified pose on the ground.[76]

Another violent entertainment was the train robbery. In 1962, the Herschends purchased a small three-car train formerly owned by car magnate Henry Ford. It had a working steam engine, open-air coach for seventy-five passengers, and caboose. The Frisco Silver Dollar Line, as it was called, wound around a few thousand feet of track through wooded areas of the property. This was the first "ride" at the park, and its success paved the way for more.[77] Multiple times a day, employees portrayed infamous bushwhacker Alf Bolin and his gang, who would hold up tourists on the train. The idea first materialized because the train needed to pause to rebuild steam, and thus the Herschends needed some way to entertain the guests while they waited. Portrayed as "ruffians" (implying a certain level of harmlessness), Bolin and his gang were "clumsy" and never success-ful in their robbery attempts, though they did fire off several rounds. In real life, Bolin murdered over thirty people.[78] Area newspapers reported on the influence of this spectacle. In October 1963, a grand-mother prepared to take her three-year-old grandson on a train trip from Springfield, Missouri, to Fort Scott, Kansas. She noticed that the boy was "unaccountably worried." Finally, he came out with it. "Granny, will I get shot?" he asked anxiously. "No, they don't shoot people on the train," she assured him, wondering where in the world he had gotten such an idea. "They do down at Silver Dollar City," he replied promptly.[79] A daily robbery also occurred at the General Store on Main Street. Bad guys wielding guns would hold up the clerk, she would run to the front porch and yell that she had been robbed, and "the chase was on." In 1965, the Herschends built an armory to house all the weaponry needed, having used 22,000 rounds of ammunition in the previous season.[80]

The Flooded Mine ride, a staple of the SDC experience since its opening in 1968, also emphasizes violence. Visitors climb into six-person barges that float on a river through the "Lucky Silver Mine," modeled after late nineteenth-century Missouri mines that used prisoner labor. Over the course of 530 feet of the ride, tourists witness animatronic convict laborers attempt to escape the flood-waters. In the 1980s, the Herschends added laser pistols to the ride, which visitors fired at targets to help the warden prevent escapees.[81]

The violence in Flooded Mine is meant to be funny. The animatronic figures have exaggerated extra-wide grimaces and grins. Their bodies have elongated, floppy limbs, more like scarecrows or rag dolls than realistic mannequins. One prisoner, waist-deep in water, continuously spits an arc of water out of his mouth like a Roman fountain. Another prisoner hangs from his wrists, modeled on a punishment used at the Missouri State Penitentiary in the late nineteenth century called "the rings." A sign next to him states, pun intended, "Sentenced to hang for 187 days." In another tableau, a grinning ward sits in a cage like a zoo animal with a sign that reads "DO NOT FEED THIS PRISONER." Two guards play poker at a table to the side of the cage, utterly indifferent to their captive.[82]

The gallows humor distances the visitors from the brutal history of convict labor, but the comedy sits in tension with the realism of the ride. Between 1964 and 1967, the Herschends purchased equipment from lead and zinc mines that had recently been shut down in Oklahoma.[83] They filled the ride's elaborate panoramas with wheels, pickaxes, jackhammers, shovels, mine cars, pumping stations, and pulleys. Boxes labeled "TNT" or "Danger—Explosives" proliferated. The punishments depicted were historically accurate to those used in Missouri prisons. This realism likens the ride to "dark tourism" sites such as prisons and concentration camps, but many of those places designate that they are not for children.[84] Flooded Mine, instead, is pitched as family-friendly, harmless fun.

In the 1960s, a decade looked back upon as one dominated by the civil rights movement, the feminist movement, the anti–Vietnam War movement, and youth rebellions against cultural norms in general, the numbers at Silver Dollar City kept climbing. Crystal Payton, author of *The Story of Silver Dollar City*, asserts a connection: "The social and political turbulence of the civil rights and anti-war movements not only did not hurt attendance, it just may have helped. . . . Headline America may have been a quarrelsome place in the 1960s, but those who didn't live in the headline world, and they were many, found respite from the fray in [SDC's] programming and experiences."[85]

We do not have testimonials from park visitors in the 1960s to back up such assertions, but it was true that SDC had attracted notice for what it had to offer beyond entertainment. A region that had always been one of the most impoverished in the United States was building a solid future via selling a specific vision of the past. In 1968, Mary Herschend won the Missouri Businessman of the Year Award (a gendered title that caused chuckles among her family).[86] She officially entered the US Congressional Record in 1969 when her district's representative in Washington, Durward G. Hall, lauded her for being "a creator and builder" who "used her womanly intuition and charm to create a city" that had become "famous for its warm hospitality and country-flavored friendliness."[87] Hall's praises implied their opposites: Herschend was a builder (not a destroyer, like rioters); she used womanly intuition and charm (not tactics from the feminist movement) to traverse the male-dominated world of business; and Silver Dollar City was hospitable and friendly (not hostile like anti-war protesters).

Mary Herschend was the kind of person that Richard Nixon courted in his 1968 presidential campaign. In his speech accepting the Republican nomination, he invoked a new imagined community: the "forgotten Americans," the "non-shouters," whom he claimed represented the majority of the country. While rioters and protesters on the Left were his obvious counterpoints, he was also invoking a contrast to his third-party challenger, former Alabama governor George Wallace, who had famously roared "segregation now, segregation forever" on the steps of Alabama's state capitol in 1963. Nixon's advisor Kevin Phillips developed an election strategy that emphasized "opposition to big government more than anything else," with racial language now coded.[88] Nixon argued that Johnson's Great Society programs robbed citizens of the dignity of hard work; he also emphasized law and order. Nixon "made no promises" to the Southern wing of the GOP to campaign in the Deep South against Wallace. Instead, Nixon focused his attention on the upper South and border states like Missouri.[89]

Missouri's Seventh District, which comprised Stone, Taney, and eight other Ozark counties, had alternated between electing Republican and Democratic representatives to the US Congress since the days of the Civil War, emblematic of its border-region-within-a-border-state status. Beginning in 1936, however, the Seventh District exclusively supported Republican presidential candidates. Opposition to Roosevelt's New Deal programs had tilted the balance. And it would turn out that 1958 was the last year the district elected a Democratic representative. Nixon needed to get out the vote here if he wanted a chance to win Missouri, a "bellwether" state that could go either way. In September 1968, Mary Herschend waited on an airport tarmac in Springfield to greet the Republican presidential nominee. She stood by his side on the dais as he gave his campaign speech. The front page of the local newspaper featured her endorsement of Nixon: "It is very necessary that all the Stone and Taney County residents get out and back this man. The future of America is at stake in this election."[90] Nixon won the district, the state, and the presidency later that year.

Nestled in the bucolic Ozark Mountains, far from the urban centers where riots and protests were happening, society was seemingly not out of control. Instead, it was contained. Every hour on the hour, Alf Bolin bungled a train robbery and hillbillies shot the pants off each other. These acts were cleansed of any stain of the real world's violent conflicts. In 1969, Hall stated that the theme park was "a reminder that despite the rush and unrest of our world today, the spirit and spice left to us by our ancestry still permeate the air and the 1880 way of life lives on."[91]

The sticking point remained that the people portraying that past were very much contemporary citizens. As the tourism industry in Branson grew, it became ever more dependent on residents continuing to perform as their own ancestors. Ella Mae and Byron Tucker were amused when outsiders came looking for "real" hillbillies. One day in the late fall of 1961, a couple from Iowa wandered into their real estate office with that goal. Ella Mae "tried to explain that, actually, they were talking to a couple of hillbillys," but the couple was not convinced by their modern clothes and normal, sober workplace. "I should maybe have kicked off my shoes and brought out a jug for Byron," she wrote.[92]

She could have directed them to downtown Branson to see the *Baldknobbers Hillbilly Jamboree*, a show by the Mabe family. There, "real" hillbillies performed, not as characters from a 1907 novel or an abandoned 1880s village, but as themselves. The Mabes were not outsiders like Harold Bell Wright, the Trimbles, the Herschends, or Heller, but rather a family with multigenerational roots in the Ozarks. "Without Silver Dollar City, there would be no Branson," publicist Lisa Rau has stated bluntly.[93] While perhaps true, it was not only *Shepherd of the Hills* or Silver Dollar City that made the city the multibillion-dollar tourist destination it is today. It was also locals who added live music, dance, and comedy to give visitors an even greater in-depth emotional experience, packaged in a powerful presentation of what conservatives saw as the most important social unit: the family. It was time for the hillbilly variety show.

3 FAMILY

The Hillbilly Variety Show

On June 30, 1967, twenty-year-old Gary Presley (no relation to Elvis) did not put on a tie-dyed t-shirt to participate in the iconic "Summer of Love." He did not participate in any of the more than 150 rebellions against racism and police brutality erupting in cities across America. He did not set foot on a college campus to protest the Vietnam War or join a meeting of the Students for a Democratic Society. Instead, he donned his grandfather's oversized overalls, plopped a broken straw hat on his head, and blacked out several of his teeth with an eyebrow pencil to transform himself into Herkimer, a hillbilly. He stepped onto the stage alongside his father and three siblings for the opening night of the *Mountain Music Jubilee* on Highway 76 outside Branson. One year later, four brothers — Bill, Bob, Lyle, and Jim Mabe — built a theater across the road to mount the *Baldknobbers Hillbilly Jamboree*, a show they had first performed in a downtown municipal building in 1959. The famed "Strip" was born.

While *The Shepherd of the Hills* and Silver Dollar City were initially the most popular entertainment attractions in Branson, the Presleys and Mabes created the model for a "Bransonized" show format that would come to dominate the Strip. The Bransonized show followed the mantra of faith, family, and flag; family was at the center. "The greatest compliment our fans have ever given is . . . letting our family entertain their families," the Presleys have said. "Our show has always been about our family entertaining your family," said Tim Mabe.[1] Numerous Branson entertainers have carried the sentiment forward through the decades, including the Plummers, the Osmonds, the Braschlers, the Wilkinson Brothers, the Lennon Sisters, the Lennon Brothers, the Lowe Sisters, the Duttons, the Brett Family, the Hughes Brothers, the Haygoods, the Petersens, and many, many more. In 2019, Missouri governor Mike Parson offered an official proclamation honoring the Mabes for sixty years of "le[ading] the way in providing clean, family entertainment for all ages to respect and enjoy." He noted at the recognition ceremony, "I came here tonight because I believe that family values are so important in our country today."[2]

What are family values? In theory, any type of family could promote any set of values it wants, but the phrase "family values" has come to represent a specific ideal: a unit consisting of a heterosexual married couple who respect distinct gender roles and raise children who obey their parents. The cohering of this phrase began in the 1960s, when many Americans reacted to social justice movements not with pride but with horror, believing that civil rights, feminism, and anti-war efforts had frayed traditional family bonds. By the 1970s, the idea that family values were under siege had gained traction. Political leaders founded institutions such as Focus on the Family (1977), the National Federation for Decency (1977; later the American Family Association), the Traditional Values Coalition (1980), and the Family Research Council (1983). Family values became rhetorical glue that held together seemingly distinct constituencies: evangelical Christians who believed in God-given biological gender roles; fiscal conservatives who proclaimed that federal programs like welfare intruded on family responsibility; anti-Communists who saw the heterosexual nuclear family as the bulwark of the American way of life; and opponents of the civil rights movement who found "family values" a useful colorblind phrase for their arguments against school desegregation. Family values thus helped weave various strands of American conservatism into an ideology

Clay Cooper Theatre marquee, Branson, Missouri, May 12, 2022. Photo by author.

that aligned with the Republican Party by the 1980s.[3] The movement needed more than lobbyists and think tanks to be successful, however. It needed broad cultural support.

One of those supports came from country music. Country music had historically attracted listeners from across the political spectrum, but in the 1960s, concerted efforts began to link the genre with the political right. Within the county music industry, the Branson family variety show has played an important and heretofore largely unrecognized role in reinforcing the family values component of a conservative worldview. Like the performers at Silver Dollar City or *The Shepherd of the Hills*, the Mabes, Presleys, and other Branson family entertainers make ideology come to life as everyday common sense. They have asserted that their performances aren't performances at all. As Branson headliner Clay Cooper would proclaim as his tagline in the 2020s, these families are just "Real People Havin' a Real Good Time!"

This process of representing family values via live entertainment has not been seamless. Americans have long stereotyped performers as sexually loose, immoral, and financially irresponsible. The jobs demand work on nights and weekends, which are normatively times dedicated to child-rearing. Many entertainers travel much of the year, lacking a fixed "home" seen as essential to the nuclear family. Performers are associated with nightlife venues deemed unsuitable for children, the elderly, or even married people. Furthermore, the theater is associated with queer sexuality. For the family values movement, heterosexual married couples and their offspring are the foundation of a strong nation; other sexual orientations represent a threat. Even the model that Branson initially presented onstage — a hillbilly family — was suspect. Stereotypes about hillbilly families include lazy and violent patriarchs, manly women, and unkempt children. Many jokes about hillbilly families involve incest and bestiality. There was a reason the country music industry tried to distance itself from the hillbilly image in 1940s. Finally, no family can perfectly match an ideological ideal. Staking one's brand on fidelity to family values is risky. Branson's performing families were not immune to the troubles of families nationwide: divorce, alcoholism, drug abuse, financial distress, and other issues. Starting in the 1960s, however, they polished themselves up as shining exemplars of family values for the rest of the nation.

The Beginning

There is a remarkable similarity in the Mabe and Presley families' origin stories. The patriarchs, Orville Presley, born in 1890, and Don L. Mabe, born in 1902, had dropped out of school in fifth and seventh grades, respectively, to work as farm laborers in the Ozarks. They both struggled financially. In 1930, Presley owned his own farm and was a retail merchant, but the Great Depression hit the family hard. By 1940, Presley was an unemployed renter who reported only $200 in annual income.[4] Mabe drove a school bus and took on additional work building roads. While this meant the Mabes were slightly more prosperous, they had eleven children to feed. Bob Mabe, born in 1930, remembers growing up poor in a house with no running water. The outhouse jokes in the Baldknobbers stage show years later were based on experience.[5]

Don Mabe and Orville Presley also shared the call to ministry. Mabe pastored at a Southern Baptist congregation, and Presley started one of the first Assemblies of God churches. Assemblies of God was a variant of Pentecostalism. The Pentecostal revival, which was galvanized by the Azusa Street Movement in Los Angeles in 1906, was notably interracial and led by a Black preacher, William J. Seymour. It combined West African and Protestant Christian religious practices; Pentecostals emphasize a relationship with the Holy Spirit, and worshippers express that relationship through their bodies — speaking in tongues, singing for hours, physically demonstrating "gifts of the Spirit," and performing "acts of divine healing and miracles."[6] Yet as Pentecostalism spread throughout the country, it adapted to the entrenched segregation that governed American life. In 1914, some 300 white Pentecostal ministers met in Hot Springs, Arkansas, to establish the Assemblies of God denomination as essentially a way to continue Pentecostal worship, but without Black leadership.[7] Presley, just across the state line in Missouri, joined this movement.

Regardless of denomination, religious services functioned as entertainment in the Ozarks. Preachers were expected to perform with charisma. Assemblies of God in particular maintained the Pentecostal emphasis on experiencing the Holy Spirit in one's body. The Presley and Mabe children sang multiple times a week in church and learned from their fathers how to captivate audiences. The matriarchs had an influence as well. Presley's wife Mamie played harmonica in the home until "eventually her arm would just give out," and Mabe's wife Hazel was known as the "funny" one in the family, teaching her sons the rhythm of comedy, such as how to time throwing flour in someone's face.[8]

The Mabes and Presleys also were influenced by the variety-show tradition of the Ozarks that dated to the post–Civil War era, especially medicine shows and Toby Shows. Though Ozark audiences for such entertainments were virtually all white, the cultural material was not. Performers mixed Tin Pan Alley songs, Broadway hits, blues, and gospel hymns. Black and white musicians throughout the Upper South played the same instruments (fiddles, banjos, guitars, harmonicas), employed similar vocal techniques, and appeared in the same types of venues. An all-white Toby Show ensemble performed Scott Joplin's ragtime hits; the Black pianist John William "Blind" Boone toured the Ozarks playing everything from plantation melodies to Beethoven. The dancing emphasized acrobatics, visual jokes such as rubber legs and pratfalls, and tap/jig dancing, all of which had shared roots in minstrel shows and, before that, both Black and white social dances.[9]

In the early twentieth century, folklorists and recording industry producers worked to segregate such cultural practices and give them new labels. Folk preservationists such as George Peabody, Olive Dame Campbell, Cecil Sharp, and Alan and John Lomax descended on the South to collect songs that they aimed to define as traditional music. They insisted that authenticity came from racially segregated groups who sang on their front porches or out in the fields, whereas those who performed for pay under tents were inherently corrupted by a mongrel, for-profit popular culture.[10] The folklore movement gained such widespread support that "the concept of authenticity grew nearly intractable roots" by the mid-twentieth century. The legacy of minstrelsy was so deeply ingrained in popular theatrical performances that many Black political leaders welcomed the idea of an authentic, pure Black culture that existed separately from commercial entertainment.[11] Other influential proponents of the folklore movement, like Henry Ford, aimed to prove that the white Southern culture had pure Anglo-Saxon or Scotch-Irish roots. Ford promoted square dancing and fiddling to combat "unnatural" and "twisted" urban culture, which he deemed had been perverted by Black, Jewish, and immigrant influences.[12] The authenticity discourse has endured. In 1959, as part of the nascent folk music revival, the bluegrass band the Osborne Brothers played a gig at Antioch College. They prepared their usual mixed repertoire, which included comedic banter, gospel songs, and country star George Jones's hit "White Lightning," but the college students reacted negatively. They wanted "authentic" folk music. The band quickly adapted, as did subsequent bluegrass groups participating in the largely urban and college-based revival movement.[13] In 1997, the director of the Smithsonian Institution's annual Festival of American Folklore in Washington, DC, reiterated the distinction that "The entertainment industry today dominates popular views of culture . . . [but] there is another world of culture created and sustained in homes, communities, places of work and worship."[14] For preservationists and intellectuals, the world of commerce and the world of the folk remain separate.

But for performers and much of their audiences, the line between commercial entertainment and folk culture remained as blurry in the twentieth century as it had under the white canvas tents of the nineteenth century. Racial distinctions, however, hardened. The emerging recording industry divided Southern musicians by race in its catalogs to appease segregationists and create distinct marketing categories. Starting in the 1920s, records by white Southern artists were labeled as hillbilly music, and records by Black Southern artists as race records. Eventually, the categories would become country music and rhythm and blues. In 1927, producer Ralph Peer recorded A. P. Carter, his wife Sara Carter, and A. P.'s sister-in-law Maybelle Addington Carter in Bristol, Tennessee. Whereas Jimmie Rodgers established country music's "rambling man," the Carters invoked "home, mother, and old-fashioned morality," a trinity upon which to base the family values mantra. It was also linked to a rural, white way of life. The Carter Family's music was dominated by nostalgia for vanishing rural America and the family values that were purportedly disappearing along with it.[15] Of course, rural America had been vanishing for so long by the 1920s that the Carters' elegiac tone was less a reaction to actual historical shifts and more an ideology: rural America was always already slipping away, and thus family values were always on the verge of disintegration.[16]

The new hillbilly category flourished on the radio. In 1924, the

National Barn Dance radio program began broadcasting out of Chicago. In 1925, the *WSM Barn Dance* (renamed *Grand Ole Opry* in 1927) broadcast live from Nashville. The name "barn dance" evoked a rural social gathering, but these shows were produced in cities. The programs mirrored the variety tent show format (popular songs, gospel, comedy), but they were advertised as traditional hillbilly music. Occasionally someone like Black harmonica player DeFord Bailey appeared on the *Grand Ole Opry*, but overwhelmingly the barn dance radio show was framed as white.[17]

The Presleys and Mabes grew up on this variety entertainment. In 1935, ten-year-old Lloyd Presley started playing a guitar that his older brother Don had gotten in a trade for a dog. He could not read music, but he learned to play by listening intently to the radio. He dropped out of school in the eighth grade, and with his brother Elwin on the harmonica, made money by performing on a flatbed truck at social events in the area.[18] Around the same time, one of the Mabe brothers began to play a rusty hand saw found in a "darkened corner of a milk barn" after recalling that he had seen such saws used as comic relief in variety shows.[19] Nobody took music, singing, dancing, or acting lessons. Bob Mabe grew up in a home that lacked indoor plumbing, but he learned to play three-string guitar from watching television variety programs.[20] Far from being isolated, anti-modern purveyors of rural, Anglo-Saxon traditions handed down from generation to generation, the Presleys and Mabes learned music and the rhythm of a successful variety show by paying close attention to popular media.

They were lucky to live near Springfield, Missouri, a major broadcasting center that briefly seemed like it would become the capital of country music. The *Korn's-A-Krackin'* barn dance show began in 1945 on Springfield's KWTO ("Keep Watching the Ozarks"), the radio station that launched the careers of Porter Wagoner and others. The show ended in 1949, but it inspired a new television program, *Ozark Jubilee*, which debuted locally in 1953. In 1954, KWTO executives recruited country music star Red Foley to headline the live broadcast from Springfield's Jewell Theatre. In 1955, ABC-TV bought the show, and *Ozark Jubilee* became the first regularly programmed country music show on a national network TV station.[21]

While successful, *Ozark Jubilee* was not enough to make Springfield stick. From the beginning, New York producers had scorned hillbilly music and attacked it as "culturally bad," largely to protect their own market share for Tin Pan Alley pop songs.[22] Their efforts were not entirely successful, as various factors — the great migration of Southerners between 1920 and 1960 and World War II, for starters — increased the popularity of hillbilly music, which became solidly identified with the working class. By the 1940s, industry leaders had renamed the genre Western music, with Gene Autry, the "Singing Cowboy," as its most iconic Hollywood figure. Guitars replaced fiddles and banjos; Western swing and honky-tonk styles dominated. Artists like Hank Williams followed after who created their own blends of hillbilly and Western sounds. In 1953, the industry settled on a new name that aimed to reflect the genre's nationwide appeal: country. Nashville eclipsed Springfield, growing in size, sophistication, and diversity in the 1950s and 1960s. The "Nashville Sound," which inflected country music with the smooth vocals and string music of mainstream pop, began to dominate. Few family groups enjoyed the success of the Carters, as individual artists became the norm.[23]

But the image of the hillbilly family as central to country music's cultural meanings endured, even if maligned and rhetorically marginalized. Branson families filled the gap left by Nashville. In the 1950s, Bob Mabe started performing on KWTO with the Blansit Trio, and Lloyd Presley formed a group called the Ozark Playboys. The Playboys played a live thirty-minute show, *Saturday Night Jamboree*, before the national broadcast of *Grand Ole Opry* on Springfield's KGBX radio. The exploding popularity of television in the 1950s, along with increased use of recorded music to cut costs, led Springfield radio stations to abandon their live programming in 1958. Bob Mabe suggested to his brothers Bill, Jim, and Lyle that they start their own in-person variety show. He recruited his friend Delbert Howard and his father-in-law Chick Allen to join. In

1959, the *Baldknobbers Hillbilly Jamboree*, named after the Ozarks' famed Bald Knobber vigilantes of the previous century, opened in a modest room with fifty folding chairs in Branson's main municipal building.[24]

With no marketing budget, audience recruitment for the *Baldknobbers* was tough at first. The Mabe wives would stand on street corners and hold homemade signs. One evening, only fourteen people showed up. Bob came out to say that they couldn't play for fewer than twenty people, but one couple who had traveled all the way from Iowa "almost cried" and said they would pay extra, so the show went on.[25] Appealing to families became a useful marketing strategy in a tourist region that had largely focused on masculine leisure pursuits such as fishing and boating on the White River. Bill joked that "if the fishermen brought their wives to the show, they got to stay and fish another day."[26] After the first year, the Mabes also performed at the new Silver Dollar City theme park and as the square-dance band in the *Shepherd of the Hills* outdoor melodrama. During winter months, they toured to high school auditoriums across the Midwest. All these efforts increased name recognition. After two years, the *Baldknobbers* moved to the Sammy Lane Pavilion, which seated 300 people, then in 1966 to a renovated skating rink that seated 600.[27]

The Presleys transitioned from radio to live performance as well. In 1962, promoter Loyd Evans invited Lloyd Presley and his four children Gary, Steve, Deanna, and Janice to perform in Springfield's Fantastic Caverns and Branson's Underground Theatre (now Talking Rocks) Cavern. The caves' cool temperatures were as much of a selling point as the entertainment. Most houses in the Ozarks lacked air-conditioning, and attending a cave show promised relief from the sweltering summer heat.

The Presleys' cave show included experiences never found in a typical theater. Herman Mead, who ran the concession stand, occasionally whipped out his pistol to shoot rats. Gary Presley recalled, "Here you are right in the middle of a gospel song, and suddenly a twenty-two pops off."[28] While theaters in the nineteenth century

Presleys' Mountain Music Theatre, original marquee, 1967. Courtesy Presleys' Country Jubilee.

could be rowdy and noisy, by the mid-twentieth century theaters were places where audiences remained quiet and ostensibly focused all attention on the action onstage.[29] To interrupt a moment of holy contemplation with a booming gunshot was a clear violation of "legitimate" theater norms. The Presleys share the rat-shooting anecdote in their 2008 promotional book *The Presley Family Story: The First Seventy-Four Years* because it adds to the narrative of their success, coming "out of the cave and into the limelight."[30] The implied amateurism of the cave performances makes their subsequent success seem even more impressive. The cave shows, however, were recorded and syndicated on radio throughout the Midwest, demonstrating that the Presleys were no mere amateurs. They handled technology sophisticated enough to get quality audio recording in a cave, even if the natural elements could not fully be controlled.

Radio play gave the Presleys a broader fan base. After a few years, they bought a ten-acre farm on Highway 76, three miles outside Branson city limits, and built a "metal box" theater with flat floors

Presleys' Mountain Music Theatre, 1967. Courtesy Presleys' Country Jubilee.

that could also function as a boat storage unit if performing didn't work out. On June 30, 1967, they premiered their live show, *Mountain Music Jubilee*. One year later, the Mabes joined the Presleys on the highway in a new 864-seat Baldknobbers Theatre.[31] As the assassinations of Dr. Martin Luther King Jr. and Senator Robert F. Kennedy rocked the nation, as cities burst into flames, as war raged in Vietnam, as presidential candidate Richard Nixon called his supporters the "forgotten Americans," a new era of Branson tourism began.

The Making of the Hillbilly Variety Show

What did these early shows look and sound like? First, both families leaned into the hillbilly persona. Even though country music had rebranded itself to distance itself from the negative stereotypes, the Presleys and Mabes determined that the benefits outweighed the drawbacks. They saw how many tourists had journeyed to Branson to see the rural folk of *The Shepherd of the Hills* and interact with characters at Silver Dollar City. As Gary Presley once stated, "When

The original Baldknobbers, ca. 1959. From left to right: Bill Mabe, Jim Mabe, Bob Mabe, Lyle Mabe, Delbert Howard, and Chick Allen. Courtesy Brandon Mabe.

you go to Hawaii, you want to see the Hula Girl. When you go to Branson, you want to see the hillbilly."[32] Unlike his racist, aggressive, Confederate-flag-waving cousin the "redneck," the hillbilly was a less confrontational white person, a figure tied to nature, simplicity, religion, and music. The folklorists of an earlier generation had written Black, Indigenous, and immigrant populations out of Ozarkian narratives, which lent the hillbilly an ahistorical racial innocence that suited new ideas about colorblindness that were developing among Southern institutions in the 1960s.[33]

An early *Baldknobbers* program states, "Each one of the group can lay claim to being a true Ozarks' 'Hillbilly' and their music reflects a heritage passed down through many generations of Ozarks' folklore."[34] Costumes and homemade-seeming instruments implied poverty and a lack of sophistication. Lyle, as character George Aggernite, wore ragged cutoff overalls and a straw hat. Jim, as Droopy Drawers, wore a necktie to his knees. They played the washtub and

Jim Mabe as Droopy Drawers and Lyle Mabe as George Aggernite, ca. early 1960s.
Courtesy Brandon Mabe.

washboard, respectively. In the Presleys' *Mountain Music Jubilee*,
teenager Gary played Herkimer, with his blacked-out teeth and
overalls. Within a few years the Presleys added Sid Sharp, a "hillbilly come to town in a suit three sizes too small and a decade out
of date."[35] Over the years, hillbilly characters such as Willie Makeit,
Stubb Meadows, Cecil, and Cecil Jr. would also grace the stages on
the Strip.

Gary Presley as Herkimer, ca. 1970. Courtesy Presleys' Country Jubilee.

Despite their Ozark roots, the Mabes and Presleys inherited not simply Scotch-Irish or Anglo-Saxon folk traditions but also West African influences and the aesthetics of commercial entertainment. Bob's father-in-law Chick Allen played the jawbone of a mule, which they jokingly called a "jackassaphone."[36] It was meant to signal hillbilly poverty, folksiness, and amateurishness, but playing "the bones" had long been part of the professional minstrelsy circuit. "Mr. Bones" typically kept the rhythm for the musical ensemble and engaged in comedic repartee. A mule jawbone was a common instrument in Black music not only in the American South (leading to a whole category of "jawbone tunes") but also throughout the hemisphere, including in Peru, Mexico, and Venezuela.[37]

Allen also jig-danced in the show. Despite the persistent myth that jig dancing is a purely Irish tradition, by the mid-twentieth century it had been a part of minstrelsy, medicine shows, and tap dance for over a hundred years, transformed by cultural mixing and theatrical adaptation. The only extant film clip of Allen's dancing is a brief segment from *The Beverly Hillbillies* that recreates a medicine show. Granny Clampett takes on the role of quack doctor and proclaims that Allen is a "famous Indian yarb [herb] specialist" who has been "gathering berries and roots and yarbs in these hills for hundreds of years." His virility in extreme old age is testament to the power of his "potions and elixirs." To prove it, he gets up to dance. As his "grandson" (a stooped, white-bearded man) plays the fiddle, Allen performs intricate, rhythmic footwork, but not in the rigid traditional Irish style. Instead, he leans forward, back slightly hunched, his arms loose and swinging to the rhythm, his feet similarly loose.[38] A well-known dancer from recent years with a similar style is tapper Savion Glover, who is Black and identifies with a lineage of Black dancers. A further twist is that Allen claimed to be part Indian.[39] The down-home hillbilly was more complicated than he first appeared. The Mabes and Presleys were keepers of tradition — just not the tradition of a pure folk culture. Instead, they kept alive the vibrant American popular entertainment tradition of the variety show, with all its racial, cultural, and stylistic crossings.

An LP recording of a live performance of the *Baldknobbers Hillbilly Jamboree* from 1968 gives a further sense of how. The emcee, Bob Mabe, opens by welcoming the audience warmly and declaring, "In our beautiful Ozarks we have down here, we like to see people and laugh. In this little hurried-up world we live in today we don't think that you live, and laugh, like you should. So we want you to do that tonight." Rather than slow down a hurried-up world, however, the show begins with breakneck speed. The group launches into an instrumental version of "Old Joe Clark," a folk tune that the group plays at an astonishing 156 beats per minute, albeit for less than sixty seconds. The emcee starts talking again, but Aggernite interrupts with a meowing sound. The audience keeps laughing as the emcee talks; clearly Aggernite is engaging in some physical antics. The emcee invites Droopy Drawers and Willie Makeit to join Aggernite onstage. The three hillbilly comedians launch into "She'll Be Comin' Round the Mountain," a Black spiritual adapted into a railroad work song. Then comes "Black Mountain Rag," a bluegrass number with virtuosic fiddling, followed by comedic banter. The comedians break into "The Crawdad Song," a Black work song first recorded on vinyl in 1929 by two white vaudevillians who performed in blackface, Honeyboy and Sassafras.[40] The Baldknobbers' energetic version includes whoops, hollers, and tub-thumping.

The evening continues apace: rollicking fiddle playing, banjo picking, and guitar strumming. Singers cover recent hits like Merle Haggard's "The Legend of Bonnie and Clyde"; comedians use malapropisms (saying "irrigate" instead of "irritate") and engage in physical comedy. The Baldknobbers even perform George Jones's "White Lightning," which Northern college students had disavowed as inauthentic when the Osborne Brothers attempted to play it. Branson audiences had no problem with it. In the second half, a little boy sings the country novelty song "Bimbo" adorably off-key. The Baldknobbers play one original song, "Heap a Lot of Livin'," that they wrote "for people from big cities." It extols the virtues of rural life, where you can "forget about your troubles," "cut a rusty rug," and eat to your heart's content. The audience claps and cheers throughout the show. At one point someone even shrieks with laughter, prompting Aggernite to comment, "I should just tell that [joke] again, he got such a kick out of it!" The spontaneous, unscripted remark creates a sense of camaraderie with the audience. The evening concludes with the emcee exhorting, "Go to church or Sunday School in the morning. Wherever you go, take the Good Lord with you."[41] Even through the crackle of an LP decades later, a listener can sense the warmth and intimacy of the evening.

The Bransonized show formula was in place, and the first aspect was variety. Throughout the evening, no segment lasted longer than two minutes, which meant that no songs were played in their entirety. Any time the emcee launched into a monologue, the hillbillies diverted the audience's attention with physical comedy. Commentators today bemoan the distractions of handheld digital devices and social media, but popular entertainers have long known that people naturally have short attention spans and enjoy jumping from one thing to another.[42] Variety also appeals to multiple generations, which helps the entertainers confidently advertise their shows as family-friendly. If Grandma doesn't like a song, or Dad doesn't like a joke, another segment will come soon. The Presleys' *Mountain Music Jubilee* was similar. Clocking in at one hour and forty-three minutes, the 1982 version included thirty-six different numbers, meaning that the segments averaged under three minutes. While most numbers were recognizable as mainstream country, the show included bluegrass, pop songs such as "Boogie Woogie Bugle Boy," the R&B song "Kansas City," and the surfer-rock twelve-bar-blues classic "Wipeout." Most were up-tempo and catchy. There was also comedy and audience interaction.[43]

Second, Bransonized shows emphasize familiarity. The term "family values" implies a host of prohibitions against what can be seen or heard when children are present: no obscenities, no mention of sex or sexuality, and no revealing clothing. A Bransonized show avoids divisive topics such as abortion, climate change, or electoral politics. Visitors expressed relief at having entertainment options where they did not have to "worry" about content.[44] But not having to worry is not just about knowing what you won't see, but also about knowing what you will. The 1968 Baldknobbers only played one original song; the rest were well known from the popular music canon. In the 1982 *Mountain Music Jubilee*, all country songs were popular hits, many from television or film, such as "East Bound and Down" from *Smokey and the Bandit* (1977) and "You're the Reason God Made Oklahoma" from *Any Which Way You Can* (1980). There were no original songs. The gospel choices, too, were popular ones, including "I'll Fly Away," perhaps the most recorded song in gospel music history.[45] Familiarity — which is different from predictability — provides a guarantee of enjoyment for one's hard-earned dollar. Predictability is boring, whereas a familiar song, coming as a surprise in the middle of a show, can trigger fond memories and create a nostalgic feeling.

A third component of the Bransonized show is affordability, which feeds into family values. Families needed a basic level of expendable income to see a show in Branson, but less than they would need to see a top country music artist. For example, in 1977 the *Baldknobbers* show cost $3 for an adult, $1 for children aged six to twelve, and nothing for children aged five and under. In contrast, a Waylon Jennings concert in St. Louis that same year was $6.50, with no children's prices.[46] At the *Baldknobbers* or *Jubilee*, you got the best songs of not only Jennings but also all of your favorite musicians, including dead ones. Nor did you have to pay for a babysitter. Like Toby Shows before them, Branson family variety shows also often included a pre-show, giving guests even more entertainment for their money.

"Clean" comedy is the fourth aspect of a Bransonized show. Music offers pleasure, but comedy brings the fun, reassuring audiences that family values need not imply stern or dour modes of living. "Clean" scatological humor (perhaps an oxymoron) is a staple of the hillbilly repertoire. In the 1982 show, Lloyd Presley, who serves as the straight-man emcee, chastises Herkimer for ordering tongue at a restaurant, saying, "How could you eat something that came out of someone's mouth?" Herkimer responds, "Well, you ordered eggs, and I didn't say nuthin'!"[47] Some jokes leaned even further into scatology. In a later *Baldknobbers* show, the emcee asks hillbilly comedian Stubb Meadows to bring out a stool for a singer to sit on. Meadows brings out a toilet and makes a face to imply that it smells; Droopy Drawers, who comes with him, licks his fingers and then rubs them on the toilet to clean it. He then licks his fingers again, making a face.[48]

Another staple of hillbilly comedy is drag, which may come as a surprise given contemporary efforts to ban drag performances in the name of family values. Many mainstream representations of drag in the twenty-first century (such as the hit reality television show *RuPaul's Drag Race*) depict it as glamorous cross-dressing undertaken by gay men with the aim of "realness," or looking more feminine (even hyperfeminine) than women. This tradition has roots in Harlem ballroom culture that dates back to the 1920s. But another lineage of drag comes from the nineteenth-century minstrel show, where white male performers dressed as Black women. Their drag was deliberately unfeminine, aiming to both debase their targets and reassure audiences that they were masculine despite their dresses and wigs. Comedians such as Milton Berle, Flip Wilson, and Tyler Perry, as well as countless fraternity brothers, have continued this tradition, though the crossing of racial lines has diminished. Men on Branson's stages over the years have made it clear that they are *bad* at drag: they wear no makeup, their costumes fit poorly, their wigs constantly fall off, and they move awkwardly. Dolly Parton was a favored target for many years. *Jamboree* and *Jubilee* hillbillies appeared as Parton with giant balloon breasts that popped or interfered with microphones, rendering her sexuality cartoonish and thus acceptable in a family show.[49]

The fifth and most important aspect of the Branson family variety show is audience interaction. The words "Jamboree" and "Jubilee" suggest a festive social gathering, not a performance. Unlike at most theaters in America, in which a voice over the speakers tells you sternly that taking photographs is strictly prohibited, the emcee cheerfully told his *Jubilee* audience, "If you brought your camera in here tonight and want to take pictures of a bunch of hillbillies enjoying themselves, that's fine. From any place in the house at any time during the show, it will not upset one thing."[50] In the dozens of Branson family variety shows I have watched either on film or in person, no one is ever told to put away a camera. The implication is that the familial bonds and values seen onstage are not some kind of carefully crafted performance that needs copyright protection. Instead, they are meant to convey a sense of musical socializing in which the audience is invited to participate.

This invitation happens in multiple ways. Performers ask audience members questions and joke with them. Emcees announce people's birthdays and anniversaries; today, much like at professional sports events, a camera pans to those audience members, who wave as they are projected onto screens on either side of the stage. They literally become a part of the show. Sometimes, performers will come offstage and touch people, patting their arms, giving them hugs, or rubbing their heads. In one *Baldknobbers* comedy bit from the 1990s, Stubb Meadows hopped off the stage and started kissing women on the cheek. At one point he approached a male audience member, then at the last second switched to smooch the man's wife, drawing laughs from all around. This level of physical interaction does not happen in more typical theater environments.

The boundary between performer and the "real" self is fluid in Branson, as it has been since the early days of *The Shepherd of the Hills* tourism. Performers sign autographs and pose for pictures after the show in costume. Famously, they stay until the last audience member leaves. While performers at other theaters around the country also occasionally greet audiences after a show (though almost never in costume), in Branson this interaction is taken to a new level: performers also sign autographs and chat with patrons at intermission, sitting on the edge of the stage. This practice breaks the famed fourth wall of performance. In theory, seeing a performer in costume but out of character shatters the illusion of the theater. In Branson, the shattering suggests that the worlds onstage and off are one and the same.

The willingness to connect with audiences has also meant revealing imperfections. In 2017, the *Baldknobbers Jamboree* included a song dedicated to a fourth-generation Mabe family member, Shane, who had died of a drug overdose at age twenty. Throughout the three-minute song, the screens flanking the stage flashed images of a young, blond-haired boy, the picture of innocence, felled by America's raging opioid epidemic. The epidemic had hit rural white Americans particularly hard; within the Ozarks in particular, almost everyone knew a family who had been affected. With their public mourning from the stage, the Mabes demonstrated that despite their glittering gowns and slick guitars, they were just like their audiences.[51]

Finally, Branson family variety shows are always trying to sell something beyond the show ticket, a practice that hearkens back to the Toby Shows. At intermission, performers promote their concession stands, sound recordings, merchandise, and even partnerships with area businesses, offering discounts on restaurants and car washes. In more recent decades, when theaters began to produce more than one show in a season, performers would advertise discounts to other shows.

All of these characteristics (variety, familiarity, affordability, clean comedy, audience interaction, and explicit merchandising) have signified "lowbrow" performance in the United States since the late nineteenth century. After the Civil War, the Second Industrial Revolution created a new class of elites with previously unimagined wealth, including families like the Astors, Vanderbilts, Rockefellers, Mellons, and Carnegies. The industrial growth also created a new, sizable middle class. The new elites created institutions of high culture, such as the Metropolitan Museum of Art, Metropolitan Opera, Boston Symphony Orchestra, and Philadelphia Orchestra. Theater owners looking to attract wealthier patrons — or, at least, middle-class audiences that included women — darkened the lights in the auditoriums and established new norms of silence. High art demanded reverence, not audience input. The new tastemakers decried variety as "broken candy" or "musical babble." Great works of art, they argued, required concentration, sustained attention, and a sense of completeness to achieve an aesthetic sublime. Originality was the key signifier of artistic value, whereas familiarity signaled a lack of creative genius. Attempts to actively advertise, especially by offering discounts or sales, tainted art with the stench of commerce and thus were to be avoided — a rich irony at institutions founded by robber barons.[52]

By the mid-twentieth century, musical theater attempted to elevate its status by moving away from variety-style revues and toward so-called "integrated" musicals, in which music and choreography supported the development of the plot. Broadway producers and theater critics declared that integrated musicals offered greater coherence and thus greater sophistication. By the 1970s, some creators like Stephen Sondheim went even further in the high-art direction by developing the "concept" musical, where all aspects of the show, including plot, were subordinate to the supposed genius of the artistic idea or central metaphor. Of course, Broadway remained a for-profit industry that relied heavily on marketing and popularity even as it tried to distance itself from populist aesthetics, and thus developed a state of "middlebrow anxiety" that has plagued it to this day.[53] As these taste distinctions became encrusted by the mid-twentieth century, Branson performers and their audiences embraced the low. Lowbrow aesthetics reaffirmed "down-home" family values as opposed to the snobbery of urban elites. They also reaffirmed a worldview in which commercial success did not signal a lack of genius or artistic originality, but rather an embrace of the value of free enterprise.

Selling the Branson Family Show

From the beginning, the Mabe and Presley family stories were as much a part of the performance as the onstage productions. They offered a vision of success based on hard work, Christian faith, and above all, commitment to family. A 1970 brochure for the *Baldknobbers* depicts each cast member in three ways: first, photographed in costume; second, in a cartoon drawing representing him engaging in a stereotypical "hillbilly" activity such as sleeping lazily under a tree; and third, photographed in a suit posing with his wife and multiple children. Audiences could rest assured that these men, despite being performers and hillbillies, were in the end family types. The caption for the photograph of the only single cast member, "Cousin Jeff," read "Wanted . . . a girl looking to get married, so I can have a family picture like the rest of the boys."[54] By the early 2000s, publicizing the families' offstage lives had migrated from brochures to the stage itself. Either at the beginning of the show or at intermission at the Presleys' theater, lighting cues draw the audience's attention to giant screens that flank the main stage, where black-and-white photographs of the family appear as a voiceover recording tells the stories of the cave and the metal box theater. The voiceover waxes nostalgic about the early years of empty folding chairs before offering data points of the show's growth, including the expansion of the theater to accommodate 2,000 seats in the 1980s. The Mabes have a similar slideshow that recounts their history and touts their success as Branson's Famous Baldknobbers.[55] The performance of family values insists on a synergy between offstage and on.

Another aspect of family values that the Mabes, Presleys, and other Branson family groups literally embody is fertility. Many shows have no fewer than four siblings performing together. The large broods signify that these families honor God's command to be fruitful and multiply. Several generations occupy the stage together, demonstrating tight-knit bonds that contrast to the isolated nuclear families of modern, urban America who are said to suffer from loneliness and anxiety.[56] The Mabe family's *Baldknobbers* began with four brothers, a father-in-law, and a friend. The Presley family's *Jubilee* began with Lloyd Presley and his four children; in the 2020s, Lloyd's great-grandson appears on the stage with his father, uncles, aunts, cousins, and grandfather. In any given year, the Duttons' show includes matriarch Sheila and patriarch Dean, up to seven of their children, the spouses of their children, and multiple grandchildren. The Haygoods are six siblings, as are the six Knudsen brothers in *SIX*. The Petersens consist of a mother, four adult children, and a close friend. The Hughes Music Show (which started in 1995) boasts of being the "World's Largest Performing Family," with over forty-five members onstage.[57] In *The Hughes Family Christmas Special* in 2018, a five-month-old played Baby Jesus. The "cuteness" of having children involved in productions tugs at the audience's heartstrings. It is also a conspicuous example of how theater can support, not inhibit, family values ideals about childbirth. Matriarch and manager Lena Hughes boasted in 2016 that theirs was "the only show in Branson, if not the whole world, that's been able to produce a live 'Baby Jesus,' from within the family for the past 20 years," showcasing the clan's consistent fertility.[58]

Another aspect of Branson's model of family values is that women do work, but in specific pathways that carefully do not challenge the homemaker ideal too much. *Jamboree* and *Jubilee* promotional materials proclaimed that the wives "put family first," but they were not housewives. Women's employment was what gave the Presleys the financial security to "take the plunge" and open their own theater in 1967. Lloyd's wife Bessie Mae worked at a utility company, and Gary's wife Pat at Branson's Security Bank. In addition to these jobs, the wives ran the theater. They sold tickets, ushered, and maintained the books. They were the first to arrive and the last to leave, while also performing domestic duties. The same was the case with the Mabes. The men performed onstage while the women sewed costumes, ushered, ran the box office and concession stands, and kept the books.

The families have also put the children to work. In the 1960s, preteen Steve Presley handed out flyers at campgrounds and slapped bumper stickers on cars during intermission; Ryan Thomas remembers opening the popcorn bags at the concession stand in her family's theater as a five-year-old in the 1980s; and many shows have teens, preteens, elementary-aged children, toddlers, and even infants (the Baby Jesus) onstage. Other kids simply have had to hang out. Isabelle Roig remembers taking the bus to her father's theater every day after school. She would sit in the green room during her father's Elvis tribute show (the *Tony Roi Experience*), eating popcorn and drinking soda. Sometimes she fell asleep. She then accompanied her parents and the cast across the street to Applebee's, where she would stay up until one or two o'clock in the morning.[59]

Women in the office and children eating out at 2 a.m. might seem antithetical to professed family values. But when the business is a family business, the norms get blurry. Branson's variety shows can claim the ethos of a long-lost agrarian life. The Mabes and Presleys were only one generation removed from family farms, where all members of the household pitched in. Historian Bethany Moreton identifies this model with the Ozarks' biggest company, which also happens to be the biggest company in the world: Walmart (formerly Wal-Mart), founded in Rogers, Arkansas, the same year that the Presleys began performing in Fantastic Caverns. The Ozark families who supported Walmart justified the company's low wages because they saw the family, not the individual, as most important. Plus, pragmatically, there were few other employment options. The Presleys tout their success as stemming from "the love and respect of family members for each other," but it was also the women's outside employment, as well as the unpaid labor of the wives and children in marketing, concessions, and management, that made it possible for the family shows to survive.[60]

In the 1970s, Branson's Strip extended to include the Plummer Family, the Foggy River Boys, the Ozark Mountain Hayride, and the Stan Hitchcock show. Bob Mabe split off from the Baldknobbers to start *Bob-O-Link's Country Hoe-Down*. Off the Strip, Lloyd Heller opened the Corn Crib Theatre in 1969 to produce his own Toby Show, a hearkening back to the original rural tent entertainment that emphasized family values. Both the Presleys and the Baldknobbers expanded their theaters multiple times; by the end of the decade, they had 2,000 and 1,700 seats, respectively.[61] On television, in contrast, a "rural purge" in 1971 led to the cancellation of *The Beverly Hillbillies, Green Acres, Hee Haw, The Jim Nabors Hour, Mayberry R.F.D.,* and *The New Andy Griffith Show*. Conservatives argued that television was now a contributing factor to the breakdown of family values, with more programs featuring violent or sexual content. They pointed to sitcoms such as *All in the Family* (1971–1979), in which foul-mouthed Archie Bunker, his feminist daughter Gloria, and the rest of the cast touched on racism, homosexuality, abortion, rape, and the Vietnam War. They also cited the television documentary *An American Family* (1973), which followed the Loud family as "their lives seem[ed] to fall apart," as potent examples of the destructive dominance of liberal ideology in American culture. Pundits declared that a "countercultural hangover" weighed down the country, and historical events such as the disastrous end to the Vietnam War and President Nixon's resignation fueled widespread cynicism about the nation.[62]

But the "rural purge" on television was only partially true, as were declarations that the nation had given up on so-called traditional values. After its 1971 cancellation by CBS, Hee Haw gained new life in syndication. Hosted by country music stars Roy Clark and Buck Owens, it featured the variety format of music, corny comedy, and gospel that had endured since the nineteenth century. Country music historian Bill C. Malone called it "hillbilly to the point of grotesque parody" and deemed its success "strange," but it was only strange if you thought audience desire for that entertainment had vanished.[63] Even though new adventures in Mayberry disappeared from the screen in 1971, Branson grew to attract more visitors from a wider geographic area. In 1981, Hee Haw show writer Thomas Lutz built the Hee Haw Theater in Branson to present live variety shows featuring stars from the television program. Appetite for earnest, goofy, heartfelt reiterations of traditional family values had not disappeared into a haze of marijuana smoke and cynicism.

As nationwide interest in Branson developed, it began to compete with Nashville as a destination for country music fans. Advertisements drew a contrast between Appalachia as tainted by capitalism and the Ozarks as a purer form of Americana. The division replicated a decades-old split in the country music industry between more commercially oriented, pop-inflected songs and "old-time," traditional-sounding music, even though Branson shows included just as many Nashville hits as Nashville itself and were just as fully invested in capitalist enterprise. A full-page ad in a Wichita, Kansas, newspaper for Branson's Oakmont Shores housing development in 1973 mentions Baldknobbers and the Jubilee as shows that produced "Just Plain REALNESS. . . . one of America's last strongholds of pure individuality and bedrock tradition. . . . It's the American life we remember in its purest form."[64] Lyle Mabe claimed that they had been offered opportunities in Nashville, but "We've always tried to stay independent. We're all family men."[65] That independence itself conveyed authenticity. A column from a 1977 small-town Missouri news-paper asserted that Branson was more "real" than commercialized Nashville. "The real music of the American people was born back in the hills," it claimed,[66] ignoring that Branson variety shows were for-profit endeavors that drew upon a repertoire of popular hits. In 1978, Chamber of Commerce executive manager Dan Throop echoed the depiction of Nashville as too "commercial" and said, "Branson is one of the last wholesome family vacation spots in the country."[67]

In truth, country music fans had long embraced the genre's ties to commerce. The way that folklorists had divided folk and popular music, or the way East Coast aesthetes divided highbrow and low-brow theater, did not mirror how Branson performers or their au-diences approached entertainment. They were not wholesome and authentic out of some high-minded rejection of the marketplace. Instead, support for capitalism *was* a wholesome American value. The independent entrepreneur *was* an ideal Jeffersonian Ameri-can. When asked how he defined himself as an artist, Gary Presley refused the premise: "I don't really . . . There are a lot of artists, so-called artists, that are sitting home in the basement playing their own instruments and nobody cares about [them]. . . . I think of us as entertainers."[68] His answer implied that artists were self-indulgent, whereas entertainers worked hard to make a living. Presley did not want to be seen as the lazy, barefooted hillbilly whiling away on his fiddle, nor as the effete *artiste* who prioritized self-expression. He performed to uphold his duty to provide for his family. The distinc-tion with Nashville was less about commercialism and more about Branson's cultivation of relationships with audiences. In contrast, the Nashville-based country music industry spent the decade of the 1960s trying to "present itself as a thoroughly professional, busi-nesslike entertainment center," which meant de-emphasizing fan relationships and making stars less accessible.[69]

In *The Presley Family Story*, author Ron Marr writes, "The Presleys view the business they've built as something far more than just a mere show. There is a far deeper meaning. . . . an honest appreci-ation of the fulfillment of a dream. . . . a dream that required hard work, sacrifice, and a deep and abiding faith in both God and family."[70] There was no better model for the family values movement than a family that worked together, prayed together, and achieved financial success by showcasing their values.

Selling family values as a brand comes with risks, however. While the Presleys have maintained the sheen of unity for several decades, not all families have been able to do so. In the 1960s, Bob Mabe divorced; in the 1970s, Lyle Mabe started showing up to the theater drunk, which became clear to audiences when he forgot his jokes. Fed up with Lyle's public humiliations, Bob split off to found *Bob-O-Link's* in 1977. Brandon Mabe (grandson of Jim, the original Droopy Drawers), who took over the *Baldknobbers* in the 2000s, also divorced. In 2014 the family started a reality television show. Pitched as the "first reality musical," *Branson Famous* followed the Mabes as they tried to "cling to their legacy" with "country-fried ambition." It focused on bickering among Brandon, his fiancée Megan McCombs, and his parents as they struggled to keep the show afloat. Critics panned *Branson Famous* as "cheesy" and "fabricated," and it lasted less than one year. Instead of encouraging self-deprecating laughs alongside hillbillies, *Branson Famous* was typical reality television, in which the audience gawked at the dysfunction of strangers.[71] Nevertheless, Branson audiences seem to have forgiven the public displays of imperfection, as the Baldknobbers continue to perform to this day.

Starting in the 1980s, the family values ethos of Branson faced a bigger foe than the Mabe family's transgressions: the celebrity headliner show. With such productions came corporatization, outside financing, and new performers who adapted the Bransonized show model without the lived experience to back it up. The Jeffersonian/Harold Bell Wright ideal of the independent entrepreneur achieving the American dream through his family's collective hard work and faith in God was in jeopardy. The unnamed fourth F threatened to overshadow family as a core value: free enterprise.

4 FREE ENTERPRISE

The Business of Show Business

> I'm so glad you came to Branson
> 'Cause it's the place where
> Dreams come true.
> Not just for entertainers,
> But for families and folks like you.
>
> *"Welcome All You Travelers," written by John*
> *Davidson, © 1992 Hidden Hills Productions*

I 've heard a number: six million in six months," said *60 Minutes* host Morley Safer in 1991 to country music star Mel Tillis, who had opened a theater in Branson in 1990. Tillis smiled faintly. "Well, that's pretty close," he stated. "But you have to work two shows a day and sign autographs." Safer continued to emphasize wealth: "People come here and spend as much as a billion and a half dollars." "Person-for-person, the richest town in the country." Even the title of the segment, "$ound of Music," suggested what Branson was all about: making money.[1]

The get-rich-quick image recalled America's mining and oil boomtowns of the late nineteenth century. In late twentieth-century Branson, the commodity to grab before it disappeared was not a fossil fuel, but land to build a theater. The *60 Minutes* segment precipitated the Branson "Boom," which turbocharged the growth that had already started to accelerate in the 1980s. Dozens of celebrity entertainers relocated to the Ozarks, eager to strike gold. Millions of tourists arrived in buses and cars to see the performances of the American dream. John Davidson, who traded Hollywood for Branson in 1992, penned a song proclaiming that ordinary people could not only see the dream but also *experience* it in Branson.[2] Mythical places — the heartland, real America, small-town America — now had a physical location. And, in contrast to the nostalgia-tinted sentiment that such places were dying or already dead, Branson was vibrantly alive.

Branson's star rose at a time when the American economy was changing dramatically. Manufacturing had reached its peak in 1979 before beginning a long, continuous decline as companies moved factories overseas.[3] In the mid-1990s, when the North American Free Trade Agreement (NAFTA) went into effect and the internet began to play a bigger role in business operations, global outsourcing accelerated further. The 1980s and 1990s were decades of widespread mergers and acquisitions, creating megacorporations that swallowed up small businesses. The trend even reached Broadway, where Disney Theatrical Group began to dominate new show production.[4]

In contrast, Branson marketed itself as a place where the individual still controlled his destiny as the master of free enterprise. With little to no government regulation in Taney County, anyone with the willingness to work hard could open their own business and succeed — at least, that was the story Branson boosters told. In reality, the barriers to entry skyrocketed during the 1980s and 1990s, leading to a new saying among locals: "If you want to make a million dollars in Branson, come to town with three million."[5] You had to have your bootstraps already firmly in place. And the well-strapped did come. From six theaters featuring six shows in 1980, the entertainment industry bloomed to forty-five theaters featuring eighty-six shows by 2000. The number of hotels and restaurants increased exponentially as well.[6] Business leaders wrote about Branson as an exemplar of the new "Experience Economy," which relied on industries such as tourism that provided in-person experiences. Such industries could not be outsourced. Business analysts claimed that the "Experience" sector was the fastest-growing part of the US economy in the late twentieth century.[7]

Branson boosters, bullish about endless growth, borrowed a phrase from the hit film *Field of Dreams* to describe the town's entrepreneurial dreamscape: "If you build it, they will come."[8] In the 1989 movie, a small-town farmer with fading economic prospects defies rationality and the advice of his brother to build a baseball diamond for ghosts. He succeeds in attracting thousands of people who are eager to experience "all that was once good in America."[9] With both agriculture and manufacturing increasingly dubious prospects for financial stability in the heartland, building an attraction that offered to take people back to the good old days seemed to be a winning strategy for fictional Iowa farmers and Branson entertainers alike.

For a while during the 1980s and 1990s, it all seemed possible. The city, with its population of merely 2,550, stretched its modest marketing dollars to compete with huge tourist destinations like Las Vegas, Los Angeles, or New York. And unlike those global cities, Branson could publicize itself to conservative Americans as a place where you could have your cake and eat it too: a success story of the new experience economy that retained its small-town feel, its small-government ethos, and its values of faith, family, and flag. Here in the Ozarks, Thomas Jefferson's ideal society of independent family enterprises in a rural setting came to life. In Branson, individuals ran their own businesses on their own terms instead of being cogs in a multinational corporate machine or buried under governmental red tape.

At least, that was the story told. From the start of the boom, Branson's American dream rubbed up against some hard realities. Problems with zoning, planning, labor, housing, traffic, and the environment quickly emerged, with little existing government infrastructure to solve them. The city also faced capitalism's existential dilemma: the imperative to grow in a world with limited resources. To survive, Branson had to expand, continuously. It had to enlarge its share of the crowded tourism market while not diluting its brand. Could it promise down-home hillbilly values and also build Broadway-style theaters? Could it build the infrastructure to support millions more tourists while still credibly claiming to be a small town? And finally, could it declare that the only color important in Branson was the green of the US dollar, while still selling a political vision identified with white Christian conservatives?

If You Build It, They Will Come

The transformation of Branson from regional tourist destination into national hotspot began with a crisis. By the late 1970s, *Shepherd of the Hills*, Silver Dollar City, Heller's *Toby Show*, and the "6 on 76" — Presleys' *Mountain Music Jubilee*, the *Baldknobbers Hillbilly Jamboree*, the *Plummer Family Music Show*, *Foggy River Boys*, *Bob-O-Link's Country Hoe-Down*, and the *Ozark Mountain Hayride Country Music Show* — had settled into a stable entertainment ecosystem. They were competitors, but publicly stated that they "worked together for a common purpose" of increasing the number of visitors to the area. As the *Springfield Leader and Press* reported in 1978, "The reason it works is just plain ol' hillbilly economics. Music brings the tourists, and tourists bring the gold."[10]

But in 1979, the Ayatollah Khomeini overthrew the Iranian government, and the United States' easy access to Middle Eastern oil screeched to a halt. At gas stations across America, cars waited in lines that wrapped around the block. Families put road trips on hold. While the 1973 oil crisis had not affected Branson much, this one threatened to decimate the now-much-bigger tourism industry more dependent on tourists from farther away.[11] Peter Herschend of Silver Dollar City banded together with Mark Trimble of *Shepherd of the Hills* and Pat Jones (father of future Dallas Cowboys owner Jerry Jones) of Exotic Animal Paradise to buy gasoline and advertise that tourists would be guaranteed to fill their tanks in Branson. The successful venture proved that intentional collective action could benefit the entire area.[12] In 1980, the three men launched the Marketing Council of Ozarks Mountain Country, often known as OMC, for further cooperative efforts.[13]

The Marketing Council consciously set out to rebrand the region, which for the past seventy years had been known as Shepherd of the Hills Country. With fading public memory of Wright's novel, "Ozarks Mountain Country" offered greater name recognition. Collective marketing was also needed to overcome Branson's geographic isolation. The isolation was both part of Branson's draw — it signaled that the town was a place apart, where rural America still existed – and a bane of its existence. Without an airport or train station, people had to arrive by car or bus. It was within a day's drive of one-third of the nation's population, whereas rival destinations farther east like Myrtle Beach or Pigeon Forge were within a day's drive of twice as many people. It took aggressive marketing and promotion to pitch Branson as worth the extra hours on the road.[14] Herschend encouraged all area businesses to put the OMC logo on their marquees and brochures, as well as to contribute financially to the collective.[15]

Cooperation was not an easy sell, for it contradicted the individualist ethos of American capitalism that was gospel in Branson. Within a year, however, the OMC could claim victory. Despite continued nationwide gasoline shortages and a recession, which caused destinations like Disney World to experience zero growth in 1980, there was an 18 percent increase in attendance at Shepherd of the Hills Farm and a 23 percent increase at Silver Dollar City. The number of variety shows doubled from six to thirteen in less than three years. The Presleys expanded their theater to 2,000 seats and filled it most nights. While good weather helped, boosters claimed that the tourism increase was due primarily to "effective advertising." From the initial three in 1979, the area businesses that contributed to the collective effort grew to 145 by 1981.[16] Tourism increased again the following year, by 17.5 percent. Revenues neared the $1 billion mark. Clearly, the $180,000 the OMC spent on advertisements had "paid for itself several times over."[17]

In 1983, one local entrepreneur observed the rising tourism numbers and took a gamble that paid off hugely. Jim Thomas, a divorced Democrat with thwarted dreams of a political career in southwest Missouri's Republican stronghold, had been near rock bottom a few years before. He and his second wife, Joy, had spent a quarter of a million dollars on a "podunk restaurant" on the outskirts of Branson that failed. They sold the restaurant at a loss and bought a bankrupt, de-franchised Holiday Inn in nearby Kimberling City but could not turn it around. With six kids from previous marriages plus two of their own, they needed money. Jim suggested another long shot: purchasing Stan Hitchcock's 1,000-seat Old Sawmill Theatre on Highway 76 near Silver Dollar City, despite no experience in the entertainment business. The Thomases brought in "third tier stars" of country music, such as Jeannie C. Riley and Tom T. Hall, and were pleasantly surprised when the shows sold out. People drove hundreds of miles to see these minor celebrities in the flesh. Touring musicians often skipped the multi-state Ozarks region, as there was seemingly not a big enough city to support filling a concert hall. What performers and their managers had perhaps discounted was that people would drive far to see them, especially if they performed in a destination like Branson that offered other entertainment options for the whole family.[18]

The success set Jim's wheels turning. If people turned out for Riley and Hall, how many more would come for a major name? A piece of land came up for sale, and he bought it to build another theater. He boldly contacted country music superstar Roy Clark's agent and convinced him to put Clark's name on the theater and for Clark to perform there three times a year. In contrast to the local family shows of the 1960s and 1970s, Clark was the prototype of the Branson entertainer to come: a nationally recognized celebrity who was ready to slow down. Clark's last Country Music Association award had been in 1980 and his last Grammy in 1982, the year before he arrived in Branson. While that meant he was still at the top of the heap when he arrived, he would thereafter only receive retrospective awards. Clark was also the cohost of the popular country-oriented television variety show *Hee Haw* and knew that entertaining audiences required more than a straight concert format. He adapted to the Branson mandate of accessibility by meeting and greeting audiences. The local family shows had been greeting audiences for years, but Clark's fame raised the stakes of such interactions. In the 1983 opening season, every show at the Roy Clark Celebrity Theatre sold out.

The Thomases decided to keep going. They quickly taught themselves the ropes of show business, from handling handlers to selling tickets to publicity. They invited other country stars to perform when Clark was not in town and put their own young children onstage in a clogging-and-comedy pre-show. Joy shrewdly noted, "Lots of times the star wasn't as fun as the variety show we had given them, but that didn't matter. They wanted to see that star. . . . when we got through, those people had two full hours of totally forgetting everything in their life."[19] All people need some form of escapism, and the early 1980s provided plenty of need, especially for blue-collar workers. The economy was in a deep recession. Unemployment hit 10.8 percent in 1982, the highest since the Great Depression. Among construction and auto workers, the rates hit 22 percent and 24 percent, respectively.[20] While the economy started to improve in 1983, the loss of manufacturing jobs continued, as did the increased corporatization of farms. The Cold War was an endless source of fear and angst. Between the big Nashville names, the entertainment value, and the modest cost of a Branson vacation, the Thomases' operation drew more and more visitors.

Side hustles became as important as the main hustle. Joy opened a gift shop in the lobby. She and Jim sold investment shares to build a hotel and opened a dinner theater. They bought another theater next door and convinced country music star Mickey Gilley to come. Soon after, another country music star, Boxcar Willie, bought the Wilkinson Brothers' Theatre across the street. With each big name added, Branson's reputation grew as a destination not just for Ozark mountain music, but for country music more broadly. While the buildings had to be up to code, "the people in Branson were very naïve," stated Joy, and the city rubber-stamped just about any construction project.[21]

Joy's most important side hustle was selling bus tours from a makeshift office cordoned off from the lobby by a bedsheet. In the 1980s, the so-called Greatest Generation was entering retirement. Their working years had coincided with four of the most prosperous decades in American history: the 1940s through the 1970s. They now had pensions, IRAs, and other savings to spend on leisure travel, but many of them did not want to drive. Motor-coach tourism for senior citizens boomed in the 1980s, and the combined efforts of OMC, the

Presleys' Mountain Music Jubilee, ca. 1980s. Courtesy White River Valley Historical Society.

Thomases, and other entrepreneurs positioned Branson to be a part of it.[22]

If the Thomases brought Nashville to Branson, Chisai Childs brought Las Vegas. She was a six-foot-tall woman from Texas with a name that humorously meant "little one" in Japanese. (She had been born in Tokyo, where her father, a captain in the US Army, was stationed after World War II.) With money from her mother's side of the family, Childs started a country music variety show in her hometown of Grapevine, Texas, but relocated it to Branson in 1981. She built the Starlite Theatre, the name spelled out in glittering gold letters on a red marquee. The show she produced and emceed, *The Grapevine Opry*, deliberately invoked Nashville's *Grand Ole Opry* but with a bigger emphasis on glamour. Childs carefully calibrated the production to emphasize wealth — and thus success — but not elitism. In the Branson family variety shows, performers had often stayed in an overalls-and-straw-hat costume for the entire production. As emcee, Childs changed outfits fifteen to twenty times, ball gown followed by bedazzled evening dress followed by glittering

The Starliters at Chisai Childs's Starlite Theatre, ca. 1980s. Courtesy White River Valley Historical Society.

pantsuit. She always ended dressed as an antebellum Southern lady, giving her the nickname "The Belle of Branson."

With a bigger budget, Childs offered more sophisticated lights and sound than other shows. She added variety acts previously unseen on Branson stages, such as magicians and mimes. She hired a virtuosic Japanese fiddler, Shoji Tabuchi, and put him in a tuxedo. Whereas the family shows had typically kept their roster of performers limited to relatives or close friends, Childs had no such allegiances and lured talent with higher pay.[23] She also lured audiences with special events that promised a personal, even familial relationship with performers. In April 1985, she invited the public to celebrate Tabuchi's birthday. The whole family would get to see the show for $7; everyone would get a piece of "Shoji's Cake," and she promised "VERY Special Guests Performing" and "Eventful Surprises!"[24]

Childs's success attracted imitators. In 1985, Janet Dailey, a best-selling romance novelist from Iowa, opened Country Music World with her husband Bill. They boasted "the only theater in the Midwest with stereo sound" (unclear if this was in fact true) and emphasized their advanced lighting technology, which set off an arms race of production values among theaters. They also recruited Tabuchi

Chisai Childs, "The Belle of Branson," ca. 1980s. Courtesy White River Valley Historical Society.

away from Starlite. A game of musical chairs began as performers hopped from venue to venue.[25]

In the end, however, the Starlite and Country Music World did not depart dramatically from the Bransonized formula. The productions were all variety shows that offered familiarity, clean comedy, affordability, and most importantly, accessibility. Childs's performers, like all the others in Branson, stayed to meet and greet the audience. Country music star Buck Trent, whom Childs recruited to Branson, was surprised when she told him to go into the lobby *before* the show. Already in his costume, his mind in performance mode, he nevertheless obeyed. He later said, "It felt like a heavyweight championship fight with a buzz in the crowd, and camera flashes going off, people asking for autographs and all that. I thought, 'Man, this is it.'"[26] He never again doubted the wisdom of building a relationship with the audience or fulfilling Branson's seductive promise of accessible celebrities.

Between Childs, Dailey, and Jim Thomas's growing celebrity empire, family shows began to feel the squeeze. The collective spirit of the early 1980s gave way to public grumbling about too much competition on Highway 76, which was now known informally as the Strip. In 1978, there had been six shows. In 1984, there were twenty. Mark Trimble of *Shepherd of the Hills* complained, "The pie is the same size as it was. . . . There are so many people hacking away at this pie down here, but it only goes so far."[27] Trimble was incorrect about the size of the pie staying the same, as the number of visitors had grown, but the tripling of venues in six years did feel significant. Vi Asselin, president of Sammy Lane Boat Lines, said that the increase in afternoon matinee shows on the Strip had hurt his business.[28] The OMC continued to push for collaboration, but it was a hard sell. Dawn Erickson of the *Branson Beacon-Leader* wrote, "'Eating each other alive' may be a phrase which is hard for Ozark Mountain Country business owners to swallow. Nevertheless, it's happening."[29]

In such a competitive atmosphere, businesses turned to promotional "stunting": kickbacks, free tickets, and more underhanded tactics. Rumors circulated that theater operators were "approaching bus tours already scheduled to attend one attraction and convincing them to go to another." Some managers lowered ticket prices below cost. One business owner likened the gimmicks to "prostitution," saying, "If the product is good, it doesn't need that kind of promotion to sell itself." Some businesses refused to cooperate with OMC and spent promotional dollars just on themselves. Others freeloaded off the marketing paid for by OMC contributors.[30] To publicly shame

these "parasites," in early 1986 OMC put out a prominent advertisement that listed all of its contributors, including theaters, insurance
agencies, stores, resorts, motels, restaurants, construction companies, and banks. It ended with a question in all caps: "ARE YOUR
NEIGHBORS SUPPORTING YOU?"[31] Pointedly, it asked readers —
particularly business owners — to look in the mirror and ask whether
they were doing enough to support the region, or if they were just
living off the hard work and financial contributions of others.

Such language was especially potent in the 1980s, when the conservative coalition under President Reagan set out to reduce the size
of government. Reagan famously popularized the phrase "welfare
queen" to invoke an image of people living extravagantly off federal
handouts instead of working hard; the phrase was racially coded to
imply that Black women in urban areas were especially fraudulent
and undeserving of support.[32] In the Ozarks, the ethos of independence from government largesse had a long history dating back to
the Great Depression, when it elected as its representative the anti-
New Dealer Dewey Short.

But OMC did not entirely want the government to wither away.
While most of OMC's funds went to publicity, in the mid-1980s it
began to spend some of its budget on lobbying the state. Herschend
declared that Missouri's tourism promotion funds should be raised
from $1 million to $12 million and said, "The travel industry has
never been perceived by the powers that be as a viable body. We
have been seen as a mom and pop organization and that's not so."[33]
Though committed to individualistic free enterprise and small government, when it came to business, OMC was all about collectivism
and state support.

Despite the struggles to unify the business community and
increase state funding, Branson continued to grow. The country
music industry began to take notice. Singer Rex Allen pointed out
in 1986, "Branson is what Nashville always wanted to be and never
pulled it off. . . . They have a real country type of entertainment
and that is important. Country music lives and thrives in places
like Branson."[34] Branson had built what Nashville needed: live per-

formance to give people the *experience* of country music. Country music was intimately intertwined with the recording industry and thus with commercialism. It had emerged out of popular performance practices like medicine shows and radio programs in which entertainment was in the service of selling goods.[35] To soften that commercial image and inject a semblance of authenticity into the lyrics of country songs, fans needed to interact with the artists. While sitting at home listening to the *Barn Dance Radio Hour* or an LP, one could imagine the social world of rural Americana. By attending a Branson show, one could experience it.

Boxcar Willie bought fully into Branson's American dream when he purchased a theater there in 1986. Born Lecil Travis Martin in Texas during the Great Depression, Martin joined the US Air Force at age eighteen and served for over twenty years before turning to country music full-time. He adopted the stage name "Boxcar Willie" and the persona of a hobo, always appearing in overalls. He was inducted into the Grand Ole Opry in 1981 and only had one top-forty country hit, "Bad News" in 1982, but achieved widespread success because of his invented persona, his television appearances, and his heavy touring schedule. Eventually he tired of life on the road and turned to Branson. He was a cheerleader of the city from the day he settled in. "I don't think there is a better part of the U.S. that a fellow can open a business or move to such as the Branson area," he told the local newspaper. Willie was unapologetic about his politics: America first, and preferably rural America. He famously turned down $20,000 a week on Broadway for Branson. He harbored a disdain for urban poverty, which he did not explicitly state in racial terms but was implied by echoing Reagan's coded language about welfare queens. Willie stated to the *New Yorker*, "Let me tell you, there's a big difference between hoboes and bums. Those folks I saw on the sidewalks of New York are bums. Hoboes were just transient workers . . . There are plenty of jobs out there if people just want to work, but they'd rather be on welfare."[36] From his stage in Branson, he hawked his merchandise with a side helping of anti-globalism: "Everything but the little binoculars is made right here in the United

Mel Tillis and Boxcar Willie in Branson, ca. early 1990s. Courtesy White River Valley Historical Society.

States of America. . . . I get sick every time I see a Honda go down the road, especially when they close down another General Motors plant." He then made a face like he had "swallowed cod-liver oil."[37] His lament about the current state of America made him a perfect conduit of nostalgia for the good old days, when being poor, home-less, white, and rural — a.k.a. a hobo — was a noble life associated with freedom, patriotism, and individual choice. He closed his Branson shows by saying mournfully, "What I wouldn't give to turn the clock back 50 years," inviting his retiree audiences to remember their young adult years with fondness.[38]

By 1990, Mel Tillis, Mickey Gilley, and Cristy Lane also called Branson home base. To succeed, they had to follow the rules of the

Bransonized show. Accessibility was rule number one. Ron Sylvester wrote, "Visitors to Nashville can see Boxcar Willie's old car in a
museum. Tourists in Branson see Boxcar and other country music
stars, shake their hands and get autographs."[39] Country stars quickly
learned that they would "only succeed" through "Ozarks hospitality." They would also only succeed if they spent time in Branson and
talked up Branson to their audiences. Audiences wanted to hear
how the performers lived the country lifestyle discussed in country
songs: eating home cooking, fishing, hunting, hanging out with
friends, and spending time with family. Freddy Fender told a local reporter that "You might see me walking around in my Harley T-shirt,"
and that his wife frequented the local Walmart. His "mid-size home"
was identical to the others on his block. Tillis extolled the fishing on
the lakes and the numerous Baptist churches. His grandson Marshall
Howden recalled, "The audience wanted to see that you went out
and shopped in the grocery stores and that you sleep in the same
bed every night and you committed to Branson."[40]

Proximity to celebrity was only the first level of appeal. The
promise of experiencing a reality sprung from the mythic universe
of country music lyrics — a small town in rural America governed by
faith, family, and flag — was an even greater draw. But the contradiction between Branson as small-town American utopia and Branson
as a showbiz mecca was about to come to a head, precipitated by a
seeming stroke of luck: free advertising on the nation's most popular
television show.

Boom

During the 1980s, even as it experienced rapid growth, Branson
had struggled to compete with tourist destinations that had
multimillion-dollar marketing budgets. On December 8, 1991, the
city caught a break with twelve minutes of free nationwide advertising worth $7.2 million: a feature segment on *60 Minutes*, called
"$ound of Music." The CBS network show was the number-one pro-
gram on television that year; approximately 40 million Americans

watched it each week. The segment was rebroadcast on May 24, 1992, to reach millions more. In the twenty-first century, with myriad streaming services offering endless ways to watch media content on one's own schedule, it is no longer possible to have such a large, captive, national audience. "The $ound of Music" catapulted Branson to becoming the number-one tour bus destination and number-two car destination (behind only Disney World) in America in 1992, with over five million visitors total. Mel Tillis joked, "Will the last one to leave Nashville for Branson please turn out the light?"[41] It was the official beginning of the boom.

The boom "startled" Nashville. The executive vice president of Nashville's Convention and Visitors Bureau admitted that "Nobody realized there was that type of national demand" for live shows. Representatives from the Hermitage, President Andrew Jackson's historic home, complained about a 7 percent decline in attendance between 1991 and 1992 due to Branson luring away tour groups. Nashville, along with many other entertainment hubs obsessed with youth, novelty, and coolness, had forgotten that older people wanted enjoyment too. Many of Branson's entertainers had not produced hit records in years. Nevertheless, there was an eager market for them, as the tour buses full of senior citizens arriving each week demonstrated. Furthermore, Branson's idyllic small-town setting, compared to Nashville's population of 577,000, reminded tourists of what country music was supposedly all about. OMC's tagline for its television commercial on the Nashville Now network was "If you like country music in the city, you'll love country music in the country — Ozark Mountain Country."[42] It worked.

It wasn't just tourists who started coming. The promise of individual entrepreneurship drew entertainers, many of whom were historically exploited by managers, agents, and recording labels. Journalist Deborah Wilker exclaimed, "In Branson there is no middle man, no anybody else. Money comes in. Money goes directly in pocket. If Loretta [Lynn] wants a blue light stage left, she shines it there, having consulted no one. If Mel [Tillis] wants a bigger amp, he plugs it in."[43] What set Branson apart, in other words, was artistic and financial autonomy. That allure brought not only country stars Loretta Lynn, Barbara and Louise Mandrell, Conway Twitty, Buck Trent, Glen Campbell, Moe Bandy, Ray Stevens, and Charley Pride, but also pop crooners Andy Williams, Tony Orlando, and Bobby Vinton. Las Vegas–based magicians like Kirby Van Burch and comedians like Yakov Smirnoff soon followed. Everyone quickly learned to "Bransonize" their shows. Boxcar Willie served as the unofficial mentor to celebrity newcomers, telling them what to say and how to act. Some called him the "godfather of wholesomeness."[44]

Jim Stafford, a modestly successful pop singer and television personality whose career had peaked in the 1970s, learned quickly. After performing at the Wildwood Flower Lounge and the Stars of the Ozarks Theatre in 1990, he purchased the 1,200-seat Lowe's Country Music Theatre in 1991 and renamed it after himself. In a taping of a live 1993 show, he barely gets through thirty seconds of a song before telling a joke and pivoting to the next bit. The audience is integrated into the show throughout. Early on, he persuades them to sing along to "Zippa-dee-doo-dah"; later, with a song he made up about women who aggressively pursue men, he commands the women to grab their husbands' knees every time he sings the line "turn loose my leg." For another song, he asks the audience to make various noises when he kicks to the right or points his guitar down, leading to a humorous cacophony as he speeds up the switching of gestures. During a segment where he plays Spanish classical guitar music, which is stereotypically serious and passionate, he wears a wide-brimmed hat with little balls hanging off it. Every few seconds, one of the balls drops down in front of his face, prompting laughter from the audience and interrupting the song. From a traditional cultural critic's perspective, Stafford's show was the epitome of lowbrow taste: no time for reflection, nothing to cause deep thought, not even the completion of a single artistic idea. Those nineteenth-century German critics who decried variety as "musical babble" were turning over in their graves. But Stafford was a wizard of popular entertainment who knew his audience, and he ran his Branson show successfully for decades.

When *The Independent* journalist Jim White traveled all the way from London in 1993 to see what the Branson fuss was all about, Stafford affirmed that it was largely about the American dream:

> This is the first time in 30 years that I can sleep two nights in the same bed. No more planes, no more tour buses, the folk just come to me. And I'm in charge of my own destiny. . . . and I take the money. It's beautiful, I've got a house by the lake, I go fishing, I play golf, my kids grow up breathing clean air. Why the hell'd I want to live in a big city like Nashville with all its big city problems?[45]

As with "welfare queen," the phrase "big city problems" by the early 1990s had a clear set of implications. In addition to smog, it meant crime, gangs, and the crack cocaine epidemic, all of which were coded as Black. Andy Williams explained that he decamped from Los Angeles because "I wanted to get away from the gangs, from the drive-by shootings. The closest things we have to gangs in Branson is the Lennon Sisters."[46] Nashville lacked Los Angeles's reputation for riots and gang warfare, but it did have a racially mixed population — enough to invoke the "big city problems" bogeyman. In the 1990 census, Nashville was 24.3 percent African American, as opposed to Branson's 0.1 percent.[47]

As Tillis tried to warn people on *60 Minutes*, Branson's American dream took hard work. The first level was the physical labor of putting on two shows a day, six days a week, for nine months in a row. And putting on a show meant *putting on a show*. As Stafford explained, "The thing I would hear people say is, 'They sang real good, but they just stood there.' These folks want to be entertained, they want something to happen. You've got to sing and dance and tell jokes."[48] Some performers, like Tillis, thrived on it. Every evening before the show, he would emerge from his dressing room, slap his hands together, and say, "All right, let's get to work." After the show, his powder-blue suit was bathed in sweat. Such clear expenditure of effort was a class-leveler, a physical manifestation of a democratic

Mel Tillis greeting fans in Branson, early 1990s. Note that he has sweated through his jacket. Courtesy White River Valley Historical Society.

ethos: you may be a celebrity, but you have to work hard to earn my dollar.

The second level of work was the emotional labor of being friendly with strangers. After each show, performers had to stay to shake hands, sign autographs, give hugs, and shoot the breeze. Never mind that it was nearing midnight and that they had arrived in the theater twelve hours earlier to set up for the matinee, perform the matinee, greet that audience for two hours, prepare for a second show, and perform that second show. The compulsory performance of friendliness extended beyond the theater. Stories abounded among locals and tourists of encountering celebrities in stores and discovering that they were just as humble and charming as their stage personas.[49]

Not all celebrities fit the bill. Willie Nelson failed in Branson during the 1992 season, despite the fact that he was the only performer on the Strip with multiple recent hits and a current recording contract.[50] But he performed to a half-empty theater. He simply sang "for ninety minutes straight," with no comedy or variety. And though he dutifully stayed to sign autographs, his bandmates disparaged the busloads of "very old" people who would "go to sleep in the front row." Nelson was also miserable, and most likely that came through both onstage and off. He had come to Branson out of financial desperation; poor management had left him millions of dollars in debt. In the middle of the season, Nelson's son committed suicide. Six days later, he was back onstage. "He was a prisoner," said a bandmate.[51] Merle Haggard had a similar experience. He performed concerts instead of variety shows and was rewarded with small, unenthusiastic audiences. "I actually had to tell people to put their hearing aids back up," he reminisced to a reporter. Haggard left Branson so depressed that he stopped playing his guitar for months. "It almost ended me. I can't say enough bad about it," he later stated.[52]

Wayne Newton, known as "Mr. Las Vegas," perhaps faced the toughest adjustment, though he did outlast Nelson and Haggard. In the early 1990s, Las Vegas began to transform from a town where singers were the stars (the Rat Pack in the 1960s, Elvis Presley in the 1970s) to a town where themed casinos (the Mirage in 1989, the Excalibur in 1990) were the stars. Many headliners decided to decamp for Branson. In 1993, Newton built a 3,000-seat, $14 million theater, bankrolled by Shenandoah South, an investment corporation consisting of local businessman Gary Snadon, Pizza Hut franchisee millionaire Eugene (Gene) Bicknell of Kansas, and Richard Gallagher of Springfield, Missouri. Much publicity and fanfare accompanied Newton's ambitious and luxurious performance space, whose façade looked like a Southern plantation mansion.

But Newton's opening night went poorly. He told some of his standard racy jokes, including "about Pennsylvania Amish towns with names such as Intercourse," and another about the sexual habits of the elderly. Jerry Davis, the president of nearby College of the Ozarks, complained vociferously. When Newton offered to donate $15,000 of the proceeds from his show to the private Christian college, Davis refused it.[53] After consulting with Boxcar Willie, Newton cleaned up his act and began raking in profits but butted heads with his investors. He accused Snadon of swindling him, won a lawsuit against Shenandoah South, and left the theater after one season.[54] He moved on to the Five Star Theatre owned by Jim Thomas, who willingly renamed the space the Wayne Newton Theatre. But Mr. Las Vegas soon clashed with Thomas as well, calling him "nothing but a country bumpkin that thinks that you can tell people what to do." He then moved on to share his buddy Tony Orlando's ostentatious Yellow Ribbon Theatre, a giant 2,000-seat space located off the Strip. Built at the height of the boom, it could not recoup its investment once growth leveled off.[55] After the Yellow Ribbon declared bankruptcy in 1997, the Vegas pals then moved to Glen Campbell's Goodtime Theatre, which they planned to rename the Talk of the T.O.W.N. Theatre (TOWN as their shared initials). Within one season, the partnership fell apart. Newton accused Orlando of owing him more than $2 million and locked him out of the theater, leaving Orlando unable to retrieve costumes and his daughters' toys. Orlando accused Newton of planting secret recording devices in the meeting rooms and lying about their debt. Newton then relocated permanently back to Las Vegas. Neither his official website nor his Wikipedia page mentions Branson at all, despite his six years performing there, including two in a theater with his name on it.[56]

Unlike Nelson, Haggard, or Newton, Shoji Tabuchi understood the assignment. When the boom began, the founding families feared that the influx of country music stars from Nashville would eclipse the local Ozark shows. Instead, their biggest competition came from an unknown fiddler born in Japan who turned out to be a consummate entertainer and shrewd businessman. Before Chisai Childs brought Tabuchi to town in 1981, he had spent fourteen years bouncing around the United States from gig to gig, playing fiddle in backup bands with the occasional solo feature. He continued in that type of role for eight years in Branson, which gave him ample opportunity to study the attributes of a Bransonized production. In 1989, he struck out on his own and opened the *Shoji Tabuchi Show* at a former automobile museum. Ron Sylvester of the *Springfield News-Leader* gave his debut performance a mediocre review. Sylvester acknowledged that Tabuchi "sure can fiddle," but he criticized the unfinished space. Workers were still laying carpet two hours before showtime, trying their best to turn a museum into a theater. Because the performers had been unable to rehearse in such conditions, the light and sound crews "consistently missed cues." Sylvester also disparaged Tabuchi as "The Japanese man with the Liberace jacket and the Moe Howard haircut."[57] The references to the flashy Vegas entertainer and Three Stooges doofus implied that Tabuchi's mash-up of gaudy costuming and simpleton personal style was tacky.

People wrote letters to the editor, incensed. "Could the person who wrote that article have actually been in attendance?" said Carla Reynolds. "The Shoji Tabuchi Show is a new and refreshing music show, loaded with a host of vibrant and extremely talented entertainers." She praised Tabuchi's "fiddle wizardry" and "exceptional repertoire." B. K. Smith, who also attended opening night, agreed. Smith "left feeling that I had been a part of something exciting and wonderful," and concluded, "The people of our area should be grateful and proud to have a theater of this caliber and even a review like that can't spoil the quality of what's there."[58]

With such tremendous popular support, Tabuchi did not stay in the automobile museum for long. He built his own theater along the Shepherd of the Hills Expressway and opened it to the public on May 1, 1990. He took a risk in building off the Strip, but tourists did not seem to mind — his entire season sold out. In a departure from the Branson standard of aluminum or concrete boxes, his ornate theater had distinctive architectural style. Amy Smith of the *Knoxville News Sentinel* breathlessly reported on the "more than a mile of flashy, purple neon that embellishes the art-deco exterior of

Shoji Tabuchi Theatre, 2005. Danita Delimont / Alamy Stock Photo.

Tabuchi's theater" and the lobby that "glitters with crystal chande-
liers." And, of course, she mentioned the glamorous bathrooms.[59] But
it wasn't just the décor that brought audiences. After all, they had
flocked to see Tabuchi even in the converted car museum. Instead,
his consummate showmanship, combined with his wife Dorothy's
production savvy, dazzled audiences.

At the start of a performance in the summer of 1993, the Shoji
Tabuchi Theatre went dark. A voice boomed in the darkness:
"SHOJI!" as lights spelled out the giant letters. A man in a bedazzled
dinner jacket bounded onto the stage, a beaming smile on his face,
his hair in a perfect bowl cut. He appeared youthful, energetic, innocent, and playful. He launched into a virtuosic violin solo before
declaring that "For me, the American dream came true." Then he
demonstrated how: through a song-and-dance number about show
business. Singing "Putting It Together" from the Broadway musical
Sunday in the Park with George, Tabuchi's bleached-blond, white
American wife bustled about the stage, interacting with ensemble
members who pantomimed making costumes, setting up photo
shoots, and handing her forms to sign. The musicians upstage —

piano, drums, guitar, dobro, bass guitar, trumpet, and trombone —
played at a frenetic pace. "Art isn't easy," Dorothy proclaimed, as
dancers broke into choreography borrowed from the "Music and the
Mirror" number in the hit musical *A Chorus Line*, leaping, pirouetting,
and kicking in front of a set of mirrors. The set pivoted, and suddenly
a group of country line dancers came forward, singing, "There's no
business like show business," from the musical *Annie Get Your Gun*,
as they held arms and torsos rigid, stamping and kicking their feet.
The men lifted and twirled their partners as Dorothy suddenly appeared on a platform in a sparkling, skintight country outfit: fringe,
belt, boots, cowboy hat. "I'll bet before the night is through, we'll play
your favorite song," she proclaimed. She was probably right, as in
the space of two hours, the cast performed parts of seventy songs.[60]

Shoji's production took the Bransonizing formula and kicked it up
a notch. Want variety? You barely had to wait thirty seconds before
another song began. But it was not just the number of songs but the
types of music, belying the claim that Branson visitors just wanted
country. After cast member Jay Wickizer came out in a red silk shirt,
cowboy hat, and silver-studded, fringed black coat to sing "Hard-
Workin' Man," the stage transformed into an Orientalist fantasy
for "Christina's Arabian Medley." Disney's *Aladdin* had just become
a box-office smash hit, and Tabuchi was quick to capitalize. Two
men appeared in whirling dervish outfits, spinning with one arm
curved up and the other arm curved down. Women twirled scarves
while wearing Bransonized versions of belly dancer costumes, with
no navels or cleavage visible. Twelve-year-old Christina Tabuchi
(Dorothy and Shoji's daughter) flew in on a magic carpet before
rubbing a giant lamp to make three genies in puffy bodysuits tap-
dance with swords. The variety proceeded unabated: a John Lennon
cover followed by Western swing, Louisiana zydeco, polka, waltz, a
1950s–1960s pop medley consisting of seventeen songs in about ten
minutes, Caribbean steel drums, and Mozart. Then Tabuchi really
got the crowd going with the "Orange Blossom Special," as his violin
mimicked the sounds of a train going faster and faster. As he sped
up, he upped the wow factor by playing behind his back, over his

head, and then, under his leg while he hopped. The audience gasped and whooped; he left the stage and came back, and the audience rose for a standing ovation as he played *even faster*.

In addition to variety and spectacle, Tabuchi brought the self-deprecating humor essential to a Bransonized show. The hometown boys may have dressed up like hillbillies and cracked jokes about outhouses, but Tabuchi recognized that such jokes from an outsider would come across as insults. Instead, he set himself, and his foreignness, as the target. "I'm from Louisiana. Can't you tell by my accent?" he said with a grin. At another point, he complained that Mel Tillis wouldn't go fishing with him anymore because "every time he turns around, I'm eating his bait." The audience burst out laughing. Tabuchi laughed too. "You don't believe that, do you?" he said, smiling. Then he added a final punch line: "I used to, but I quit."

Tabuchi would not have flourished had he simply emphasized his foreignness. Instead, his show concluded by reiterating that as an assimilated immigrant, he was the ultimate example of the American dream. The final segment began with the lights coming up on Dorothy. She offered testimony about her husband: the man who arrived in the United States with $500 in his pocket and the "biggest dream of his whole life." Through hard work (washing dishes, washing cars) and faith ("not once did he think about giving up his music or leaving"), his dream came true. She concluded, "Shoji and I know that without a doubt, everything that we have, everything that we are, and everything that we will be in the future we owe to God without a doubt. We also feel with all our hearts that we live in the greatest country in the world. And that is the United States of America!" The audience cheered wildly. Dorothy disappeared as the ensemble entered the stage in gospel choir robes to sing "I Will Follow Him." The *Baldknobbers Hillbilly Jamboree* and Presleys' *Mountain Music Jubilee* had often ended with a gospel number. The *Shoji Tabuchi Show* instead segued from gospel into "America the Beautiful," and finally, "The Star-Spangled Banner." The audience rose to sing along. The Tabuchi family, a Holy Trinity of father, mother, and child, appeared on a platform that levitated above the ensemble.

Technological spectacle built up the climax. Laser lights flashed, an American flag waved, fireworks burst on a giant projector screen, and in the final moment, red, white, and blue confetti rained down on the stage.

For almost the entirety of the 1990s and into the early 2000s, the *Shoji Tabuchi Show* was considered one of the most popular shows in town, if not *the* most popular.[61] He declared that he had achieved the American dream doing it the Branson way. He also offered something unique to many of his audience members: a feeling of absolution. His audiences consisted largely of the World War II generation, many of whom had lost friends and relatives fighting the Japanese in the Pacific. In Branson, rather than hold on to their antagonism, they warmly embraced a man with a thick Japanese accent.

Bust

Despite the successes of Tabuchi and others, the Branson business community was beginning to worry that the boom was turning into a bust. The first problem was traffic. All popular tourist destinations are by definition crowded, but the lack of planning exacerbated Branson's overcrowding woes. Few regulations governed the city's entertainment industry. If you owned land, you could build pretty much whatever type of business you wanted. You could have as many entrances and exits to that property as you wanted. Your show could start at any time you wanted, and everyone wanted to start at 2 p.m. and 8 p.m. Every afternoon and every evening, thousands of cars and buses attempted to turn off Highway 76 and into theater parking lots around the exact same times. It infamously took two hours to travel two miles down the Strip. Every visiting reporter mentioned the traffic, as did every tourist when they returned home to tell their friends and family about Branson.

Traffic thus became a huge potential liability. Nobody wanted to go on vacation to sit still in a car for hours, especially not senior citizens with hip problems or families with young kids, and especially not after driving hours to get there in the first place. And if people were talking about traffic, that meant they weren't talking about the shows, the attractions, or the restaurants. Pete Herschend said dramatically in 1992, "If we don't work to solve this, much of the Branson miracle will simply cease to exist."[62] Widening the two-lane highway seemed infeasible because of the hilly topography. Some raised the idea of trolleys or elevated light rail, but funding never materialized, given the stigma of mass transit as a liberal government project.[63] Instead, building more roads became the answer. In 1992, Governor John Ashcroft declared the traffic an "economic emergency" and fast-tracked a $140 million, eighteen-mile highway loop project, called the Ozark Mountain Highroad.

Ashcroft faced opposition from several groups: environmentalists who worried about slashing through hillsides, local landowners who vowed they would not sell, and most importantly, business owners along the Strip.[64] The reason why a carnival has a midway is to funnel people down one lane and see all the goods on offer. Slow traffic did not bother Strip business owners; traffic gave people in cars more time to read the marquees. A bypass road meant bypassing eye-catching signs about where you could eat, sleep, or see an extra show. Furthermore, traffic suggested popularity.[65] But Herschend, whose business was not on the Strip and who was good friends with Ashcroft, prevailed. The Missouri Department of Transportation held a public hearing without allowing any opponents of the Highroad to comment. Boxcar Willie decided to remedy that situation by showing up with "his own portable microphone and speaker," arguing loudly with officials, and getting ejected.[66]

In the end, nobody won. The Missouri Highway Commission approved the project in November 1992, but the northern half of the loop was not completed until June 2003, meaning that environmental problems and disruptions to civic life dragged on for over a decade, all without solving the acute traffic problems. The initial $18 million cost ballooned astronomically, leading some locals to acerbically call the project "Silver Dollar City's $200 million driveway."[67] Few people ever used the Highroad, and the southern half of the loop was abandoned altogether.

Labor was also a major issue. City officials had not developed any affordable housing, and thus some entertainment industry employees were living in tents in local campgrounds. Headliners might have cleared millions in months, but ushers, ticket takers, and cleanup crews made near-minimum wage and were unemployed from when shows closed after Christmas until they opened again in March or April.[68] Leaders dreamed up several projects to extend the tourist season year-round, but aside from Jim Stafford's "Hot Winter Fun" shows in January, Branson essentially remained closed three months of the year. Workers' efforts to improve wages failed repeatedly, even when the boom brought an influx of tradesmen and theater professionals, labor pools with traditionally strong union membership. In September 1993, stagehands at Andy Williams' Moon River Theatre held a vote to join the International Alliance of Theatrical Stage Employees (IATSE). Four voted for, three voted against, and four were contested ballots; in the end, the unionization attempt was defeated. A handful of workers at the Grand Palace planned a unionization vote, but some of their fellow employees went public with their opposition. They claimed that a union would result in the loss of creative freedom, personal freedom, and the freedom to settle issues directly with managers. In the end, the National Labor Relations Board dismissed the unfair-labor-practice claim against the theater, and the unionization effort died. Unfair-labor-practice charges were also filed against the Wayne Newton Theatre but settled.[69] The only successful unionization effort came from government workers. In March 1994, for the first time in the city's history, employees in the Public Works Department voted to join the Teamsters Local No. 245 of Springfield. Wages were the most salient issue. While their entry-level pay was comparable to public works employees in other Missouri small towns, the Branson ones "probably do about ten times the amount of work," said one worker, given that four to five million visitors a year utilized the city's infrastructure.[70]

These services could often not keep up. Twice in 1992, the overwhelmed sewage treatment plant spilled wastewater into Lake

Taneycomo, causing health concerns. A whistleblower complained to government officials that building codes were being violated left and right in the rush of new construction. The state's top building safety regulator, Shirley Cramer-Benson, opened more than 200 investigations into Branson theaters, restaurants, and hotels in 1993, leading to a rash of negative publicity. Cramer-Benson was fired soon thereafter — despite having served in the role for nineteen years — which she claimed was in direct retaliation for her investigations.[71]

With problems sprouting like weeds, the 20 percent growth in 1993 slowed to 3.7 percent in 1994. Theater owners complained about the increasing competition and worried that it hurt Branson's reputation as a place where American dreams came true. Jim Thomas dismissed such concerns. "The town is no longer a 'field of dreams,'" he admitted, but that meant "we must now get down to what the American system is all about — free enterprise and competition. . . . Branson is becoming a better place because it has become competitive."[72] The OMC, led by the Herschends, decided that the solution to the problems created by overgrowth was even more growth. "The key to continued development is reaching an ever-widening market," stated Kathy Oechsle, a sentiment that OMC shared. The Marketing Council aimed its next round of advertisements at "upscale" families in Dallas/Fort Worth, Chicago, Minneapolis, and Houston.[73] But it lacked resources. In 1995, the city's paltry marketing budget of $1.7 million was the equivalent to the cost of one sixty-second ad during the Super Bowl. Even with the OMC's additional $2.5 million, the numbers paled in comparison to Las Vegas, which spent $52 million, and Disney, which spent $60–80 million each year.[74]

Some hoped that the arrival of a new big name would attract new customers: Dolly Parton. The Herschends had developed a relationship with Parton back in 1976 when they built a second Silver Dollar City in Pigeon Forge, Tennessee, six miles from Parton's hometown of Sevierville. Pigeon Forge had been incorporated in 1961 as part of its bid to become a tourist destination, modeled like Branson on selling hillbilly culture as entertainment. In 1986, the Herschends officially partnered with Parton and renamed the Pigeon Forge theme park Dollywood. While infused with Parton's persona, it retained the fundamental aspects of Silver Dollar City, including an emphasis on live performance, craftspeople making and selling goods, and an earnestness that gave a feeling of authenticity despite the clearly manufactured environment.[75] The Herschends' family business was becoming a family empire. Together with Parton, they opened the Dolly Parton Dixie Stampede Dinner Show in 1988, first in Pigeon Forge, then in Myrtle Beach, South Carolina, and finally in Branson in 1995.

Branson's *Dixie Stampede* show started at 5:30 p.m., "allowing guests to get to other shows," because "Dolly's philosophy is that she doesn't want to compete with her friends."[76] The production recast the brutal Civil War as a "friendly rivalry" between the North and South, and the marketing and publicity emphasized the Confederacy. The theater looked like a Southern plantation mansion, and "Dixie" was in the title. Producers described the show as "recreating the charm and romance of the Old South, and the chivalry and honor of a bygone century." Inside, the auditorium was set up like a rodeo, with a sand-covered stage area in the middle and seating all around, divided in half between the "North" and the "South." Each side cheered on horseback riders competing to win points through virtuosic tricks, like riding upside down or jumping through a fiery hoop. A hillbilly comedian provided comic relief, and audience members came down to participate in certain events, such as a chicken-catching race or toilet-seat horseshoe. Throughout, waiters in Civil War uniforms appropriate to their side served a multicourse dinner: soup, a whole squab, sliced pork tenderloin, corn on the cob, and a pastry dessert. Local critic Ron Sylvester considered the meal a "social equalizer" because all patrons were required to eat with their hands.[77]

But the evening was only an experience of equality if you were white. In between the horse-riding, chicken-catching, and pig-racing competitions, the show told the *Stampede's* version of American history. In it, the South offered refinement and civilization. At one point, a gazebo descended from the ceiling, carrying women in antebellum ball gowns and gentlemen in tailored suits. They stepped off to waltz in the dirt arena, the lilting strains of violins playing a nostalgic tune. Grace, beauty, the good life — all transmitted without recognition of what made those attributes possible, namely, enslaved labor. For the reconciliatory final number, Dolly Parton's recorded voice declared that the competitions had all just been in good fun. The division between North and South was all just a misunderstanding, because in the end audience members were all Americans. The audience cheered and sang along to a patriotic song.[78] This depiction of the South — as misunderstood defenders of states' rights and heritage — had been ingrained in American culture for so long that the *Dixie Stampede* did not register as controversial or diminish Parton's reputation as an icon for people across the political spectrum.[79]

With the 1995 tourism season starting off slowly, local performers expressed hope that this new attraction, which premiered midseason in July, would jump-start tourism.[80] The *Dixie Stampede* did succeed wildly, selling out every performance. But whether it helped other shows was an open question. Producers decided to add a second show per night at 8 p.m., thus voiding Parton's stated commitment not to compete with fellow entertainers. Tour companies now included the *Dixie Stampede* as a "guaranteed" show alongside Shoji Tabuchi, meaning that it took a slot that would have otherwise gone to other shows.[81]

The *Dixie Stampede* did arguably capture tourists who would have gone to rival destinations like Pigeon Forge, but the Herschends and Thomas also aimed at even bigger fish: New York and Las Vegas. These efforts began in 1993 when Branson brought the Broadway musical *Pump Boys and Dinettes* to town, with its full original cast, as well as a version of *Oklahoma!* starring Rudy Gatlin of the Gatlin Brothers.[82] They continued in 1994 when the Herschends built a 4,000-seat theater called the Grand Palace that won the Country Music Association's "Venue of the Year" Award. The publicity caught the attention of the Radio City Rockettes, which had been contemplating finding a second venue for their *Christmas Spectacular*. The Rock-ettes management was impressed how "Branson worked together to promote Christmas as an entire community" and felt that Bran-son was a cultural fit for their approach. Their *Spectacular* included a nativity scene; it was an all-ages, "clean" show; and it celebrated America. Advertising promoted the Rockettes as "coming home," given that the organization had started in 1925 in St. Louis as the Missouri Rockets before decamping to New York and developing their signature production in the early 1930s. In 1994, the Grand Pal-ace became the first place the Rockettes performed their *Christmas Spectacular* outside of Radio City Music Hall. They replicated the whole experience, complete with live exotic animals and the famed scene with the Rockettes as wooden soldiers. It was a huge gamble, costing $1 million to produce, but it paid off. Thousands of eager fans flocked from hundreds of miles around for a chance to see this famed American tradition that had heretofore only existed in New York City.[83]

While the Rockettes' success signaled that Branson's bid to compete with New York or Las Vegas was serious, stumbling blocks remained. The biggest one was not the city's location or its traffic problems or its marketing budget, but its identity as a bastion for Christian conservatism. As the long culture war in America flared up again in the 1990s, Branson struggled to balance its desire for limitless growth with the fact that its values of faith, family, and flag, promoted as universal, were not seen as so universal after all.

5 FAITH

The Culture Wars

> We are the most politically incorrect
> community in the world. God likes this,
> and so do millions of tourists.
>
> Don Gabriel, "The Branson Manifesto," ca.
> 2006

In 1990, the Plummer family faced a choice. Big country music stars were moving into town, threatening the livelihoods of mom-and-pop variety shows like theirs. Real estate prices were skyrocketing. After seventeen successful years on the Strip, it seemed to Darrell and Rosie Plummer like the right time to cash out and retire back home to Knob Lick, Missouri. Their daughter Melody agreed and decamped for Texas. Their son Randy, however, refused to leave. He thought back to 1971 when he first set foot in Branson, a wide-eyed teenager watching the Presleys and the Mabes perform. Randy recalled, "I felt the presence of God so strong here. Really, I mean I remember that to this day. How I felt . . . I just felt like God's hand was on this area so much." The Lord had called him to the Ozarks, and he was not going anywhere.[1]

Others who arrived in Branson experienced God's hand as an oppressive force, one sometimes intertwined with racism and homophobia. After the 1990s boom, shows started to hire professional dancers, singers, and musicians from outside the area, advertising in industry publications on the coasts like *Backstage* and *Backstage West*. Melissa Calasanz and Heather Castillo of Los Angeles landed jobs with the *Andy Williams Show* in 1996, and the culture shock was immediate. Some things were minor, like the lack of fresh produce at grocery stores. Others were major. "I had never seen more hypocrisy in my life when it came to hometown values," Calasanz said.[2] A married leader of a Sunday morning show-service groped her; a proudly born-again Christian magician snorted copious amounts of cocaine backstage. When Castillo, who was white, went out on the dance floor at a country music bar with a Black castmate, someone tapped her on the shoulder and told her they needed to leave, immediately. Her biggest head-spinning moment came the day she decided to check out Eureka Springs, a popular tourist destination fifty miles south down Highway 65. As soon as she crossed into Arkansas, she saw something that made her heart stop. It was a commonplace, seemingly innocuous "Adopt-a-Highway" sign. This one, however, was adopted by the Ku Klux Klan. Castillo turned around. "I think that going to Japan and dancing for an all-Japanese audience was less of a culture shock," she said.[3] In Branson, she felt like she had landed in another country.

What kind of country was it? Were the Missouri Ozarks "God's country" or "Hee-Haw Hell"? Was Branson "a perfect American town" or "a neon nightmare"? The *60 Minutes* exposure had been both a blessing and a curse, bringing not only more tourists, but also more outside scrutiny. In the 1990s, polarized descriptions of the city began circulating nationally and epitomized the culture wars that were engulfing the United States.

On two things, both sides could agree. First, faith, especially evangelical Christianity, was everywhere in Branson. Ozark Mountain Country was not just in the Bible Belt; it was the *buckle* of the Bible Belt. The scope of Christian entertainment was remarkable. Branson was not just one outdoor Passion Play or one Creation Museum; it was an entire industry with dozens of theaters and hundreds of performers who openly and proudly affirmed their faith. It brought together not only evangelical Christians, but also Mormons, Anabaptists, and Catholics, groups with a history of antagonism. In Branson, they shared an investment in live theater as a place to spread the gospel of Jesus Christ. As the twenty-first century approached, Branson's reputation became self-reinforcing: the more it was known as a center for Christian entertainment, the more Christian performers and tourists came, and the more its reputation became true.

Second, both sides agreed that the scope of Christian community-building had political implications. If one wanted to find the heart of the new Religious Right, they just needed to go to Branson. The two sides disagreed about whether that political future was a dream or a nightmare. The culture wars entered a new phase in 1979 after Jerry Falwell established the Moral Majority, an organization that aligned evangelical Christians with the Republican Party and helped push Ronald Reagan to the presidency. In the late 1980s, the Family Research Council trademarked the phrase "Faith, Family, and Freedom," which was soon taken up by Republican politicians. New terms such as the Christian Right and the Religious Right began to circulate as a nod to the growing intertwinement of faith, conservative ideology, and political party affiliation. In 1990, evangelical leader and onetime presidential candidate Pat Robertson turned his Christian Coalition into a voter mobilization organization that distributed election guides to churches. In the 1994 midterm elections, these efforts helped the Republican Party capture both the House and the Senate for the first time since 1953.[4]

The media depicted the opposing sides of the culture wars with broad strokes. One side was evangelical Christian, white, and conservative. They opposed abortion, LGBTQ rights, affirmative action, and gun control; they favored prayer in school, low taxes, and limited government, except for supporting the military. The other side was secular, multiethnic, liberal, and in favor of the exact opposite agenda.

Of course, such archetypes failed to capture the complexity of reality. Many evangelical Christians were neither white nor conservative. Many conservatives were not evangelical or even religious. People's stances on the issues did not always neatly line up with their "side." And even if someone was evangelical, white, and self-proclaimed as conservative, that didn't automatically mean they supported the KKK adopting a highway in Arkansas. But journalists in the 1990s who wanted to find a ground zero for stereotypical cultural warriors had a field day in Branson. They depicted the city as an anti-modern cancer eating away at progress. For them, the city's brand of Christianity was inextricably intertwined with racism, homophobia, nativism, and the lowest common denominator of American culture. And "brand" was the right word — they saw religion in Branson as a cynical marketing tactic rather than as a deeply felt spiritual practice.

But for several entertainers and millions of tourists, Branson was a "haven."[5] It was one of the few places they could take their families on vacation and feel assured that their values were respected. They felt besieged by what they considered to be the country's increasingly secular agenda. In their eyes, most entertainment hubs in the United States — Las Vegas, Los Angeles, New York, even Disney World — promoted secular liberalism. In contrast, Branson was a place where they felt safe saying "God and country" together. It modeled the future they wished to see for America, one with Christianity at the center.

Branson's place in the culture war reflected national trends. Evangelical Christianity was on the rise in the late twentieth century but seemed continuously "embattled."[6] Conservatives won nationwide political office and passed legislation that achieved the Right's economic goals of deregulation, lower taxes, and the weakening of the welfare state. But they failed to shift the culture. Throughout the 1990s, 2000s, and 2010s, the push to ban abortion, halt the multiplying legal protections of LGBTQ rights, and reinstate prayer in schools fell short again and again, with the tide only turning in the 2020s.[7] Continued failure fueled resentment, but the earnestness that defined Branson entertainment stubbornly persisted. Whether such earnestness was authentically felt or simply savvy branding, the result was the same. When journalists scorned Branson as a place for "has-beens," the city took the insult and flipped it on its head. The fact that many Branson entertainers were past their prime but flourishing demonstrated the Christian concept of rebirth and the American ideal of the second chance. The city's ethos of resurrection made it seem possible that by extension, the nation could be born again.

People like Melissa Calasanz were caught in the middle. She was not a cultural warrior for the Left or the Right; she was a performer who needed a job. So, despite the hypocrisy she encountered, she stayed at Williams's Moon River Theatre for four years. While not unionized, she received decent wages and good benefits. By her account, Williams treated her and other employees well. She also had a much lower cost of living than she would have had in Los Angeles. She lip-synced her way through gospel songs and pirouetted her way through rousing patriotic numbers. She painted her face white and put on a red sequined showgirl dress to sing "The Lullaby of Broadway" in Japanese. She befriended locals, whom she found to be some of the most genuinely kind people she had ever met. She helped closeted friends find men to hook up with in literal closets. She only left when Williams developed nodules on his vocal cords and could only offer his dancers part-time contracts.[8]

The internal conflict Calasanz felt was reflected on a citywide level as the new millennium approached. Despite the entertainment community's attempts at unity, the national scrutiny caused fissures. Some leaders felt humiliated by the negative media and wanted to change the city's image. Others wanted to lean into being the vanguard of the Christian Right. As conservative leaders nationwide began to articulate the three F's slogan in the early 1990s, so too did people in Branson, seeing it as a natural fit with what was already happening onstage. A third faction wanted to maintain Branson's Christian foundation but detach it from political agendas or culture wars. Whether such separation was possible was an open question.

Indeed, how *could* a city dedicated to theatrical entertainment be designated as God's country in the first place? For hundreds of years, Christian ministers had declared that performers lacked industriousness and virtue, leading to sloth and moral decay. Theater was suspect because it trained people in the art of deception. Dance was suspect because of its physical intimacy, displays of the body, and obvious intimations of sexual intercourse. Attending theater was not seen as much better than performing onstage. Even spectatorship purportedly inflamed worldly passions, leading patrons down the road of sexual impropriety and taking time away from work, family, and religious contemplation. While congregations incorporated music as part of worship, many banned dancing or participation in theater.[9] Thus from one perspective, it is head-scratching to think of Branson's Strip as a place divinely blessed.

At the same time, Christianity in the United States has long been intensely theatrical. In a country with no state church, religious institutions have competed in a marketplace-like environment for worshippers.[10] No one is required to attend your service, so if you want people in pews and dollars in the collection plate, you had better offer something interesting to watch or hear. And ironically, the lack of government-supported arts institutions has meant that historically, Americans turned to churches to fulfill not only their spiritual needs but also their desire to be entertained. British writer Frances Trollope, traveling in the United States in the 1830s, bemoaned the dearth of theaters and noted with astonishment that instead people went to debates about Christianity to amuse themselves.[11] While the rise of radio, film, television, and digital media in the twentieth and twenty-first centuries has offered a plethora of opportunities for diversion, the precedent established in the nineteenth century that religion would entertain has endured.

Evangelical Christians were particularly adept at religious entertainment. Evangelicalism is difficult to define but is generally understood to include four basic principles. The first is *conversionism*, or the belief that you cannot simply be born as a Christian but must actively choose to accept Jesus Christ as your Lord and Savior, and thus be born again. The second is *biblicism*, or belief that the Bible is the inerrant Word of God. The third is *crucicentrism*, the idea that Christ died on the cross for humanity's sins. The fourth and most central to the entertainment question is *activism*: the belief that true Christians must serve God by spreading the Gospel (or "Good News") to others, using whatever gifts God has given them. Those gifts could include singing, dancing, or acting.[12] This activism is embedded in the very name: an evangelist is one who evangelizes.

Starting with George Whitefield (1714–1770), evangelical preachers of both the First and Second Great Awakening heavily employed theatrical techniques to share the Good News. Whitefield used his skills as an actor, particularly "good elocution, a trained memory, [and] the ability to project intense emotion," to command audiences of thousands.[13] He theatrically reenacted Bible stories as part of his sermons, turning staid recitation into enthralling, entertaining performance. For rural Americans who lived on isolated farms, the once-a-year tent revival or camp meeting was a major source of entertainment, social engagement, and emotional release. Nevertheless, a sacred/secular divide persisted until the mid-twentieth century, at least in rhetoric. Devout Christians were supposed to focus their efforts on salvation for the afterlife, not worldly matters. The enormous popularity of Billy Graham, who preached to thousands in football stadiums and conferred with President Dwight D. Eisenhower, heralded a major shift. By the late twentieth century, evangelicals regularly adapted popular culture phenomena, including rock music and musical theater, as forms of ministry, and engaged in electoral politics as part of their mission.[14]

Branson's designation as God's country gained traction after the publication of *The Shepherd of the Hills* in 1907. Wright believed in the lived experience of Christianity rather than abiding by doctrine handed down by ordained ministers. In *The Shepherd of the Hills*, no characters attend church, and yet Wright portrayed them as exemplars of lived Christianity. The tourists who flocked to Branson in the 1910s and 1920s came to find not just the inspirations for the characters, but also a sense of divinity in the hills. In a sentiment to be repeated for the next hundred years, local taxi driver Pearl Spurlock told her customers that Branson had "God's special favor."[15]

In the 1960s and 1970s, *Shepherd of the Hills*, Silver Dollar City, and the family variety shows all were examples of Wright's lived Christianity. Performers' faith was so central to their identity that it was woven in seamlessly. Pete and Jack Herschend of Silver Dollar City became born again during their young adulthood in Branson, and their faith guided their decisions about the theme park thereafter. They believed, after St. Francis of Assisi, in "preach[ing] the gospel always, using words only whenever necessary" — meaning that people would rather be led to Jesus Christ via Christianity in action than via exhortation from a pulpit. Pete stated, "Sometimes people will never know why they feel good about this place. There are people who are Christians who spot it rather readily in the feeling of the park. . . . People who are not Christian say this place has a special feeling. People often write back and say this is where they met the Lord."[16] Not everything was indirect. Silver Dollar City included a Wilderness Church that, from the beginning, conducted Sunday services for both employees and guests. There was also a staff minister and weekly Bible study. From its inception to at least the early 2000s, it was the only theme park in the country to have these religious offerings.[17] The Mabes and Presleys, descended from preachers, wove gospel into their shows, as did virtually every other family show.

While the area had always drawn Christian audiences, the idea to *market* Branson as a specifically religious destination began in the early 1980s. In 1982, Burke Christian Tours out of North Carolina started their first motor coach tour to the Ozarks, billed as "Ozark Mountain Holiday." The main highlight was *The Great Passion Play*, in Eureka Springs, Arkansas, which that year overtook *The Shepherd of the Hills* as the number-one outdoor drama in the United States. *The Great Passion Play* — first produced by notorious antisemite Gerald L. K. Smith — told the story of Jesus Christ's last days on earth and claimed to be "historically accurate and true to Holy Scriptures."[18] The next day's itinerary featured *The Shepherd of the Hills*.[19] In response to where the tourism market was going, director Keith Thurman revised the script in the 1980s "to emphasize Christian tones more blatantly." For example, at the end, the ghosts of two dead characters appear holding hands, signaling that they have been reunited in Heaven — something that never appeared in Wright's book. Thurman also eliminated the mild cussing of the original script (which had an occasional "hell" and "damn") after receiving complaints from visiting church groups.[20] The two productions combined to attract almost half a million people a year.[21]

Other Branson-area ventures caught on. In 1985, Silver Dollar City began to organize Young Christian Weekends. After taking in the crafts, the saloon shows, and the rides, young Christians could attend a "youth-appealing Saturday evening music ministry," and "youth seminars" that included topics like "Sex and Dating" and "Christ and the Athlete."[22] And in 1988, the Marketing Council decided to defy nature and add a fifth season to winter, spring, summer, and fall: Christmas. Billed as "Ozark Mountain Christmas," the Marketing Council convinced Waltzing Waters, Wilderness Safari, the Presleys, and 76 Music Hall to stay open through December. The city's annual Adoration Parade was incorporated into the marketing of the new season. The parade had begun in 1949 when artist Steve Miller and furniture store manager Joe Todd hatched a plan to create a twenty-eight-foot-high nativity scene on the top of Mount Branson, a hill that overlooked downtown, as a "Christmas card" for residents and visitors. Miller worked on design, while Todd secured funding from the Chamber of Commerce. At dusk on the first Sunday in December, the nativity scene was lit. Then residents paraded in a loop around the downtown area, looking up at Mary, Joseph, and the Three Wise Men greeting Baby Jesus.[23] While religious, the Adoration Parade had the elements of spectacle, ritual, and tradition that also worked for tourism purposes. In the parade's fortieth year, OMC marketed it as the symbolic opening of the Christmas season. Doing so reminded tourists that the city's overarching goal was to "put Christ back in Christmas." The first year of Ozark Mountain Christmas, sales tax receipts in Taney and Stone counties increased 264 percent over the year before, and it became a permanent fixture of the Branson tourism industry.[24]

After the *60 Minutes* segment in December 1991 precipitated the boom, marketing to Christians increased. City boosters created the *Branson Church Getaway Planner* to help groups organize their trips effectively; they encouraged pastors to plan retreats there. The boom was even publicized as an act of God. *Charisma* magazine proclaimed in 1993 that "Behind all the music, money and tourism is a larger, quieter story. God is using Branson to attract hundreds of people to His Son."[25] At least one gospel number was obligatory in every Branson show, including for the not-particularly-religious

Andy Williams. Some performers and local preachers established a new type of production, the "show-service." In the very same theaters that charged patrons to see performances of gospel music on Saturday nights, visitors could come for free Sunday mornings to listen to much of the same material. Barbara Fairchild started a show-service in the Wayne Newton Theatre. At Jim Stafford's Theatre, pastor Dewey Aitchison started the *Branson Gospel Hour*, which included singing by country music star Glen Campbell, a born-again Christian. Tourist Seth Golding testified that he found Jesus at this Gospel Hour. Lured by the promise of hearing Campbell, he was equally struck by Aitchison's sermon. The event "opened some doors that really hadn't been opened to me before," Golding stated. He returned to Branson a few months later to have Aitchison baptize him in Table Rock Lake, and Glen Campbell sang at his wedding.[26]

The boom also brought Mormon entertainers to Branson. The Church of Jesus Christ of Latter-day Saints (LDS, or colloquially known as the Mormon Church) had long supported theater, dance, and music as means of worshipping God. Unlike many evangelical Christian denominations that approach the body as a repository of sin, the LDS church embraces the body as a "divine gift" that can be cultivated to become closer to God. Marty Hughes of the *Hughes Brothers Show* reflected, "Music is really a whole body celebration, isn't it? And when you show that through dance, it's a representation of God's gift of vibrations. It's really an amazing thing to dance. It's a celebration in the scriptures and it's a celebration of life. It's a celebration of fertility."[27] Early LDS leader Brigham Young (1801–1877) was well regarded as an actor and infamously finished building a theater in Salt Lake City decades before he finished building the temple. Furthermore, the LDS faith tends to be all-encompassing, meaning that one's professional and social worlds are contained within the religious community. Dancing, music-making, and theater are not sinful activities done sneakily on a Saturday night across the street from the church — they are done within church-sponsored recreational events.[28] Mormons in the twentieth century looked to musical theater as an example of American values in action and self-consciously adapted the genre as a means to show themselves to be fully American rather than religious pariahs. To this day, Brigham Young University and the University of Utah have some of the nation's top musical theater programs.[29]

Mormons also connected to Branson's exceptionalism-within-American-exceptionalism. Senator Mike Lee of Utah once joked that "Mormons sort of have an extra chromosome" when it comes to American patriotism. The religion was founded on American soil and, according to the Book of Mormon, Jesus came to visit his followers in America after his death and resurrection. The nation is thus imbued with divine special favor. Furthermore, founder Joseph Smith claimed that Missouri was to be the site of a "new Zion" to which Jesus Christ would return. Thousands of LDS members settled in Missouri in the 1830s, including Smith himself in 1838. Locals fearful of this seemingly strange and blasphemous new religion ran him out within the year, but many Mormons ended up staying despite the threats of violence. To this day, Missouri has a spiritual significance for the LDS church.[30]

The first Mormon performers to come to Branson were the Osmonds. Andy Williams, who had launched the Osmond family to fame on his television variety show in the early 1960s, told them he was finding great success in his new Moon River Theatre. The Osmonds' careers had faltered in the 1980s, and with debts piling up, Branson seemed worth a shot. Thirty-eight Osmonds piled into cars to make the journey from Utah and open the Osmond Family Theater in the former *Bob-O-Link's* space. The eclectic variety of their musical style — often seen as a cause of their fall from the charts, as nobody could figure out if they were pop, rock, country, or what — worked perfectly in Branson. They hired eighteen dancers to perform in their show, which was an unheard-of size for an ensemble at the time. The Osmonds were a hit, and in turn, they praised Branson and its visitors. They told journalist Jeanne Laskas that "Branson is a place to which people come not just to hear music but to confirm their convictions about America and God." One Osmond said, "America is going down the toilet" but that Branson was "moral majority land."[31]

The Osmonds' success encouraged more Mormon entertainers. The Hughes Brothers arrived two years later in 1995. Marty and his four brothers grew up surrounded by music in Salt Lake City. Symphonies, concertos, marches, operas, jazz, Broadway tunes, popular music — the Hughes parents' taste was diverse, and something was always playing on the record player. Father Gary played the accordion, piano, and guitar. He also had an impressive vocal range and sang the National Anthem at President Nixon's first inauguration as a member of the famed Mormon Tabernacle Choir. Matriarch Lena (Nilsson) Hughes, who emigrated from Sweden at the age of one, played the clarinet and was first chair in the Utah all-state orchestra as a teenager. Gary and Lena met at a Mormon Church "fireside," or event geared toward young adults to build a sense of religious community. These firesides would often feature performing families, including the night both Lena and Gary attended. Lena heard this "amazing big voice" behind her during a singalong number, turned around, and the rest was history. They married in 1966 and started having children soon thereafter. Lena always dreamed of having a performing family like the ones she saw at firesides. She put her oldest, Marty, in front of an audience at age three for an Independence Day celebration. He wore a top hat and carried a cane as he performed a tap dance to "Baby Elephant Walk," a Grammy-winning instrumental song by Henry Mancini. Marty dropped down to one knee for the grand finale, and the audience rose for a standing ovation. He never forgot that rush of energy from an appreciative audience, and it instilled in him a love of performing.[32]

Eventually Gary and Lena's five sons formed an act to perform at state and county fairs. The older boys sang and danced to everything from rock to pop to Broadway; the youngest, age six, did impressions of Michael Jackson. "I think the family that prays together and the family that sings together, stays together," said Marty years later.[33] Like many Mormon performers from Utah, the brothers found their way to Vegas, but producers there told them they would find more success in Branson. Though they had never heard of the town, they decided to check it out after a recording session in Nashville. They did a one-week audition at Silver Dollar City, landed a contract for the summer of 1995, performed with the Osmonds in the fall, then opened their own show for Christmas.

What the Hughes lacked in financial capital they made up for in hustle. They brokered agreements with ticket resellers and timeshares; they sang at restaurants; they participated in Branson community events to alleviate suspicions that Mormons were not "true" Christians. They switched their repertoire to emphasize country music but simultaneously kept their impressive ballroom dance routines to differentiate themselves. They did three shows a day, six days a week — a morning show, an evening show, and a Wild West show in between. "We were the hardest-working guys in town," Marty boasted, but the overwork caused his brother Jason to develop nodules on his vocal cords, from which he never fully recovered.[34] Owning their own theater seemed like a healthier way to make the Branson dream happen. Instead of performing three shows a day, they could do one show a day and rent out the space to other groups. In 2000, they bought the Roy Clark Celebrity Theatre from Jim Thomas.

Marty Hughes was grateful for Branson and the opportunity to "go into the entertainment business through the back door." He called Broadway a "cesspool" that had "ruined a lot of [Mormons'] moral lives."[35] Jason Hughes's professors at Brigham Young told him to leave college and take his prodigious talent straight to New York. Jason demurred, choosing to get married first and see what his brothers wanted to do. Marty felt like he could breathe and fully be himself in Branson. Even in Utah, people had approached him after shows to chide him for saying onstage that his brother was going on a mission. In Branson, Marty said, "that wouldn't matter." If he wanted to do a benefit concert for somebody going on a mission, other faith leaders in Branson would help. The back door had drawbacks. In the 1990s, Jason had hoped that Branson could be a launching pad for a national career and successful recording contracts. It never happened. In the 2020s, Marty expressed a tinge of regret that the Hughes Brothers were "still not an international name."[36] But for deeply religious performers, faith could win out over fame. Just as the Osmonds paved the way for the Hugheses, the Hugheses paved the way for other Mormon families, such as the Duttons, the Bretts, and the Knudsens. Lynn Knudsen and five of his brothers had been performing on the Disney–Vegas–cruise-ship circuit, but nothing had felt quite right. In Branson, they could live the dream of family entertainment in an environment that was friendly to their values. They started their a cappella show *SIX* at the Hughes Brothers Theatre and sixteen years later were still going strong.[37]

Other faith-based entertainers came to Branson not in hopes of gaining fame, but of resurrecting it. It was these figures that sparked culture war conflagrations the most. Anita Bryant, an "unabashed villain" of the political left,[38] was one of them. Born in 1940 in Barnsdall, Oklahoma, her career as a Christian entertainer had started at age two when her grandfather taught her "Jesus Loves Me" and persuaded the local Southern Baptist preacher to let her sing in church. She won the Miss Oklahoma beauty pageant in 1958 and came in third at the Miss America pageant the following year, which led to national fame as a pop singer. Throughout the early 1960s, she toured with Bob Hope to entertain US troops abroad and won awards from the National Guard and the Veterans of Foreign Wars for her service. She became the official spokesperson for the Florida Citrus Commission and appeared in advertisements for Coca-Cola, Kraft Foods, Holiday Inn, and Tupperware. She was popular across the political spectrum, singing at both the Democratic and Republican national conventions in 1968, a remarkable feat in that divisive year. By 1970, 75 percent of the American television-viewing public knew who Anita Bryant was.[39]

As she ascended to celebrity status, Bryant did not shy away from expressing her faith. She published books on Christian parenting (she was married with four children) and Christian cooking. She also was openly patriotic and sang the "Battle Hymn of the Republic" at the Super Bowl. Former President Lyndon B. Johnson was so taken that he requested that she perform it at his funeral, which she did. Her fame traveled internationally. London's *Daily Mail* reported in 1973 that Bryant was "The Real Mrs. America" and "the original folk heroine . . . an antidote to Watergate. Anita Bryant is in the process of giving back America its self-respect."[40] She avoided wading into divisive political waters. Instead, she stayed in her lane of patriotic Christian homemaker who happened to have a multimillion-dollar career as an entertainer. In some ways, nothing could be more American than that.

In 1977, the tide turned. That year, Bryant launched a crusade to repeal a local ordinance prohibiting discrimination on the basis of sexual orientation in her home of Dade County, Florida. Bryant claimed that gay teachers "recruited" children to a homosexual life-style, which, according to her beliefs, was a sin. She was successful in getting the repeal passed. With the backing of Jerry Falwell, Pat Robertson, Jesse Helms, and other male leaders of the Christian Right, she started a "Save the Children" campaign nationwide. Some considered it the first organized backlash to gay rights and an inaugural moment in the family values movement. Bryant gave speeches and published *The Anita Bryant Story: The Survival of Our Nation's Families and the Threat of Militant Homosexuality*. Her actions galvanized activists from the other side. At a televised press conference in Des Moines, Iowa, a protester smashed a pie in her face. After taking in the shock, her face covered in whipped cream, she began to pray for her assailant: "Father, I want to ask that you forgive him, and that we love him, and that we're praying for him" — at this point she broke down in tears and tried to continue between the sobs — "to be delivered from his demon lifestyle" — but could not get any further.[41] It was the beginning of the end. She received death threats, kidnapping threats, bomb threats, and endless hate mail that included human feces and voodoo dolls. Sponsors dropped her, late-night talk-show hosts mocked her, and in 1980, her marriage dissolved, which caused religious conservatives to turn against her as well.[42] Bryant's precipitous fall at age forty could have been where

Anita Bryant, ca. early 1990s. Courtesy White River Valley Historical Society.

the story ended. But after ten years in the metaphorical desert, she married her childhood friend Charlie Dry and published a book, *A New Day*, in which she proclaimed that those who kept faith would discover God's power to redeem and heal. She also described how God led her to Eureka Springs, Arkansas, where locals helped her renovate a theater.[43]

After the *60 Minutes* special on Branson came out, Bryant moved her show to the Strip. She also was conveniently escaping piles of debt and back taxes owed in Eureka Springs. From the spring of 1993 to the winter of 1997, thousands of tourists in Branson applauded her as she resurrected her Mrs. America persona onstage, wearing a US military jacket over a floor-length, bedazzled evening gown. Bryant Bransonized her show, singing not only her own songs, but also covers of Hank Williams, Patti Page, and 1950s rock 'n' roll hits. Her male musicians played instrumental bluegrass numbers and wore drag to perform as the Anderson Sisters, an irony seemingly lost on Bryant and her audience members. She engaged in audience interaction, bringing older men to the stage to sing duets. Her patriotic section was impressively grand, as she sang the theme song of every branch of the US military and asked everyone who served in that branch to stand as she did so. This segment was quickly copied by other performers on the Strip. Bryant's second act departed from the standard Branson show with a lengthy Christian testimony section, in which she told her story from her "glory days" to her fall to her redemption via God's grace.[44]

Bryant praised the Christian ethos of the town. "I'm excited about the camaraderie that has come together with a lot of people here in Branson," she said in 1996. "There is a move of God that is happening that people are starting to care about each other here. I saw that when people went over to Wayne Newton's theater for the National Day of Prayer." When asked if Branson boosted her career, she said "certainly."[45] Branson did not give her enough of a boost, however. In May 1997, Bryant and Dry filed for personal bankruptcy, with debts of over $1 million. They owed Missouri, Arkansas, and the federal government hundreds of thousands of dollars in unpaid taxes.

Like a cat with nine lives, Bryant banked on her reputation as a devout Christian and charmed her way into opening yet another theater in Pigeon Forge, Tennessee. There, ministers "would come and cry with her" and "fans would take her hand and pray after the show," but once again, she failed to pay employees as debts piled up further. Performers, ushers, and box-office workers faced eviction or car repossession. Some were so poor that they "stole popcorn

and candy from the theater's concession stand so they could eat."
Dancer Ashley Matthews stated, "They [Bryant and Dry] were always
telling us God's going to come through. They would attach his name
to everything and if we didn't believe them, we didn't have faith."
After that theater closed in 2000 and Bryant declared bankruptcy yet
again, employees gave up on ever recovering thousands of dollars
in back pay. Meanwhile, Bryant and Dry remained ensconced in a
gated community in the Smoky Mountains.[46]

Bryant was not the biggest name to come to Branson to find
redemption. That honor belonged to Jim Bakker. In the 1980s, the
televangelist and his wife Tammy Faye sat atop a massive empire
they named PTL (Praise The Lord) Ministries, which included a
television program and a theme park similar to Silver Dollar City,
called Heritage USA. The empire came crashing down in 1987 after
church secretary Jessica Hahn accused Bakker of rape, which led
to further revelations about PTL's financial mismanagement. In 1989,
a jury found him guilty of mail fraud, wire fraud, and conspiracy,
and he was sentenced to forty-five years in prison. Celebrity lawyer
Alan Dershowitz helped secure his early release by encouraging
the judge to enact a prohibition against fundraising that "would
guarantee that Mr. Bakker would never again engage in the blend of
religion and commerce that led to his conviction."[47] In 1994, Bakker
left prison, with the condition that he not conduct a ministry on
television for the remainder of his reduced sentence.[48]

It wasn't long after the expiration of that sentence that Bakker
relaunched his televangelist career. In 2002, he chose Branson to do
so, with the enthusiastic support of locals. Some named religious
reasons. "God's forgiven him, so why shouldn't I?" said Reverend Cecil Todd of Branson's Revival Fires Ministries. Others were more business minded. The presence of a nationally famous (albeit disgraced)
televangelist "could aid their own ministries and bring Branson national TV exposure," a journalist summarized. When Bakker and his
family arrived in September 2002, volunteers helped them unpack
and cleaned their bathrooms. In 2003, he began broadcasting *The
Jim Bakker Show* daily at Studio City Café in Branson with his second

wife Lori, who also saw this opportunity as a second act. The new Mrs. Bakker had had five abortions between the ages of seventeen and twenty-one before becoming a born-again evangelical in 1989 and an anti-abortion crusader. After five years, wealthy developer Jerry Crawford, who credited Bakker for saving his marriage, built a Christian community called Morningside, thirty miles south of Branson, specifically for Bakker and the taping of his show. Like Disney's Celebration in Florida, it was a planned community that had "a surreal indoor streetscape of Italianate store facades," condos, and of course, a giant chapel. In the 2020s, Bakker was still broadcasting from Morningside and still getting into trouble with the law for false advertising, such as when he attempted to sell a "silver solution" to cure the COVID-19 virus in March 2020.[49]

Critics pointed to Branson's ready embrace of people like Bakker and Bryant as evidence of the town's moral hypocrisy. In the early 1990s, national and international media outlets commissioned journalists to trek down to the Ozarks. They wrote scathing commentary not only about the performers onstage, but also about the audiences and the town itself. Virtually nobody had anything positive to say. Instead, they depicted Branson as the exemplar of everything that was wrong with the conservative side of the culture war.

The first problem, they felt, was simply taste. Di Webster of Melbourne, Australia's, biggest newspaper, *The Age*, felt affronted by the carnival atmosphere of the Strip, with "theatres, shopping malls, pinball parlors, mini-golf courses, water slides, kewpie doll shops, bunjee jump and fast-food outlets" all jumbled together. She called it a "neon nightmare" and "hee-haw hell."[50] As noted earlier, variety and commercialism had long been hallmarks of lowbrow culture. Even when tastemakers and artists began embracing lowbrow aesthetics in the 1960s, they did so with irony and distance, such as Andy Warhol and his Campbell's Soup cans. If art wanted to be Art, it had to be anti-capitalist, or at least critique the presumed emptiness of consumer culture. In contrast, Branson entertainers embraced a capitalist mindset in earnest. Webster declared that "hip coastal dwellers" were "embarrassed" by Branson; she cited one Los Angeles

The Branson Strip, a late twentieth-century carnival midway, with "the Tallest Texan" outside of Bob-O-Link's Theatre to advertise the Texans show, ca. late 1980s. Courtesy White River Valley Historical Society.

college student who looked at Branson's 1993 vacation guide and said, "It's like when your mother tells you not to watch the horror movie but you can't stop."[51]

Gary Indiana of the *Village Voice* was less critical of the lowbrow taste and more of the people, both onstage and in the audience. He began his 1993 article with an anecdote about an "obese" family that "waddled" out of an RV that had caught on fire. He called Branson tourists "lumpen," "fantastically corpulent," "plump," and "dropsical-looking." He said that they had "plaque-encrusted arteries" and observed that the lobby at one show was "packed full of white people spilling out of their K-mart leisure-wear, snacking." He characterized the Osmonds as "pretty hefty," and John Davidson as "remarkably thicker and older than one remembers him." It becomes clear that Indiana thought that being fat was worthy of ridicule, especially if one was white and working class. The article's title, "Town of the Living Dead," suggested that Branson was ghoulish and irrelevant. It was Indiana's thesis that the performers and audience members had struck "a satanic bargain": he saw the tourists as "profoundly out of whack with the trajectory of American popular culture," but performers treated them like they were at the center of all that was good and true in the nation. In return, tourists treated the performers "as if they were, currently or ever, major stars."[52]

An article with even greater traction was published the following year in *GQ*, a popular national men's magazine. Jeanne Marie Laskas put her thesis on the first page: "If Branson, Missouri, Midwest vacation Mecca, is a reflection of some part of our national soul, let's get the hell out of here."[53] Everything about Branson horrified Laskas, starting with what she considered its bad taste. The lowbrow Strip had "everything squashed willy-nilly" with what she said sarcastically was "a lot of exciting neon." She despised the uncoolness of the performers ("even Lawrence Welk is building a place in Branson, and he has been dead since 1992") and, perhaps most damning of all, wrote that the Wax and Historical Museum was "perhaps Branson's truest house of art. . . . it stands as a pure reflection of the soul of [the] culture." This soul was macabre, dreary, and devoid of aesthetic value: "Wood paneling, a low ceiling, the smell of mildew, dripping air conditioners. . . . Everything is old. Everything is dusty." The more time Laskas spent in Branson, she noted, "the more I feel like an outsider, part of the bad world, a dirty blotch on the landscape of this, the good world."[54] Branson's relentless promotion of itself as real America and her home — the liberal Northeast — as a "disgusting place . . . of satanic rap music, murder, drive-by shootings, moral decay, Beavis and Butt-Head and other evils embraced by Hillary Clinton" gave her "the funny urge to act out." John Davidson's patriotic number, in which she noted he wore a "white-and-blue jacket with fringe and sequins," made her "about to hyperventilate."[55]

Joe Queenan was perhaps the most vitriolic. In his book *Red Lobster, White Trash, and the Blue Lagoon: Joe Queenan's America*, he tore Branson apart. It was the last stop on his tour of America's lowbrow culture, and he stated, "This was, at long last, the bottom of the pit." He called the city a "Mulefuckers mecca," an "elephant's graveyard for washed-up shitkickers," and a "cultural penal colony." He gleefully ridiculed Tony Orlando, Bobby Vinton, Shoji Tabuchi, and the tourists who loved them.[56] Other media outlets were less cruel, but still adopted a mocking tone. *Life Magazine* stated in 1994, "Branson is not beautiful, educational or, God forbid, cultivated. Branson is one thing: fun."[57] The article concluded, "If you are still not sure whether Branson is right for you, take the Bobby Vinton test. The crooner once said proudly that he moved to town for one simple reason: 'I'm not hip anymore.' If you're proud to say the same, you'll have a whale of a time."[58]

Though the critics mostly focused on the aging crooners, they also attacked the local family variety shows and the hillbilly archetype in particular (i.e., "Mulefuckers mecca"). Prior to the boom, most of Branson's audiences had come from within a three-hundred-mile radius, presumed insiders to rural white culture, who laughed knowingly with the hillbilly. Were these new audiences now laughing *at* the hillbilly? Some felt that no matter how much one might profit off stereotypes of hillbillies as lazy and ignorant, the psychological damage of debasing oneself was too great a price to pay. Others disagreed. Jerry Lee, a local entertainer whose childhood home did not have electricity until 1947, saw no problem with trading in hillbilly stereotypes. It was "simply making a living the same way hillbillies have from the time they moved into these unforgiving hills: by getting creative."[59] Some shows made modifications. In 1996, the *Baldknobbers* dropped the word "Hillbilly" from the title of their show, and the Presleys' *Mountain Music Jubilee* became the *Presleys' Country Jubilee*. Gary Presley stopped blacking out his teeth when he portrayed Herkimer. But comedians still told jokes about outhouses, chigger bites, and squirrel hunting.[60]

Indeed, Gary Presley and others laughed all the way to the bank. Their shows offered a product that millions wanted. The coastal perception that Branson visitors were unhip and "out of whack with the trajectory of American popular culture" was itself out of whack with the trajectory of American popular culture. In 1990, conservative commentator Rush Limbaugh became the most-listened-to talk-show host on the radio, and he remained a dominant force for the next thirty years.[61] In the 1994 midterm elections, 60 percent of the

600 candidates for national, state, and local offices who were supported by self-identified religious conservatives won their races.[62] In 1996, Rupert Murdoch established the Fox News Network. In 2002, Fox News became the top-rated cable news network and stayed there for over twenty years. Church membership had been on a steady, uninterrupted decline since the 1970s, but the percentage of Christians who identified as evangelical increased dramatically in the late twentieth and early twenty-first centuries, drawing millions away from mainline Protestantism.[63]

Even attitudes about highbrow and lowbrow culture were starting to shift. In 1997, architectural critic Ada Huxtable, an old-guard cultural aesthete writing for the *New York Times*, glumly threw up her hands and admitted defeat: America had fully embraced Vegas's love of the fake and the surreal. John Seabrook argued that American culture had entered a "nobrow" phase, where nobody cared about notions of taste and everyone was a "cultural omnivore" who appreciated Bach and Britney Spears in equal measure.[64] The exception, however, was country music. On the one hand, country music was ascendant, with the most dedicated radio stations in the country in the 1990s. A 1995 survey determined that 37 percent of the population, or about 70 million people, listened to country music every week—significantly more than any other genre.[65] Garth Brooks was the third-best-selling artist of the decade, behind only pop stars Celine Dion and Mariah Carey. On the other hand, "anything but country" persisted as a response to the common question "What kind of music do you listen to?"[66] Those writing about Branson seemed to miss the "nobrow" memo, as not only the town's country music shows, but also every other aspect of its tourism industry, faced withering criticism for its lowbrow taste. Vegas had cleared the bar; Branson had not. The derision only reinforced the paradoxical status of country music listeners, Branson visitors, and conservatives writ large by the end of the millennium: numerically populous but still culturally marginalized. The white working class—Branson's primary demographic—remained targets of disdain as "America's perpetual bigot class."[67]

The savage criticism did not cause a massive drop-off in Branson tourism. While the pace of growth slowed in the mid-1990s, the number of visitors kept climbing. In 1995, John Hopper Tours, based in Nashville, reported that "no customers expressed concerns" about the negative media attention. The editor of *Destination*, a publication of the American Bus Association, stated, "It's obvious that whatever impact the negative publicity may have had, it didn't slow our operators' ability to make money marketing Branson."[68] Locals reaffirmed their commitment to the audiences who took time off work, saved up money, and planned a vacation to come see them. As Lisa Rau, publicist of Silver Dollar City, said in response to Queenan's depictions, "While we hate to see anybody attack Branson . . . we certainly have a product that people in middle America love."[69] But underneath proclamations that the cruel words didn't matter, an us-versus-them narrative hardened. Branson's tourists and entertainers now knew explicitly that people made fun of them for being old, fat, religious, Republican, earnestly patriotic, members of the white working class, and, most damning, lovers of the only remaining vestiges of lowbrow culture still deemed unacceptable to the mainstream. Choosing to visit or work in Branson took on a politicized edge, a willing act of defiance against a seemingly liberal cultural norm.

In recognition of the new political power of the Right's religious base and Branson's role as a mecca for it, President George H. W. Bush decided to hold his first reelection campaign stop as the official Republican nominee at Silver Dollar City. In August 1992, he arrived straight from the Republican National Convention in Houston, Texas. Political operators named several benefits of this visit. As a stand-in for the "heartland," Branson helped Bush "ditch his image of wealth and appeal to middle America." It also was a direct challenge to his opponent, Bill Clinton, who was from nearby Arkansas and running in part on his down-home charm. Bush's rally of over 17,000 cheering supporters on a hot afternoon demonstrated that the incumbent could "come into Clinton country and raise a crowd." In the *Branson Tri-Lakes News*, advertisements from businesses that welcomed President and Barbara Bush to "God's country" filled four full pages. Sponsors included restaurants, motels, realtors, banks, *Shepherd of the Hills*, and multiple theaters. The Herschends offered free shuttle service from the parking lot of the Grand Palace to the rally. The Baldknobbers Theatre, Jim Stafford Theatre, Moe Bandy's Americana Theatre, and the Presleys' Country Jubilee Theatre served as rally ticket outlets. Stafford, Boxcar Willie, the Baldknobbers, and Glen Campbell performed as openers for the rally. Some did so purely for "public relations" reasons. Others, like Campbell, took a stand: "It is a statement — I'm for Bush, I'm a Republican and I'm for the party."[70]

While the Ozark counties of Missouri voted solidly for Bush, Clinton won the state and the nation.[71] After Clinton's victory, Jim Stafford incorporated a bit into his show where he asked Democrats in the audience to cheer. He was met with absolute silence (one reporter called it "the sound of one hand clapping"). When Stafford asked Republicans to cheer, the crowd roared. "Well, where the hell were you guys?" he asked.[72] Campbell and Williams both discussed their Republican Party affiliation from the stage; Mel Tillis and others regularly performed at Republican fundraisers. Yakov Smirnoff hung pictures of himself with Ronald and Nancy Reagan in his lobby. The Osmonds had a portrait of the Reagans over one theater door entrance and George H. W. and Barbara Bush over the other. Williams had the same two portraits in the center of his sweeping staircase in the Moon River Theatre lobby.[73]

The Herschend family took on an important role in linking the city to the Christian Right through their relationship with Pat Robertson. Robertson, the son of a US senator, believed in the power of popular media to spread Christianity and influence public policy. He established the Christian Broadcasting Network (CBN) in 1961 and started the television program *The 700 Club* in 1966, which is still broadcast daily on CBN to this day. *The 700 Club* is a variety show that mixes "news and commentary, interviews . . . music, prayer, and ministry."[74] Robertson also founded CBN College in 1977 (later renamed Regent University) and ran for president in 1988. After dropping out of the

Republican primary, he turned his attention to another organization he founded, the Christian Coalition, to support conservative, religious candidates for public office. In June 1998, the *700 Club* came to Silver Dollar City for a two-day taping of their show. "It's a very good match for us," said Deborah Howse, the public relations manager for CBN. The two shared a "family emphasis" as well as, of course, a foundation in Christian faith and the use of variety entertainment as a form of ministry. It was not the *700 Club*'s first time in Branson, as they had come to tape segments on the city's Christmas season two years earlier. Robertson's cohost Terry Meeuwsen made candy with SDC employee June Ward, who delighted in tricking Meeuwsen into believing that SDC had a corn syrup well. The week of his visit, Robertson had "stirred up controversy" by stating that a "Gay Days celebration" in the city of Orlando, Florida, would lead to God's retribution in the form of hurricanes and other natural disasters. Pete Herschend said he "didn't think twice" about still inviting Robertson. Herschend stated, "He stands for families being together. So do we. Why wouldn't he be here?" Hundreds of fans came to watch the taping and angled for a chance to greet Robertson. According to Ward, visitation at SDC shot up after the airing of the episodes. Robertson also benefited from being surrounded by supporters during the week of controversy. "I really think Branson is the heartland of America," he stated. "I'm among friends. It's like coming home."[75]

Robertson was not the only national Christian Right celebrity to visit Branson. In 1999, local evangelist Cecil Todd hosted a four-day Revival Fires Celebration at the Grand Palace to commemorate his fifty years of ministry. Jerry Falwell came as a featured speaker. Falwell had honed his religious faith as a student at Baptist Bible College just up the road in Springfield. While in town, he spoke to the *Springfield News-Leader* and defended his role in shifting evangelical Christianity toward active political engagement. Those who say that evangelicals should "stay out of politics" is "how the country got in trouble in the first place, because conservative Christians were not involved," he stated.[76]

Branson leaders put their money where their mouth was in terms of defending the town's Christian values brand. In the early 1990s, Las Vegas began to lose its monopoly on legalized gambling in the United States. By 1995, Native Americans had built casinos on reservations in nineteen different states, and six more states licensed riverboat casinos. For Branson's impoverished neighbors, gambling seemed like a no-lose way to expand the tourist economy in the region. Rockaway Beach, on the shores of Lake Taneycomo, had been a thriving leisure spot in the 1950s before the construction of Table Rock Dam altered the water temperature of Taneycomo to an unswimmable fifty degrees year-round. Rockaway Beach, Reeds Spring, Kimberling City, and Hollister struggled in the shadow of Branson's boom. But again and again — twice in 1994, then in 1999, 2004, 2008, and up to the present — Branson's Board of Aldermen passed resolutions to reject gambling, seeing it as counter to the area's family-friendly, religious brand. Despite being outspent by pro-gambling lobbyists, they successfully mounted campaigns year after year to lead Missouri voters to reject ballot measures that would allow gambling on the White River.[77]

During the 1990s, therefore, Branson solidified its reputation as a nationally important, culturally significant home base for the Christian Right, a reputation that attracted both fervent critics and fervent supporters. But the political polarization of the country had not reached its apogee. While Branson's support for Republican politicians was explicit in the 1990s, condemnations of then-president Bill Clinton were less common. Attacking the president came across as unpatriotic to Branson audiences. Instead, attacking his wife Hillary emerged as a more acceptable practice. Throughout Branson in the early 1990s, bumper stickers read "Don't blame me, I didn't vote for President Clinton. Or her husband."[78] Branson's hillbilly comedians appeared as the First Lady, using the purposefully-bad-drag tradition to depict her as unnaturally masculine and improperly ambitious.[79] Later, in the mid-2000s, hillbilly comedians Droopy Drawers Jr., Stub Meadows, and Hargus Marcel appeared in the *Baldknobbers Jamboree* as the Dixie Chicks, a female country music group that faced conservative backlash for their criticism of then-president George W. Bush. The impersonators stumbled on-stage in crooked wigs and stuffed button-down sweaters, appearing more like low-class housewives than the stylish Chicks. They spoke briefly in high falsettos before exiting, no song to be heard. The bit relied on purposefully shoddy cross-dressing to indicate that the Chicks were pathetic and ditzy — and thus incapable of coherent commentary on politics.[80]

This foray into a specific political controversy was a gamble. The third tenet of Branson's Holy Trinity — flag — was a point of particular pride. Ever since landing in the national public eye in the early 1990s, Branson had struggled to reconcile promoting itself as a neutral flag-waving town with its reputation of being a hotbed of the Christian Right. That reconciliation would prove even more difficult in the twenty-first century.

6 FLAG

The Most Patriotic City in America

> We were celebrating God and country
> before it became fashionable.
>
> *Presley Family, 2008*

When Eddie Stovall arrived in Branson in 1995, he stood out. He wore gold earrings, he sang doo-wop instead of country, and he was tall and Black. Stovall was part of a re-formed Platters group, which had had its heyday in the 1950s with hits like "The Great Pretender." They came to Branson to perform in what was supposed to be a one-off classic car show, but a promoter convinced them to stay for a season at Mutton Hollow Entertainment Park. It was a total "culture shock" for the only Black group in town aside from country music star Charley Pride. They were used to a home base in Los Angeles and international audiences, not a sea of white tourists in a wooded hollow. But Branson embraced the Platters, and in turn, the Platters embraced Branson. They moved on up to headline at Roy Clark's Celebrity Theatre in 1998 and were one of the most successful groups in town for years.[1] Decades later, Stovall was still performing six nights a week in downtown Branson. Something had happened that first season to make him feel particularly at home in a seemingly unlikely place: Branson's Veterans Homecoming.

Stovall had enlisted in the military at age seventeen. He had spent his youth shuttling between his mother's apartment in New York and his grandmother's home in Alabama. In the rural South, he fell in love with the music of Elvis Presley; in the Bronx, with the sounds of doo-wop. Other kids played basketball at recess or after school. He sang on street corners, in hallways, even in bathrooms with his makeshift quartet. "I wanted to be a teenager so bad, I could taste it," he said with a smile. The youngster was entranced with the romance emanating from the beautiful harmonies. He knew he wanted to sing for the rest of his life, but impulsively he enlisted in the army after a friend's cousin came home from being stationed in Korea. "He glorified that army. Oh, he glorified," Stovall stated. "He made us think that was the best place in the world." Unfortunately for Stovall, after a year of training and a year of fighting in Vietnam, he returned home to anti-war protesters. Nobody granted him a hero's welcome.

After leaving active duty (he remained in the National Guard for fifteen more years), Stovall embarked on a professional singing career and joined the groups that he had looked up to as a child, such as the Drifters, the Coasters, Hank Ballard and the Midnighters, and of course, the Platters. As he toured the globe with these groups from the 1970s to the 1990s, the musical zeitgeist shifted from disco to punk rock to hip-hop. But it turned out that millions of people still had the same attachments to the romantic promise of the 1950s as Stovall. In Branson, audiences eagerly attended the shows he produced. Above and beyond that musical bond with his appreciative audiences, the Veterans Homecoming celebration in 1995 was everything Stovall had never experienced as a young man. "The whole town just turned out," he said. "We had guys that ran across each other that hadn't seen each other since Vietnam," and "helicopters flying over the place all day long." "It was a big deal," he said. "It was a real big deal. Finally, they made us feel welcome."[2]

Honoring veterans is key to how Branson embodies the third F: flag. In October 2022, Mayor Larry Milton made an official proclamation declaring Branson to be "The Most Patriotic City in America." In addition to stating that "The city of Branson is all about faith, family, and flag," he added that "We love our veterans, we honor our veterans, and there's no city in America who holds our veterans in the highest esteem as Branson does every single day."[3] Milling about every theater lobby are men and women in hats that indicate their branch of the military or what war they fought in. At almost every show, a pause occurs, usually in the second half. The house lights come up, and the emcee stands center stage to declare that America's greatness rests on the shoulders of its military. At some theaters, the emcee asks all veterans to stand and be honored. At others, they ask the different branches (Army, Navy, Air Force, Marines, Coast Guard) to rise one by one, so that each can garner its own recognition. Easily a full third of the audience stands at such moments. It is a theater experience unlike any other in the United States.

While Branson entertainers had long included patriotic numbers in their performances, it was not until the 1990s that veterans specifically became a focus. Tony Orlando's presence was one major factor. His most iconic track, "Tie a Yellow Ribbon Round the Ole Oak Tree," debuted in 1973. In the song, the protagonist is returning from three years in prison and hopes that his lover has tied a yellow ribbon around an oak tree to signal that she is still devoted to him. Too anxious to look out the bus window, he asks the driver to do so instead. The whole bus erupts in cheers, as there is not one, but one *hundred* yellow ribbons tied around the oak tree. "I'm comin' home," the singer concludes joyfully.[4] The lyricists' source for the yellow ribbon idea is disputed (and was even the subject of a lawsuit), but Library of Congress research suggested that it was a folk tradition dating back to the nineteenth century, when a woman who wanted to show her allegiance to a man away at war or in prison would wear a yellow ribbon or handkerchief.

The song took on broader significance during the Iran Hostage Crisis of 1979. The wife of an American diplomat in Tehran suggested that US citizens looking for a way to support hostages' families should "tie a yellow ribbon around the old oak tree." The phenomenon caught on, and when the hostages came home in 1981, they were greeted by thousands of yellow ribbons from cheering supporters.[5] By the time Orlando christened the Yellow Ribbon Theatre in Branson in 1992, the song was synonymous with support for people involved in military conflict, particularly veterans. In 1993, he organized a special Veterans Day performance at the theater that recognized twenty-eight former Iranian hostages and two thousand veterans plus their families. Building upon this momentum, Branson began to stretch Veterans Day to Veterans Homecoming Week, billed as the largest Veterans celebration in the nation, with over sixty events that included a parade, a film festival, reunions, and special free shows.[6] Also in 1993, as we have seen, Anita Bryant incorporated the official songs of all branches of the military in her show. Many Branson performers took this page from Bryant's playbook. By the late 1990s, almost all shows explicitly honored veterans.

In addition, Branson began actively marketing to veterans. Very few tourist destinations treat veterans as a niche segment. In 1997, the Branson Veterans Task Force nonprofit corporation was formed. In addition to organizing Veterans Homecoming Week, it sponsored thirty-six activities during the Memorial Day weekend and thirty-four special events during the July Fourth weekend. By the dawn of the millennium, the task force ensured that events happened every single month. They began hosting an annual Military Reunion Planners Conference that helped tour operators put together packages for veterans' groups. "There is no competitive market doing this," said co-chairman Debbie Ikerd.[7] On Veterans Day in 2000, the Veterans Memorial Museum opened on Highway 76. The brainchild of sculptor Fred Hoppe Jr., the museum exhibits uniforms, weapons, and other memorabilia from World War I, World War II, the Korean War, the Vietnam War, and the Persian Gulf War.[8]

At the dawn of the new millennium, Branson's dedication to veterans positioned the town as neutrally patriotic, not partisan. The 1990s culture war flames had cooled. Two decades later, however, Branson became embroiled in yet another round of the culture wars. Mayor Milton's declaration in 2022 that Branson was "The Most Patriotic City in America" threw down the gauntlet at a time when defining patriotism was a subject of furious debate. Between two world-changing political events — the terrorist attacks of September 11, 2001, and the insurrection at the US Capitol Building on January 6, 2021 — Branson's live entertainment industry underwent dramatic changes that had economic and political consequences. The early 2020s were a time of open conflict, both in the nation as a whole and in Branson itself. The polarization threatened the city's brand as a place of friendliness. How had the city's consensus fallen apart?

September 11

Branson's dedication to veterans helped it weather a rough transition as the 1990s boom years came to an end. Tourism across America was in decline. Millions of retirees had seen their pension funds disappear when the dot-com bubble burst in March 2000. On September 11, 2001, terrorists hijacked four planes and almost three thousand people lost their lives. The heightened fear of airplane travel combined with families' tightened budgets meant that leisure travel declined even further. But Branson, long known as a budget-friendly destination reached via America's highways, bucked the trend and saw increased tourism. Its patriotic ethos strengthened its attraction. In the wake of the attacks, patriotism had become practically mandatory, and it was criticizing the country that was suddenly in bad taste. Entertainer Bucky Heard stated, "After September 11, the way people looked at Branson changed. People used to make fun of us — that we dropped the flag at every show, that we were hokey. To me, the rest of America could take a lesson from Branson."[9] In many shows, performers simply continued what they had been doing. As the Presley Family stated in 2008, "We were celebrating God and country before it became fashionable."[10]

An important ambassador of Branson's patriotism was the comedian Yakov Smirnoff. Smirnoff had been a rising comedy star in the 1980s who specialized in jokes about differences between America and the USSR. He is even credited with inventing, or at least popularizing, a type of joke now known as the "Russian reversal": "In America, you can always find a party! In Soviet Russia, the Party always finds you!" He had come to the United States as an immigrant who spoke no English after an austere childhood living in a communal apartment with nine other families in Odessa, Ukraine. Kind neighbors in New York helped his family, the owner of the Comedy Store in Los Angeles gave him a chance to perform, and he

Framed photo of Yakov Smirnoff with President Reagan, hanging in the lobby of the Yakov Smirnoff Theatre in Branson, Missouri. Photo by author, 2023.

built a successful career as a stand-up comedian. The deprivation and oppression he faced under Communist rule, in contrast to the freedom and opportunities he experienced in America, turned him into a staunch patriot. On July 4, 1986, he received his citizenship in a ceremony at Ellis Island, at which he wore a tuxedo and clutched a miniature Statue of Liberty. Decades later he posted on his Facebook page about that day, "It was a dream come true for this immigrant. 🇺🇸💙🗽 I thank God everyday for my life and getting to live as a free man in America. What a country!!!"[11]

In Smirnoff's telling, he had a major hand in ending the Cold War. He met President Ronald Reagan at a party in the mid-1980s, and the two developed a warm friendship. Reagan invited Smirnoff to the White House multiple times, where the two men traded jokes and laughs. In 1988, right before Reagan left for a historic summit with

Mikhail Gorbachev, the president's speechwriter called Smirnoff. "President Reagan wants some jokes," the speechwriter said. Smirnoff obliged. Apparently, the first two days of the summit were dour affairs, with each world leader pronouncing the superiority of his respective economic and political system. But on the third day, Reagan cracked a joke. Gorbachev laughed. Soon thereafter, Smirnoff claims, the Berlin Wall fell.[12]

If indeed Smirnoff contributed to the fall of the USSR, his triumph was simultaneously his demise. In December 1991, David Letterman cruelly put "Yakov Smirnoff's career will end" as #1 on his list of "Top Ten Things that are going to happen now that the Soviet Union has collapsed."[13] Within six months, the prophecy came true. Booking agents across the country canceled Smirnoff's contracts. Ever resourceful, he packed his bags for Branson. He began performing in 1993 at the Cristy Lane Theatre and opened his own venue in 1997. He dutifully Bransonized his stand-up comedy routine by adding spectacle and variety. He hired a troupe of Russian dancers who energized the stage with virtuosic kicks, stamps, whirls, and backflips. At one point he rode out of the wings on a white horse to sing a song he composed, "From Red to Redneck," a humorous ditty that gently poked fun at the Ozarks. He also drove onstage in a red Ferrari.[14] Thousands cheered, night after night, year after year. His success confirmed the competing sides of the Branson narrative: that it was a place for washed-up has-beens, and that it was a place of second chances where the American dream lived on.

Through Smirnoff, Branson forged a direct connection to the 9/11 attacks. As he recounted to Branson journalist Jason Wert several years later, the comedian went into "shock mode" after watching the World Trade Center towers fall and sat down in front of an empty canvas to paint. His creation, "America's Heart," depicted a giant American flag in the shape of a heart. In front of the heart was the New York City skyline with the Statue of Liberty at the center, standing strong. As he finished the painting in the wee hours of the morning, a thought came to him: this had to exist as a mural at Ground Zero, and it had to go up before the one-year anniversary

of the attacks. When he flew to New York with his proposal, however, city officials rebuffed him. He even tried to broker a deal with
a politician running for statewide office and was rejected. "That's
when I realized I don't have a shot. If politicians won't take your
money, you have a problem," Smirnoff joked.[15] Undeterred, he began
appealing to owners of buildings near Ground Zero. He figured out
which façade — a damaged one covered in scaffolding — would be
the perfect canvas for his dream mural and assured the owner he
would cover all permits and costs. Smirnoff soon realized he would
have to talk to the steelworkers' union, as they were the ones who
"could get things done."[16]

In August 2002, he met with four workers in the basement of the
damaged building. Smirnoff described the scene as if from a "mafia
movie": the tough union workers, "swearing in four different lan-
guages," laughed at his idea and rejected his offer to pay whatever it
took. As they turned to leave, the leader happened to see Smirnoff's
mock-up of the mural lying on the floor. He stopped in his tracks
and turned around. A miraculous change of heart occurred: not
only did the union workers agree to put up the mural, but they also
agreed to do so for free. When Smirnoff asked why, the union leader
responded, "I want to be able to drive by this building with my son,
and I want to tell him I helped to put this in the skies."[17]

The weekend before the anniversary, fifty steelworkers worked
twelve-hour shifts to hang the mural without the city's knowledge.
At the bottom of the mural was a statement Smirnoff wrote after
the attacks: "The human spirit is not measured by the size of the
act, but by the size of the heart." Smirnoff later found out that when
government officials had toured the site on Friday, in advance of
anniversary events, they had worried about the all-gray backdrop
surrounding the site. "It looked like there was no hope," said a producer who coordinated camera shots for the broadcast. By Monday
morning, the mural was miraculously there. It formed an iconic
backdrop, a vibrant canvas of red, white, blue, and green against
steel-gray buildings, for the television coverage of the anniversary
ceremony. For the eighteen months that the mural remained on the

scaffolding, Smirnoff chose to remain anonymous. He did not want anyone thinking it was a joke.[18]

Smirnoff exemplified the earnestness of many Branson entertainers. While cynical, coke-snorting, adulterous grifters certainly populated the Strip, others were like Smirnoff, whose patriotism and devout Christian faith drove their desire to perform as a form of ministry — to inspire twin loves of nation and Jesus. For a while, it worked pretty well. After the boost of 9/11, Branson began achieving a magical balance of welcoming new tourists without alienating its base of conservative retirees. The glamorous Radio City Rockettes performed down the street from the hillbilly comedians in the *Presleys' Country Jubilee*; a local production of the Broadway show *Joseph and the Amazing Technicolor Dreamcoat* enjoyed a successful run alongside up-and-coming Mormon entertainers like the Brett Family. In 2004, there were a record 116 shows in forty-seven theaters. While some worried about dividing the economic pie too much, others affirmed a more-the-merrier ethos. "It's all the big hubbub that makes it exciting," stated Ann-Margret, the famed actress who joined Andy Williams's show that year. "If we're going to attract new visitors, the diversity fits," added Dan Lennon, marketing director for the Chamber of Commerce. Branson became a destination for aspiring performers in a variety of genres. "It's been proven that a show can come to Branson with performers no one's ever heard of and build a following and be successful," said producer Joe Sullivan, pointing to Shoji Tabuchi as an example.[19]

One show that flourished in this have-your-cake-and-eat-it-too moment was *Celebrate America*, a musical that premiered in 2004 at the Mansion Theatre. September 11 had inspired not only Smirnoff, but also a Branson producer named Gene Bicknell, who made his millions in Pizza Hut franchises. In response to the terrorist attacks, the Kansas City entrepreneur wrote this show, which was a Bransonian mishmash of genres: part "book musical" with a plot; part revue; part slideshow. Bicknell wrote some original songs, but most musical numbers were well-known popular hits. Publicity from the opening recounted: "The story revolves around a little girl named Abigail Appleberry . . . who lives in a small fictional town called Promise. Abigail's father is deployed in Iraq. To help her understand why her father must serve, Abigail's grandfather narrates a journey through time, starting with the signing of the Declaration of Independence."[20] Bicknell billed the show as "a history lesson" that covered over two hundred years in two hours: the Revolutionary War, Western expansion, the Civil War, the 1904 World's Fair, immigration to Ellis Island, World War I, the Great Depression, and World War II. A video montage then "rocket[ed]" the audience from the 1950s through to September 11, 2001. In the finale, Abigail's father returned from the Iraq War and the ensemble sang "America" and "Yankee Doodle Dandy." Abigail's grandpa, played by Bicknell himself, explained that America's freedom was unique and hard won. While religion did not figure prominently in it, Celebrate America implied that the United States was a Christian nation. The emcee who introduced the show declared that "God and country are welcome on this stage," to which audiences shouted, "Amen!" Also appearing in the Mansion Theatre at the same time was a pageant about the life of Jesus called The Promise, which used the same cast members as Celebrate America — a fact the emcee also pointed out. Celebrate America ran seven days a week, ten months of the year, for five years.[21]

The criticisms one could lodge at the show feel entirely predictable from the perspective of the 2020s. Celebrate America contained no mention of Indigenous genocide and no serious reckoning with slavery. In its segment about the Civil War, Confederate and Union soldiers bond at a campfire over their similarities, including "a profound sense of patriotism" — ignoring the fact that the Confederacy was an act of treason against the United States. Celebrate America also glorified the white pioneer experience. The only immigrants it celebrated were white, European ones. Subtlety and complexity were not key features: Abigail Appleberry who lived in a small town called Promise was about as heavy-handed as could be. It offered no new or fresh perspectives.

Scholars and activists had been putting forth critiques of this celebratory narrative for more than a century, starting with Frederick Douglass's famed 1852 speech, "What to the Slave Is the Fourth of July?"[22] But such ideas had not saturated the American mainstream in the early 2000s. Calls to tell the "horrible history" of Thanksgiving appeared in the New York Times in 2019; most Americans' awareness of replacing Columbus Day with Indigenous Peoples' Day did not happen until 2021, when President Biden made an official proclamation to recognize the latter.[23]

Back in 2004, Bicknell did not think his narrative was shopworn. Instead, he felt it was urgent. Dating back to the opening of Silver Dollar City and The Shepherd of the Hills in 1960, Branson entertainers had mournfully declared that Americans did not know their history and that live performance had to step into the breach. Even cliched ideology needs reproduction to survive. Celebrate America was important for maintaining a story of American greatness, reiterating that master narrative as the one, true, authentic history of the nation. Nevertheless, the musical flew under the radar as a mode of history making. During its five-year run, it never received critical attention, or any attention at all outside of Branson.[24]

Instead, the occasional mention of Branson in the national media during the early 2000s was generally positive. Lauren Wilcox of the Washington Post was cautiously appreciative of the town's "unglued sincerity," a phrase that implied she thought of Branson as wacky but harmless. Unlike those in the 1990s who called Branson a "cultural penal colony," Wilcox wrote, "So what if Smirnoff cranks himself into [an] emotional state for every performance? This is show business." She further averred that Branson's flag-waving ethos was "old-fashioned, moral patriotism rather than political."[25] In this early 2000s moment, in the wake of 9/11, Branson's brand of patriotism came across as nonpartisan.

Roger Cohen in the New York Times also considered Branson's patriotism as universal. He traveled to the Ozarks on the eve of the 2008 presidential election between longtime Republican senator John McCain and young, upstart Democratic senator Barack Obama. Cohen met Branson's mayor Raeanne Presley, wife of Steve Presley of the *Presleys' Country Jubilee*. He was charmed. "I never imagined that a Republican mayor from Bible-belt Missouri would revive my faith in American democracy, but Raeanne Presley did just that," he marveled. Cohen praised her as a "brisk, pragmatic, funny, no-nonsense Republican Midwesterner with little tolerance for debt, delinquency, dumbness or dereliction of duty." He expressed admiration for the town's theater industry, which attracted more than a thousand times its population. If that ratio existed in New York, Cohen said, the Big Apple would get eight billion tourists a year. Branson's spirit of can-do optimism and cheery patriotism "gave [him] hope, in these sobering days, for a nation aching to unite behind a new start and an uplifting endeavor."[26]

Just as Cohen was finding hope in Branson, the foundation was starting to crack. Its tourism industry was one of the many casualties of the Great Recession that hit the United States in 2008. Over the next four years, Branson lost a million annual visitors. The Branson/Lakes Convention & Visitors Bureau (CVB), an arm of the Chamber of Commerce established in 2006 to focus on the tourism industry, noted in 2011 that while America's higher-income families soon rebounded, almost half of Branson travelers earned less than $50,000 a year. That demographic was still struggling.[27] Then on February 29, 2012, a mere two weeks before the start of Branson's tourism season, a tornado ripped through downtown, significantly damaging the new Hilton Branson Convention Center Hotel before winding its way down Highway 76 to damage theaters, churches, restaurants, and hotels. City officials tried to downplay the impact for fear that tourists would be scared off.[28]

In the midst of this difficult period, Branson decided to hit "re-fresh" on its marketing. "Our updated brand strategy is to more clearly position Branson as a *wholesome, intimate and authentic alternative* to Las Vegas, Orlando, and other tourism destinations," the CVB declared. The CVB created a "muse" named Christi, the "person we're designing Branson for." Christi was a white suburban Midwestern mom who volunteered at her church and had a "strong sense of values." But Christi was not provincial — her dream trips

Branson's Convention and Visitors Bureau (CVB) marketing campaign image, 2012.

included New York City and Paris. Thus the CVB aimed to position Branson as an attractive destination for people who envisioned themselves as Christian, conservative, worldly, and middle class, not as the stigmatized white working class. Central to this marketing campaign was the live entertainment industry. The slogans for 2012 were *"Branson. It's Your Show"* and *"Entertainment that brings us together."* The CVB, perhaps paying attention to the national business community's declaration that the "Experience Economy" was the future, leaned into the idea of families making memories together. Experiences such as viewing performances counted more than consumer goods. The 2012 Vacation Guide listed "Live Shows" first in the three draws of Branson, the other two being "Pristine Lakes" and "World Class Attractions." The happy family on the brochure cover appeared above an image of the Strip with marquees promoting Jim Stafford, the Hughes Brothers, SIX, #1 Hits of the Ozarks, and Mickey Gilley. Table Rock Lake and the Ferris wheel were relegated to the backdrop.[29]

In 2014 tourism numbers slowly started to climb back to pre-Recession levels, but it was not clear that residents had fully recovered.[30] In 2013, Mayor Presley had won reelection handily with 74 percent of the vote, and in 2015 she was up again, facing fellow Republican Karen Best, a former educator. All signs indicated that Presley would remain at the helm. But a week before the election, on April 1, 2015, Sir Richard Branson, the billionaire owner of Virgin Airlines, announced he was going to move his US headquarters to Branson. He posted the news to Virgin.com, sent it in an email newsletter, and created the hashtag #BransontoBranson on Twitter. It was an April Fool's joke that Presley agreed to go along with. She tweeted, "Welcome Richard. Amazing things happen when you Believe!"[31] Her capitalization of "Believe" hinted at the religious undertones: Christian faith in God had been rewarded with economic bounty. Residents believed the news, especially after Presley's tweet. The executive director of the local private airport posted on Facebook, "I have my staff looking into gate availability, but it may be tough given Virgin's aggressive service rollout. In the meantime, we are anxious to see what incentives Virgin America can offer the airport and the community."[32]

When Sir Richard revealed his ruse, residents were crushed. The past six years had battered Branson, and they were not in the mood for a practical joke. When it became clear that Presley was also in on it, they were furious. Despite Branson's billion-dollar tourism industry, in 2015 Taney County had a poverty rate of 19 percent, compared to the national average of 13.5 percent.[33] The Ozarks had always been one of the poorest regions in the country, and people wanted better. Tourism provided seasonal jobs, often without benefits. Backup performers who came from out of town touted the city's affordability as one reason why they stayed. They considered the wages decent in comparison with what they would make elsewhere in the country.[34] But there was a tier of local service workers — motel housekeepers, ushers, and waiters — who received very low hourly rates. Backup dancers might go take a gig on a cruise ship during Branson's off season, but locals could not just up and leave. The affordable housing crisis of the 1990s had never been solved, and an increasing number of workers lived in motels; the meth crisis that had ravaged southern Missouri was transitioning rapidly into an opioid addiction crisis. Presley's rival Best commented, "People were ecstatic with the possibility of jobs coming through town, good-paying jobs with full-time, year-round jobs and full benefits. Once they found out it was a joke, they lost a sense of hope."[35] And hope was one of Branson's trademarks.

Residents also lost pride. News of the prank made its way into the national press, including *Newsweek*. Ghosts of the 1990s cultural critics returned. Yet again, the city and its residents were the butt of a joke. They were made out to be naïve and foolish to think that a cosmopolitan billionaire would want to create jobs in the Ozarks. Best had campaigned on a platform that such hopes were not foolish. She aimed to lure companies like Google and Expedia to the area. She wanted to promote the airport. She notably did not prioritize the live-show sector.[36] Best defeated Presley, albeit by only 162 votes, less than a week later, and "absolutely" believed that the prank made the difference.[37]

The internecine squabble mirrored the cracks developing in the national Republican Party that year. When business tycoon, reality television star, and former Democrat Donald J. Trump announced he was running for president as a Republican in June 2015, many took it as a joke. But Trump, a billionaire from New York, positioned himself as a populist upstart running against an entrenched elite of Republicans and Democrats alike. He handily won his party's nomination and went on to defeat Democratic nominee Hillary Clinton in the general election. The results prompted much commentary, analysis, and soul-searching about political parties, their ideologies, and their definitions of what it meant to be "for the people."

In Branson, confusion reigned over who was the populist and who was the elitist. Although Presley arguably represented an entrenched local elite of entertainment families that looked out for themselves, for many residents it was the newcomer mayor that represented the dangerous elitism that destroyed local family businesses. Best's victory failed to erase Branson's anxieties about marginalization. In fact, it heightened them, as she brought in a marketing team of outsiders that de-prioritized live entertainment in favor of adventure attractions like zip-lining and resorts like Big Cedar Lodge that attracted a higher-income clientele. "Branson is having an identity crisis," stated a reporter in early 2017. New advertisements featured water and trees, not show marquees. The CVB's new social media hashtag, #NotYourGrandmasBranson, bothered residents. "They are so afraid of being an old person's town, they have totally decided to throw out the baby with the bathwater," complained Americana Theatre owner Chris Newsom. He continued, "Every other state, every other tourism board, when they don't have anything to advertise, they default to lakes and outdoors."[38] To dismiss the shows as outdated risked destroying Branson's competitive advantage. Concerned theater owners started a secret Facebook group, Save Our Shows, and demanded that the Board of Aldermen create a Blue Ribbon Task Force to figure out how best to support live entertainment.

The CVB responded that their marketing efforts were working. Branson theaters collected 15.5 percent more in tourism tax in 2016 than in 2015. Visitation reached almost nine million people in 2016, a record high. But critics pointed out that a few highly successful theaters that had their own marketing obscured the fact that the show industry overall was struggling and under-supported. The percentage of visitors who saw shows had held at around 80 percent for all the years that Branson had recorded such numbers. But under Best's tenure, it declined to 72 percent and stayed there. The Board of Aldermen was unsympathetic and voted to support the CVB's marketing plan 6–0. Alderman Mike Booth suggested that the quality of the shows, not the marketing, was the root of the problem. In a public meeting, he told a parable about a dog-food company: "It started with a brilliant marketing plan. It earned increasing sales. Then it became clear that customers' dogs didn't like the food. The company crashed." Unsurprisingly, many entertainers found Booth's comparison to unpalatable pet food "offensive."[39]

The entertainers were not wrong that the new marketing de-emphasized the shows. In contrast to the 2012 marketing plan, the 2018 plan argued that Branson needed to attract business tourists through hosting trade shows and conventions. It also suggested hosting sporting events, such as cheerleading competitions and youth baseball tournaments. It offered no mission for Branson or any sense of what made it distinctive beyond being "wholesome." Christi, the Midwestern Mom Muse of 2012, vanished.[40]

The CVB's lack of support for live entertainment exacerbated the pernicious influence of the timeshare industry, which first established a foothold in Branson in the early 1980s. Representatives lured customers with offers of free show tickets in exchange for listening to ninety-minute pitches on purchasing a share of a vacation property, with a lump payment up front and yearly fees. Customers often did not realize that they were purchasing a lifetime commitment that could not easily be sold or transferred. In some cases, the promised properties had not even been built yet. In 1984, Missouri attorney general John Ashcroft announced action against three timeshare companies in Taney and Stone counties and called for "legislation regulating the timeshare industry" to curtail rampant deception of consumers. For a pro-business conservative such as Ashcroft to call for government regulation signaled how dire the situation was. Branson city attorney Peter Rea declared that "time sharing will someday become an embarrassment to the city."[41]

Rea underestimated the problem. In the 1990s, timeshares became more than an embarrassment; they became a vampiric presence that drained blood out of Branson's entertainment industry. The Ozarks Marketing Council dissolved in 1997, and Branson's

Chamber of Commerce and CVB seemed less successful at collective marketing strategies.[42] While established shows like the *Presleys' Country Jubilee* could finance their own advertising, smaller ones could not. Timeshare corporations induced theaters to sell chunks of tickets below cost, with the threat that if the theater owners refused, the timeshare agents would promote other shows instead to their thousands of captive customers. Theater owners hoped that the auditoriums full of timeshare audiences would eventually generate enough buzz to not need the timeshare customers to fill the seats. But because the theaters had sold tickets to the timeshare companies at such low margins, they often never recouped costs and thus could not save enough money to do their own advertising. They remained stuck in a cycle of dependency. Other third-party ticket resellers emerged and drove similar hard bargains. Repeatedly, Branson entertainers declared that timeshares and ticket resellers were the biggest threat to their livelihood.[43]

But the CVB was not necessarily wrong that the shows no longer fit the nation's cultural climate. While indeed in the 1990s coastal critics had lambasted Branson entertainment as outdated and culturally retrograde, that decade was also a moment when "conservative was cool" and country musicians had finally reached pop star status. The dozens of aging celebrities had a robust audience of retirees who welcomed the chance to finally meet the people they listened to on the radio in their young adulthood. But those celebrities began to die or move away in the early 2000s, as did those audiences. No new celebrities, not even past-their-prime ones, made Branson their home.

Instead, so-called tribute shows began to fill the empty theaters. Some were impersonation shows in which a performer "paid tribute" to a specific artist with costuming, hair, makeup, movements, and vocal style. Other tribute shows paid homage to a specific genre or decade of music. In 1995, there were only two tribute shows and over thirty celebrity-headlining shows. By 2021, the numbers had reversed: two celebrity shows (Mickey Gilley/Johnny Lee and Yakov Smirnoff), and an astonishing thirty-six tribute shows: *Dean Martin &*

Friends, 50 Years of Kenny Rogers, Patsy to Patsy, Elvis Live!, Back to the Bee Gees, Awesome 80s, and dozens more. In the early 1990s, Loretta Lynn had performed for two seasons and even put her name on a theater that seated 1,455 people. In 2008, the unknown Jo Dee Marie Williams performed a Loretta Lynn tribute in the 280-seat Owen Theatre.[44] The symbolism of this shift loomed large. Branson as a city of second chances for living entertainers was one thing; Branson as a city of tribute artists was another. Did the lack of originality signal the decay of the American dream? Had Branson finally earned the moniker of a "living mausoleum"?[45]

Exacerbating the artistic problems was a new challenge to Branson's version of patriotism. In 2014, a white police officer shot an unarmed Black teenager in Ferguson, Missouri, about four hours away from Branson. International protests ensued and morphed into a sustained activist movement that went by the name Black Lives Matter, or BLM. While certainly not the first political movement to demand an end to racism, BLM mounted a more rigorous critique of how white Americans conceived of their past. In particular, BLM protesters demanded that the United States reckon more explicitly with the legacies of slavery. They called for the removal of Confederate memorials and flags across the South, many of which had gone *up* during the Jim Crow and civil rights eras as deliberate counters to demands for equal rights. This call skyrocketed after a white supremacist, Dylann Roof, shot and killed nine Black Americans at Emanuel African Methodist Episcopal Church in Charleston, South Carolina, in June 2015. A few days later, Walmart, Amazon, eBay, and Sears declared that they would stop selling the Confederate flag. South Carolina governor Nikki Haley called to remove the flag from the South Carolina State House, and within a month the legislature had complied.[46]

In this context, Branson's "old-fashioned, moral patriotism" began to look less benign, as its flag-waving ethos included waving the Rebel flag. Missouri had never officially seceded from the Union, but the Confederate States of America included a star for both it and Kentucky (another non-secessionist border state) on various flag designs. Under the guise of the Ozarks' Southern heritage, the Confederate battle flag appeared throughout Branson. It was on display in the General Store window in Silver Dollar City; it waved onstage in popular shows such as *Country Tonite*, *Jennifer in the Morning*, and even *Celebrate America*; it was displayed proudly at the Dixie Outfitters Store, which opened on the Strip in 2005.[47] As the name suggests, the Dixie Outfitters Store sold Confederate memorabilia of all kinds, from flags to bumper stickers to key chains to bikinis. For a decade, the store didn't make any waves. Nobody seemed to see it as antithetical to Branson's declared allegiance to the United States and its military veterans.

After the AME Church massacre in South Carolina, the *Springfield News-Leader* investigated Dixie Outfitters. Co-owner Anna Robb unapologetically stood up for the Confederate battle flag, calling it a symbol of "Southern Heritage" rather than slavery. She further clarified that it represented "faith, family and freedom" — aligning Branson's three F's motto with the Confederate States of America. The *News-Leader* uncovered that her father-in-law was Thomas Robb, who had taken over from David Duke as the head of the Ku Klux Klan in 1989. Thomas Robb was also a pastor of the Christian Revival Center in Arkansas, a so-called church whose website declared that its primary belief was that "the Anglo-Saxon, Germanic, Scandinavian, and kindred people are THE people of the Bible — God's separated and anointed Israel."[48] When pressed, Anna Robb declined to comment on her father-in-law and claimed she no longer had any ties to the KKK, though she admitted she had attended meetings in the past. She also noted that sales were up from a dozen orders in one day to 300 in one hour after the giant chain stores stopped selling Confederate flags.[49]

The Dixie Outfitters story did not carry farther than Springfield and Kansas City in 2015, but Branson could not stay out of the national eye forever. In 2017, the reckoning came for *Dolly Parton's Dixie Stampede*. Journalist Aisha Harris of *Slate* witnessed the show at the sister location in Pigeon Forge, Tennessee, and her diagnosis was unambiguous. She described it as "a lily-white kitsch extravaganza that play-acts the Civil War but never once mentions slavery" and concluded, "Dolly's Dixie Stampede has been a success not just because people love Dolly Parton, but because the South has always been afforded the chance to rewrite its own history — not just through its own efforts, but through the rest of the country turning a blind eye."[50] Within months, Parton announced that the show's name would be changed to *Dolly Parton's Stampede* in both Pigeon Forge and Branson (the Myrtle Beach location had closed in 2010). The official press release claimed that "Dixie" had merely meant to identify the show's physical location in the South, not to defend the Confederacy. Seemingly overnight, everything was rebranded as *Dolly Parton's Stampede* — cups, t-shirts, signs, tickets, website, hashtags — as if Dixie had never existed. Commentators on the *Branson Tri-Lakes News* website protested the name change, saying the Stampede was "giving in to the PC crowd" and that "PC culture hits Branson." Others called Branson's mayor or took to social media, saying they would never return. But the *Stampede* did not suffer any lasting damage. Thousands of tourists still fill its twice-nightly dinner shows on the Strip six days a week, ten months of the year.[51]

While Parton acquiesced in changing the name of her show, Branson unified in counterprotest to Colin Kaepernick, a Black quarterback for the San Francisco 49ers. In the season opener of the 2016 National Football League season, he kneeled during the National Anthem rather than standing with hand over heart. He went on to kneel during all sixteen games of the season, stating, "I am not going to stand up to show pride in a flag for a country that oppresses Black people and people of color."[52] Kaepernick's support for racial justice caused a sustained, nationwide backlash that lasted well into 2018. The negative responses drew upon a racist history of characterizing Black Americans who protest injustice as ungrateful rather than as patriots strengthening democracy through the exercise of free speech. In Branson, the backlash did not explicitly invoke race but folded in Christian nationalism. Billboards and murals popped up declaring, "We Stand for the Flag and Kneel for the Cross." While perhaps such a phrase could still be interpreted as in line with the

Billboard painted on the side of the Pierce Arrow Theater, Branson. Photo by Kit Doyle, 2022.

more neutral "God and Country" rhetoric of the early 2000s, the giant mural on the side of the Pierce Arrow Theater featured a soldier with an assault rifle doing the kneeling. This more openly violent and aggressive image was replicated on t-shirts and other memorabilia for sale throughout the city.

Anti-Kaepernick sentiment emerged onstage as well. In the concluding number of the *Presleys' Country Jubilee* in 2018, emcee Jay Wickizer recited Johnny Cash's "Ragged Old Flag," which the country singer had written in 1974 during the Nixon-Watergate scandal. The song's narrator wanders into a town square and notices that the courthouse is "kinda run down" and that the flag outside of it is worn out. An old man schools the narrator on why he is proud of that "ragged old flag." He lists the wars of the past two hundred years and the types of "abuse" and "dishonor" the flag has faced but concludes that "she" is "in good shape for the shape she's in."[53] Thirteen years after Cash's death, Wickizer added a new lyric near the end: "And you know it really is a shame / When folks won't stand up for her at a football game." Crowds at the *Presleys' Country Jubilee* burst into applause.[54]

The controversies over the *Dixie Stampede* and Kaepernick's knee were mild kerfuffles compared to what was to come. Black Lives

Black Lives Matter protesters gathered along 76 Country Boulevard in Branson near Dixie Outfitters, June 21, 2020. © Sara Karnes, USA Today Network.

Matter protests surged once again after the murder of George Floyd in Minneapolis in May 2020. It became the largest protest movement in American history, with an estimated 15 to 26 million people participating between May 26 and July 3 of that year.[55] That included in Branson. In mid-June, a small but determined interracial crowd gathered on Highway 76 across from the Dixie Outfitters Store and peacefully marched from the store to downtown. They returned on a second weekend, holding signs that read "I DIDN'T SERVE MY COUNTRY TO WATCH MY BLACK BROTHERS AND SISTERS BE MURDERED IN THE STREETS" and "HILLBILLIES ARE SICK OF THIS TOO!" This time, they were met with counterprotesters in the Dixie Outfitters parking lot who shrouded themselves in Confederate flags.[56] An observer took a video of a blond woman in an army-camouflaged "Make America Great Again" hat. She started out sitting on the back of a black truck with a giant Confederate flag draped over her lap. Pointing her finger at the protesters, she asserted, "I will teach my grandkids to hate you all." She then stood up, spread the flag open, said "suck on this," turned around, and shimmied the flag across her back, as if drying herself off with a

Counterprotesters hold Confederate flags in the parking lot of Dixie Outfitters in Branson, June 21, 2020. © Sara Karnes, USA Today Network.

towel. She ended her performance by turning back around, raising her fist, and proclaiming, "KKK Rules." The observer posted the tirade to social media, where it reached 2.4 million views on Twitter (now X) within two days.[57]

Branson held an emergency town meeting that evening. Residents expressed consternation about the negative image the video conveyed. One said, "The world is watching Branson and aware of where our community stands at the moment on symbolic racism and hatred. Is this what we want for Branson, or can we make the change and move forward as a community to make Branson truly welcoming for people local and tourists alike? This is our chance to do what's right." Another added, "Cleaning up 76 Blvd by removing all visible Confederate memorabilia from the entertainment district is imperative. Zoning regulations need to be reevaluated. Change needs to happen in this town." Mayor Edd Akers suggested that "outside influences" had come to spread hate. It turned out, however, that the woman in the video was a Branson resident. She later apologized, claiming (to the disbelief of most) that she had "blacked out" during the protest and didn't know what she was saying, and that she didn't really know what the Confederate flag meant.[58] In contrast, Dixie Outfitters doubled down, posting to Facebook, "These socialists & antarchists [*sic*], that hate America, hate Christian values. Came to our town, While we were closed, trying to instigate violence. . . . They will not be happy, until they have taken all of the freedoms you enjoy! Until every bit of American pride and patriotism is gone. . . . This is not about our little T-shirt shop. . . . this is about FREEDOM!"[59]

The protests ended by July 2020, and the Dixie Outfitters Store not only stayed in business, but also moved to a bigger location on the Strip in the zone between downtown Branson and most of the theaters. The Hughes Brothers, Country Evolution, Pierce Arrow, and Grand Jubilee shows, as well as the Coral Reef Mini Golf and Fantastic Caverns, placed their brochures in the store's entryway, signaling their tacit approval of the store's ethos. In December 2022, the Trump Store opened 1.5 miles down the Strip, next door to Jerry Presley's God and Country Theater and across the street from Grand Country Music Hall. The two stores overlapped in many of their items: stickers in support of the Second Amendment that prominently featured assault rifles, "Don't Tread on Me" flags with a coiled rattlesnake, and t-shirts that stated, "Jesus is My Savior. Trump is My President."[60] The fact that the latter was for sale during Joseph R. Biden's presidency suggested a belief that Trump was still the rightful leader of the United States. That false belief led to an insurrection in Washington, DC, on January 6, 2021, in which thousands of Trump supporters violently stormed the US Capitol Building in order to prevent Congress from certifying the election results. Five people died, 174 police officers were injured, and four officers who had faced the surging crowd committed suicide within the year. As of May 2024, some 1,424 defendants had been charged with crimes relating to the insurrection.[61] Patriotism had taken on a new cast, as the political divides within the country deepened.

Taney County had voted solidly Republican for sixty years. Many national pundits declared that Trump did not represent conservative or Christian values and thus was a radical break from Republican norms. Nonetheless, local residents did not waver. Trump won 77.2 percent of the vote in 2016 and 77.8 percent of the vote in 2020.[62] That year a meme popped up on social media that exemplified the polarization of the nation, which many feared was on the brink of a second Civil War. It was a satirical "letter" from (Democratic) Blue States to (Republican) Red States announcing secession. The Blue States divvied up America's assets and, predictably, the Red States gratuitously came up short in every category. For the comparison of respective tourist attractions, the letter stated, "We get the Statue of Liberty. You get Branson, Missouri."[63] The CVB's efforts to remake Branson's image as an apolitical destination for outdoors recreation had failed. Instead, just like Harold Bell Wright a century earlier, it was the poster child for the conservative side of the culture war.

Branson's version of American history, which had flown under the radar for so long, also now fell into an ideological camp. In 2019, journalist Nikole Hannah-Jones published a special issue of the *New York Times Magazine* called *The 1619 Project*, whose aim was "to reframe the country's history by placing the consequences of slavery and the contributions of black Americans at the very center of our national narrative."[64] Published on the four hundredth anniversary of the first group of enslaved Africans to arrive in Virginia (though not the first time enslaved Africans arrived on the continent of North America), Hannah-Jones claimed that the nation and its incomplete path toward full democracy began in 1619, not in 1776. She did not reject patriotism, but rather recast the primary actors who best embodied patriotic ideals: not the slave-owning founding fathers, but rather Black people like her father, a military veteran who fought to fulfill the promise of American democracy.[65]

A group of professional historians wrote to the *New York Times* with concern about "the factual errors in the project and the closed process behind it" that had led to a "displacement of historical understanding by ideology."[66] Their positioning of historians as above ideology was misleading; *Times* editor Jake Silverstein correctly argued that both journalists and historians understood that historical inquiry was a matter of interpretation, revision, and competing

claims. But the *Times* was not entirely clean, either. The main publicity photo promoting the project featured a smiling group of high
school students holding up a quote in bright yellow: "We've Got to
Tell the Unvarnished Truth," a statement in direct contradiction to
Silverstein's assertion that journalism was an interpretive claim.[67] He
initially refused to change any of the essays, but eventually relented
to soften Hannah-Jones's most contentious argument that protect-
ing slavery was *the* primary motivation for colonists (implying *all*
colonists) to initiate the American Revolution.[68]

Another group responded to *The 1619 Project* with their own project. In September 2020, President Trump established the 1776 Commission, an advisory committee to support "patriotic education."
College of the Ozarks president Jerry Davis — the one who had refused Wayne Newton's money back in 1993 — was one of the eighteen
members. His participation tied Branson to the backlash against the
Hannah-Jones version of US history. In a news release, Davis stated,
"Some in our nation seek to erase any distinct sense of American
identity or American Exceptionalism from our hearts, minds, and
history books. . . . We must reinforce American ideals and values at
this critical time in history."[69] The College of the Ozarks was founded
as the School of the Ozarks in 1906 as a private Christian institution
and aimed "to encourage an understanding of American heritage,
civic responsibilities, love of country, and the willingness to defend
it."[70] Davis saw his service on the 1776 Commission as an extension of
the college's principles to the nation.

The commission released *The 1776 Report* on January 18, 2021, and
it was promptly rescinded by President Joe Biden on his first day
in office two days later. An even larger groundswell of academics
denounced it, particularly its benign interpretation of slavery and
its listing of progressivism alongside fascism and Communism
as anti-American principles.[71] Overall, the *1776 Report* was widely
ridiculed and seemed to have little impact in the public discourse.
In contrast, the *1619 Project* has lived on through its podcast, book,
six-part docuseries available on the streaming site Hulu, and education website, funded by the Pulitzer Center. *The 1619 Project* reading

guides reached over a million people and its educational programs over 40,000 in its first five years.[72] The uneven afterlives of the two reports — one ridiculed and vanished, the other validated as truth and moved into the mainstream of how American history gets taught — suggested that the *1619 Project* had won the culture wars.

But had it? The critics of the *1776 Report* ignored a small section called "The American Mind," which stated, "Americans yearn for timeless stories and noble heroes that inspire them to be good, brave, diligent, daring, generous, honest, and compassionate. . . . It is up to America's artists, authors, filmmakers, musicians, social media influencers, and other culture leaders to carry on this tradition by once again giving shape and voice to America's self-understanding."[73] Amidst the ahistorical, polemical, and hastily written text of the report, this paragraph revealed an understanding of human psychology that the political left, particularly its academics and journalists, seemed to ignore as the fractious 2020s unfolded: you cannot simply strip away myths. Unvarnished truth is important, but nations, especially the United States, need myths to cohere their diverse populations. As of the 2020s, the political left still could not figure out a way to retell America's past in a way that would unify the country.[74] Could Branson?

7 FUTURE

The City on a Hill

In the early 2010s, when Branson's celebrity headliners were dying out and the Great Recession was causing a pinch, a group of concerned citizens banded together to form Ozark Mountain Legacy. It was a modern-day revival movement, grounded in Christian faith, to ensure the region's economic and spiritual survival. After conducting surveys and hosting "catalyst group" discussions, the co-founders determined that the Missouri Ozarks had five core values. Faith, family, and flag were obviously three of them. The fourth was friendship. As co-founder John Baltes defined it, friendship went beyond perfunctory pleasantries. Instead, it was a statement on the sanctity of human life: "We, in our hearts, collectively feel that people are important and we treat them accordingly. That's a different level of hospitality. That hospitality is an act of love."[1] Baltes traced this approach back to the early Mabe and Presley shows of the 1960s. "You got to know them as real people. You saw their hearts. They built relationships. They built trust. . . . that's why I think this area grew. It was this understanding that this [is] authentic. The people who come here are real, and the people who are performing are real. . . . you can't fake that."[2] Baltes's sentiments echoed what many argued had set Branson apart from its earliest days: the authenticity of its performances of hospitality, which went beyond superficial friendliness to make genuine human connections.

Ozark Mountain Legacy's fifth core value was future. It represented the Legacy's collective sense that Branson needed to become more intentional about maintaining the first four qualities. Rather than tie the five F's to a political party, Ozark Mountain Legacy framed them as the springboard for making the southwest Missouri Ozarks a destination of hope for a nation deeply wounded and divided. "God has a purpose for Ozark Mountain Country," Baltes said; Branson was both literally and spiritually a "city on a hill."[3]

The phrase dates back to Puritan John Winthrop, who in 1630 declared to his parishioners that New England "shall be as a city upon a hill" with the "eyes of all people . . . upon us."[4] He meant it as a warning: do right by God, otherwise God's enemies would dismiss their audacious experiment as a failure. In the mid-twentieth century, politicians including John F. Kennedy and Ronald Reagan invoked the famous phrase to promote the idea that the United States could be a beacon of hope and promise for the rest of the world. In the twenty-first century, Ozark Mountain Legacy sees the region as fulfilling that role for the rest of the nation. But invoking "a city on a hill" also carries undercurrents of Winthrop's original warning. There is the sense that if the Ozark Mountain Legacy cannot succeed in its mission, people will point to Branson to discredit religious faith as a foundation for building a stronger America.

Driving down Branson's Strip of West 76 Country Boulevard in the 2020s, you can choose to see what you want to see. Do you focus on the shuttered motels and the signs offering to liquidate your time-shares and decide that Branson is in decline? Or do you pay attention to new attractions like Splash Country's indoor-outdoor water park and determine that its tourism industry is simply changing? Do you see all the crosses and think that Branson has gone off a religiously extremist deep end? Or does the plethora of churches fill you with hope that Branson is at the center of the movement to rebuild Christianity in America? When you turn from 76 Country Boulevard onto Shepherd of the Hills Expressway, do you mourn the faded neon of Shoji Tabuchi's abandoned theater as a testament to the decline of live performance in our digitized world? Or do you look farther down the Expressway at the majestic Sight & Sound Theatre arising

out of the hills and affirm that theater still retains its power to transform lives?

Branson's next role in the national drama of the long culture wars
is not entirely clear. Three potential trajectories stand out. The first is
that Branson could settle into being a modestly successful regional
destination for families to enjoy shopping, boating, fishing, golf, zip
lines, and the occasional show. It would be blandly indistinguish-
able from other lake-oriented Midwestern tourist spots. The second
trajectory is that Branson could become a stronghold for Christian
nationalism, taking the city's longstanding God-and-country ethos
and sharpening its political edge. The third threads the needle:
Branson could continue to be a unique destination defined by the
faith, family, and flag brand, but such a brand could be welcoming
to all. For believers in this third potentiality, the political genie can
be put back in the bottle.

In all of these futures, the role of performance is up in the air. In
March 2020, the COVID-19 pandemic shut down the live entertainment industry nationwide. All concert touring stopped. Las Vegas
shows closed for a year. Broadway was shuttered for more than
fifteen months. Regional theaters offered virtual-only productions
well into 2021. Dozens of theater companies closed their doors permanently, and when those that had survived reopened their doors
in 2022, audiences failed to return. Theaters shrank their seasons
massively, producing 40 percent fewer shows than in 2019. The ram-
ifications for musicians were more ambiguous. Live music concerts
regained popularity, especially for top megastars like Taylor Swift
and Beyoncé, but the ecosystem for up-and-coming singers to connect with audiences in smaller venues had been severely disrupted.[5]

Unlike in the rest of the country, in Branson live entertainment
opened back up for business a mere eight weeks after the shutdown
orders. Nonetheless, the theaters struggled. The existential threat of
COVID-19 exposed rifts about the meaning of freedom and fueled
Republican-on-Republican, internecine war undergirded by years
of the entertainers' growing resentment against local government.
In June 2020, with no vaccine in sight, Taney County health offi-

cials begged the city of Branson to enforce a mask mandate. The local hospital was overwhelmed with COVID-19 cases, as were major hospitals in Kansas City and St. Louis. With theaters, hotels, and restaurants fully reopened in Branson, the potential to cause massive disease outbreak was high. Yet while theater owners agreed to socially distanced seating, they balked at mask mandates.

Yakov Smirnoff led the anti-mask crusade. Two months into the pandemic, he had decided to move back to Branson after an eight-year sojourn in Los Angeles. He felt the Ozark city would provide more freedom of opportunity. "I think Branson overall is kind of like a test run for the rest of America," he said. "I think we're in the new frontier."[6] But Branson disappointed him. At a July meeting of the Board of Aldermen, he spoke out against the proposed mask mandate. "I'm hoping that you can make this an island of freedom and choice in the sea of hatred and fear," said Smirnoff. He compared the mandate to Soviet-era repression and warned, "It becomes a police state. You are empowering everyone to become an informer."[7] Smirnoff was not alone. Several entertainers saw the mandate as an affront to their independence and an economy killer, and they gathered at the Hughes Brothers Theatre to discuss what to do. Theater owner Clay Cooper stated, "If we do mandate this, we won't have to worry about the virus because there won't be any damn people left to spread the virus."[8] For years, Branson entrepreneurs had run their businesses as they saw fit, with little to no government regulations, zoning laws, or restrictions. Over the protestations of Smirnoff, Cooper, and others, the Board of Aldermen voted 4–1 to approve the ordinance.

The repercussions were swift and merciless. In the next election, the incumbent mayor was defeated. As the first order of business, new mayor Larry Milton repealed the mask mandate. The following year, all aldermen who had voted for the mandate were ousted, as were the city manager and chief financial officer. "It's like 'Game of Thrones' down here right now," said a local waiter, referencing the violent television drama in which political rivals murder each other to gain power.[9] Cooper was now an alderman. Marshall Howden, the grandson of singer Mel Tillis, also now had an alderman seat. The "Branson establishment" had finally been overturned, and the city could get back to the business of supporting show business.

But had the horse left the barn? The first vision for Branson's future continues the path forged by the Convention & Visitors Bureau starting in 2017 that downplayed live performance. Visitation numbers shattered records in 2021, 2022, and 2023, with well over ten million tourists each year. The 2024 season listed 125 shows, more than ever.[10] But shows no longer run twice a day, six days a week, ten months a year. Instead, some run only four times a week, or even once a week. Several only exist during the Christmas season, not the full ten months of the tourist calendar. Furthermore, the number of theaters has been cut in half, from fifty-two in 2007 down to twenty-six in 2024.[11] Outside corporations rather than local families own many of the theaters that remain.

Several entertainers speak gloomily about the future. Whereas entertainers used to promote each other's shows, in the 2020s "you just don't have that camaraderie anymore," said Jerry Presley, second cousin to Elvis and owner of the God and Country Theater.[12] Eddie Stovall echoed the sentiment. "There was a time when this was a place to behold. It seriously was a place to behold . . . The street was all bright lights, and it was hard not to get starry-eyed." He recalled major events that used to bring the community together in the 1990s and early 2000s. Entertainers would gather for after-hours parties at Moonshine Beach. The annual "Cruisin' Branson Lights" event would bring tourists to sit along Highway 76 and watch star performers like Mel Tillis and Doug Gabriel slowly ride down the Strip at midnight, culminating in a big concert in the Walmart parking lot. Every summer ended with a big block party downtown where people would "dance the night away" as a band played on the back of a flatbed truck.[13] "They don't do anything like that anymore," Stovall said in 2022, his smile fading. Audiences at Stovall's shows steadily dwindled in the 2010s even as overall tourism numbers climbed upward. Stovall showed me photos of his group performing in front of large, adoring crowds in Singapore and Sri Lanka. "That's what I'm used to," he said. "[Then] I come back home to this, thirteen people." When asked why the decline had happened, he simply said, "Politics got in the way."[14]

While Stovall did not define what he meant by "politics," for many entertainers the local government's continued lack of investment in live performance remains the most potent problem. Several complain that Branson has been unable to recruit big-time entertainers to replace the Mickey Gilleys and Tony Orlandos. This could be a city management problem, or a matter for the CVB, but there is also the global aspect: some believe that there are simply fewer big names to recruit. With Spotify, Netflix, YouTube, and TikTok transforming how Americans consume entertainment, fewer living singers have deep enough catalogs to put on a show full of recognizable hits. With the splintering of popular culture into distinct segments, each group following their own algorithmic playlist or watchlist, there are fewer common cultural touchstones upon which to base a popular tribute show. This shift has upended Hollywood and the music business, and thus, downstream, it has also upended Branson. Jerry Presley predicted in 2022 that there would be no more shows on the Strip within five to ten years.[15]

But one should not foretell the death of the Branson entertainment industry too soon. The forms of live performance may change — movie theaters did decimate vaudeville — but the human need to experience art in the presence of others remains. In Branson, there are still possible futures for live performance.

One is in the service of Christian nationalism, an ideology whose exact parameters are subject to debate. In general, a Christian nationalist believes that the United States was a Christian nation at its founding, that the truth of the country's Christian origins is under threat, and that the threat must actively be countered. Some Christian nationalists want to designate Christianity as America's official religion, whereas others hold that the government should "advocate Christian values." Christian nationalism is generally seen as racialized, as its calls to return to a better past are synonymous with returning to a past where native-born white people dominated.[16] The

Will corporate chains like Planet Hollywood, with its giant King Kong, take over the Strip? Ilene MacDonald / Alamy Stock Photo.

line between a God-and-country ethos and a Christian nationalist one can get blurry, and in no place more so than in Branson.

Some new shows that have emerged after 2016 stride confidently across that line, such as the *Freedom Journey Show*. Creator Darren Myers rejects the Christian nationalist label, most likely because of its racist connotations, but the production goes beyond Branson's standard exhortation to love Jesus and the flag.[17] Instead, *Freedom Journey* espouses the primary tenets of Christian nationalist ideology: America owes its freedoms to Christian faith, the threat of tyranny is near, and everyone must stand up to fight to restore the nation to its Christian foundations. Myers grew up in Lebanon, Missouri, and received his BA in music education at Baptist Bible College (now Mission University) in Springfield in 1989. He became a youth pastor and church music director, eventually in Rolla, Missouri. A few years into his tenure, in 2008, he decided to put on a Patriot Day Rally in a local park. The modern-day pageant, which he held on the anniversary of 9/11, included a military band, a kids' choir from the church, speeches by historical reenactors, and quotes from founding fathers displayed on giant outdoor screens, topped off at the end with fireworks. The quotes emphasized the role of Christian faith in the nation's founding. As Myers explained it, "Our rights come from God, and the whole purpose of government is to protect our God-given rights." When God drops out, he stated, the tyranny of government fills the vacuum and destroys freedom.[18]

The event was a success and occurred annually for seven years. It taught Myers that even though "these ideas are under attack . . . there is a lot of hunger for that message."[19] In 2015, he left his position as a pastor to travel the country, helping churches stage similar multimedia productions. Myers claims that his mission has never been partisan and points out that campaigning politicians cannot participate in his events. It was more about a "30,000-foot view" that "in this big spiritual war, there are people who are against freedom." As he sees it, his job is to fight back.[20]

When Myers's sons moved to Springfield and his parents to Branson, he and his wife decided to "test the waters" about building something more permanent in the area. He was disconcerted by American history museums in Washington and Philadelphia that he felt "left out the faith part" and wanted to create his own institution. He wanted to model the "experiential" approach of the Lincoln Museum in Springfield, Illinois, where, he noticed, nobody looked at the glass case with Lincoln's hat, but everyone crowded around the hologram theater. Critics disparagingly compared the Lincoln Museum to Disney for prioritizing spectacle above education, but Myers found it compelling. He also wanted to draw upon his years of experience as a music director and event organizer to develop a show. He envisioned a space that could encompass a museum, bookstore, coffee shop, children's colonial village play area, and theater.[21]

As it so happened, the *Freedom Journey Show*, modeled after his multimedia pageants, came before the museum. In 2017, Myers decided to rent out a small Branson theater for Veterans Week. To his surprise, the 110-seat space filled up for all five shows, and attendees asked if he was going to do it again next year. After three years he decided to fulfill the dream of his own space. Myers formed a 501(c)(3) nonprofit called Freedom Encounter, and in April 2021, along with an unnamed financial partner, purchased Tony Orlando's Yellow Ribbon Theatre for 20 percent of the asking price.[22]

The version of the *Freedom Journey Show* in the 2023 season began with a voiceover narration that explained the long history of tyranny in the world, starting with Nimrod in 2247 BCE, illustrated by a timeline on a projector screen. The large stage was bare — no people, no sets, no props, no musicians. When the timeline reached the Puritans, holograms of actors in colonial garb talked about escaping England to pursue religious freedom. Occasionally, members of the Myers family came onstage to sing patriotic songs, then left again to let the holograms continue the story. Ben Franklin talked about the American Revolution and the role of God in it, then Frederick Douglass discussed slavery and the Civil War, and so forth. Darren Myers came to the stage to discuss the journey of faith and freedom in the twentieth century. He read quotes from leaders such as Dwight D. Eisenhower, Ronald Reagan, and Margaret Thatcher to support the idea that the United States was a Christian nation at its founding and could only succeed as a nation by following biblical principles. Interspersed were homemade videos from Russian refugees, testifying to the freedom they experienced in America. They did not mention the war against Ukraine that had been ongoing for over a year or Vladimir Putin's authoritarianism, but instead emphasized the dangers of Marxist Communism, that old Cold War bugaboo. In the end, the Myers family came out to sing again with a giant American flag behind them.[23]

The production, as a piece of theater, did not work. It violated the basic principle of "show, don't tell," with too much didacticism and not enough inspirational, virtuosic, or aesthetically pleasing performances. Most likely for that reason, I was one of only six guests in the 2,000-seat auditorium when I saw the show in May 2023. It turned out that one was an employee and two were the parents of a performer, so I was one of three paying audience members. Even for a Branson production struggling in the pandemic aftermath, the number was shockingly low.

Whether that signaled Christian nationalism's lack of cultural or political power, however, was not obvious. If the *Freedom Journey Show* were on Broadway and only six people had shown up, it would have closed immediately. Instead, two years later, it was still running. The massive theater, with its formidable overhead costs, was not in financial distress and seemed well maintained — functioning lights, air-conditioning, bathrooms, and concession stand; the seats and the stage were in good condition. Myers takes no salary for running Freedom Encounter full-time. The 501(c)(3) received $353,148 in cash donations in 2023 — certainly not a large amount compared to the millions raked in by political action committees, but not nothing — and had zero liabilities, given that a private, limited liability corporation actually held the mortgage. The goal is to raise $5.5 million in order to make the dream of the museum and kids' colonial village come true.[24]

Despite Myers's declarations that Freedom Encounter is nonpartisan, in 2022 he spoke at the Reawaken America two-day rally at Branson's Mansion Theatre alongside Eric Trump, son of Donald Trump, and MyPillow creator Mike Lindell, who claimed that the 2020 election was stolen. Myers originally offered to host the rally at Freedom Encounter, but with 3,000 attendees, it needed a larger venue. "We're in a fight for the soul of our nation," Myers said to the crowd, after which Eric Trump took the stage. Trump stated that coming to Missouri was like a "homecoming" because they were in "friendly territory." He accused the Democratic Party of "weaponiz[ing] education" and using federal agencies to persecute conservatives before concluding, "We don't worry about this state, you guys have our back 100 percent and I promise you we have yours. And I promise you guys we're going to go get these bastards."[25] He delivered. In 2024, Donald Trump won the presidency handily.

As demonstrated by the thousands of attendees at the rally, places like Freedom Encounter have drawn like-minded people to Branson. One such person is Kim Fletcher. She was a stay-at-home mother of eight, living in Virginia, when the attacks of September 11, 2001, altered her life trajectory. Her husband had been working at the Pentagon that day, and when he came home alive, something changed. "I have been patriotic my whole life," Fletcher said. "But I didn't realize what it really meant to be a patriot. . . . That was the day I went from being patriotic to being a patriot and committed myself to doing everything I could in my power to make sure that my children were free." Around the same time, she began homeschooling her kids, which opened up a "whole new world" that she felt had been denied to her in her public school education. In particular, she felt she was learning things about American history she never knew. For example, she had heard of Davy Crockett, but did not know that he was a US senator, or that he had fought and died at the Alamo — which, in her mind, meant he was an unacknowledged American hero. She also had not carefully read Section Eight of the Constitution, which dictates what government can spend money on — and thus what it cannot. Every time she brought up a new piece of knowledge to her mother, her mother replied, "Oh yeah, I know that story. We learned it in school." Fletcher developed a sense that something had been taken away. "When did they stop telling me what America was really about?" she asked herself. Combining her resurgent patriotism and her determination that "everybody needs to have this, the heritage and the history that's been stripped from us," she founded Moms for America. The organization aims to teach moms American history and to "empower" them to defend liberty by teaching their children, voting, and even running for office themselves.[26]

Fletcher never named the "they" she claimed were taking away American history, but her actions on January 6, 2021, signaled one group: the millions of Americans who had elected Joseph R. Biden to the presidency in the 2020 election. Moms for America cosponsored the "Save America" rally on the National Mall on the day that the US Senate was set to certify the election results. Outgoing president Donald Trump spoke to the crowd: "All of us here today do not want to see our election victory stolen by emboldened radical-left Democrats. . . . They try and demean everybody having to do with us. And you're the real people, you're the people that built this nation. . . . We fight like hell. And if you don't fight like hell, you're not going to have a country anymore . . . we're going to walk down Pennsylvania Avenue. . . . And we're going to the Capitol."[27] At that point, thousands indeed marched on the Capitol and violently took over the building. They assaulted police officers, attempted to capture senators, and erected a gallows while chanting "Hang Mike Pence," the vice president who rejected Trump's request to overturn the election results. Fletcher was subpoenaed by the January 6 Commission and gave a deposition about her role. She had stayed on the lawn to pray instead of breaching the Capitol and saw nothing antidemocratic about the attempts to stop the certification. Instead, she believed that trust in government had been completely broken because "the infiltration of those trying to destroy our country, shred the Constitution, and tear down our public are pretty much complete."[28]

Like Myers, Fletcher believed that the fight was a spiritual one. When the COVID-19 pandemic turned her husband's job into a remote position, Fletcher decided to search for a new headquarters for Moms for America that would fit its ethos. Her son suggested she check out Branson. As soon as her daughter drove them into the area, "I got this internal explosion, like a flutter, instant excitement." She felt attuned to a spiritual awakening. As a military wife, she had moved often. Branson felt different. "You see God everywhere" in Branson, she said, as well as "founding fathers painted on murals." Branson was a place where God and country were intertwined. Fletcher stated, "This isn't just about trees and hills and the beauty and majesty of the area. This is about the spirit that dwells here. . . . I've been all over the world and I've never experienced anything like this." She relocated the headquarters of Moms for America to Branson, and her household along with it.[29]

Fletcher expressed faith in the power of theatrical performance to transform the world. "You go into these shows [in Branson] and you just leave changed," she said. She aimed to bring that power to Moms for America. "How do we touch hearts? It's through a story," she said. "If all we do is focus on elections and public policy, we're going to lose everything." She talked excitedly of partnering with Freedom Encounter. "People just get it here in Branson," she concluded.[30]

While Freedom Encounter and Moms for America are clearly Christian nationalist, other newer Branson organizations are more subtle. One is Sight & Sound. Sight & Sound bills itself as "Christian Broadway" and produces original musicals that "bring the Bible to life." While a giant American flag flies in its parking lot, the shows never explicitly mention the United States or contemporary politics. Glenn Eshelman founded Sight & Sound Theatre in Lancaster, Pennsylvania, in 1976. The name comes from the book of Matthew, in which the disciples ask Jesus why he speaks to the people in parables. Jesus replies, "In seeing, they do not see. In hearing, they do not hear." Thus the people need stories to open them to the Truth, "with a capital T," of God.[31] In 2004, Peter and Jack Herschend of Silver Dollar City pitched Sight & Sound on opening a second location in Branson and brought the executives down for a site visit. When Eshelman set foot on the hilltop where the theater would be built, he immediately felt the hand of God, like Harold Bell Wright, Randy Plummer, and countless others. "This is where the Lord is asking us to go," he said. "We knew we were called to Branson."[32]

In 2006, construction that reportedly cost over $36 million began. Publicity emphasized the large scale of the endeavor. The structure would be 339,000 square feet, the largest building in Branson; the theater would seat 2,000; the stage would be 300 feet wide (claimed to be the largest in the United States), wrapping around the audience on both sides. A typical Broadway stage is 38–45 feet wide.[33] Because most Sight & Sound productions featured live animals, the grounds included a fenced outdoor pasture, an indoor stable, a "special grinder system" for waste treatment, and an indoor training arena.[34] Set apart from the neon marquees, glittering octopus, scowling King Kong, and giant meatball that lined Highway 76, the imposing temple-like structure with three domes rose majestically from a wooded hillside, leading locals to nickname it "Little Jerusalem."[35]

Sight & Sound fit into Branson "culturally, theatrically, and spiritually."[36] While one version of Christianity is about asceticism, Sight & Sound's chief creative officer, Josh Enck, preferred extravaganza.[37] From his perspective, spectacle did not detract from a spiritual

Sight & Sound Theatre, Branson, Missouri. Courtesy Sight & Sound Theatres® Branson, MO.

experience, but rather enhanced it. He cited God as the model. The goal of the shows was "not just to inform or educate, but to inspire," because "inspiration is at the core of who God is. Look at his creation! He inspires us with the sunrise, with the sunset. . . . it's our duty to inspire the next generation with the things of Christ and Truth."[38] The emphasis on spectacle is also aimed at attracting audiences who "do not have a relationship with Jesus and may be experiencing the Bible for the very first time." As Enck explained, "We repeatedly hear from them how their experience was not what they expected. They express sheer awe at the scope of the productions, the innovation, the live animals. . . . They didn't realize how entertaining and how relevant the stories from the Bible were."[39]

The debut production in Branson, *Noah*, which ran from 2008 to 2011, was indeed spectacular. In act 1, the forty-five cast members constructed the exterior of Noah's Ark onstage, which included eleven pieces that weighed more than 100,000 pounds each. The curtain opened on act 2 with the interior of the ark spanning the entire 300-foot wraparound stage, which made the audience feel like they were *in* the Ark. Over 100 live animals and 200 animatronic ones filled the four-story set. Soon, the flood began. Dark-blue and white patterned laser lights swept over the audience to simulate rocking back and forth in the ocean as the sounds of thunder and pouring rain boomed from the surround sound. The "whole auditorium gasped." One person stated that it was like watching a show and being on a ride at the same time.[40]

Branson audiences and local critics responded positively. The sold-out audience for *Noah* enthusiastically applauded "a new level of entertainment in a city where nearly 100 shows of all formats already fill stages day and night." Other shows got similar responses: *Joseph* in 2012, *Jonah* in 2014, *Moses* in 2016, *Samson* in 2018, *Noah* again in 2020, *Jesus* in 2021, *Queen Esther* in 2023, and *David* in 2025. Reviewers made secular comparisons. "As good as anything you would see on Broadway," said a patron from Michigan about *Noah*. "Definitely Broadway Worthy!" wrote a woman from St. Louis. By the time *Jesus* came to town, commentators asserted not only equality, but superiority: "I have been to numerous Broadway shows and nothing compares to this," wrote a patron from San Antonio, Texas. Craig from Lancaster, South Carolina, went even further: "We've seen some really great shows from Broadway to Vegas and Orlando to London but none as spectacular as *Jesus* at the Sight & Sound theater in Branson."[41]

But spectacle is only one-half of the equation; story is the other. As in Broadway musicals, Sight & Sound performers use song and dance to tell stories. Musical numbers connect audiences to biblical teachings on emotional, sensory, and embodied levels that are difficult to access simply with dialogue. Sight & Sound's creative teams eclectically draw on a variety of traditions, eschewing authenticity in favor of popular aesthetics. For example, in *Noah*, a rousing dance number communicates the family's joy when the rains stop after forty-one days. Instead of attempting an ancient Mesopotamian folk dance, Noah's sons and their wives break into a mid-twentieth-century-style American square dance with choreographic references to other hit stage shows that were popular when *Noah* was originally being developed in the mid-1990s. Dancers click their heels like Irish performers in *Riverdance*. Then they bring out brooms, with which they rhythmically sweep, jump over, and soft-shoe much like the performers in the Broadway show *STOMP*. Yet in *Noah*, only four songs further the plot or develop the characters. The other eight are prayers to God. These numbers do not draw on Broadway vocal conventions, but rather a variety of contemporary Christian musical styles: *a cappella* barbershop quartets, solemn hymns, praise and worship songs as seen in twenty-first-century megachurches, Christian rock, and Black gospel music.[42]

Sight & Sound's political messages are indirect. In interviews and press releases, representatives never mention contentious social issues such as abortion, LGBTQIA+ rights, or elections. At the same time, in arguing for the relevance of ancient Bible stories to the present, they gesture toward a worldview. In the summer of 2020, a season racked by the COVID-19 pandemic and nationwide protests against racism, Sight & Sound debuted *Queen Esther* in Lancaster, which then came to Branson in 2023. The musical depicts the biblical story of Hadassah, an orphaned Jewish girl in the Persian Empire who navigates a perilous path. Captivated by her beauty, King Xerxes decides to make her his queen. Hadassah conceals her Jewish identity and assumes the name of Esther. She struggles to maintain faith in God as she faces people in Xerxes's royal court who wish her community harm. Eventually, she learns to trust in God that she was "made for such a time as this" (Esther 4:14) and bravely saves the Jewish people from a harmful government.

In a September 2020 interview, co-creator Kristen Brewer asserted that the show, like its title heroine, was "needed 'for such a time as this.'" Brewer did not mention specifically why but stated, "You read the book [of Esther] and you realize there's always going to be a plan of attack on the people of God. One of the lines of the show is 'God has a plan, there is an enemy, and we have a choice.' And those three things work together to sort of create our current circumstances."[43] Brewer offered a call to action, vaguely suggesting that evangelical Christians were under attack in the 2020s, including from their government, much as Esther and the Jewish people had been in fifth-century BCE. *Queen Esther* galvanized viewers to "make a choice" to stand against secularism and the perceived concomitant social ills.

When Branson's local government tried to take a stand in the most recent culture wars fray, it demonstrated the complexity of the city's position. In 2023, conservative activists across the country came after drag queens. The culture wars that spring eternal revived the proposition made famous by Anita Bryant in the 1970s that LGBTQ+ adults, particularly drag queens, were attempting to "groom" children for sexual deviance. Tennessee and Montana moved to ban drag performances on public property, and the Pentagon banned drag performances on military bases.[44]

Branson decided to take a different route. On July 10, 2023, the Planning & Zoning Commission recommended that the Board of Aldermen pass an ordinance restricting drag performance to a specially designated "adult entertainment" district downtown. In what appeared like a smart move, the Board of Aldermen did not ban drag altogether. As Mayor Larry Milton pointed out, such a ban would be inconsistent with the Constitution, a document that Branson residents and visitors revere deeply. Milton observed that the courts had blocked every attempted drag restriction elsewhere, given that such bans were obvious violations of the First Amendment's right to freedom of speech.[45] Thus, he argued, restricting rather than outlawing drag seemed wise.

The backlash came from people who saw the new law as a capitulation to left-wing political correctness. Milton tried to explain that the resolution aimed to be the best compromise that honored faith, family, and flag equally. But his explanations seemed to fall on deaf ears. In the comments section of the *Branson Tri-Lakes News*, one constituent wrote, "Never would think Branson would get sucked into this wokeness. This is a family community that doesn't need to have this shoved in their faces." Another stated, "I'm not a resident, just a frequent visitor to your area. Please, please, please find a way to keep this woke nonsense out of your community. Keep the Branson area clean and wholesome." A third wrote, "Stop this garbage or you WILL lose the kind of family tourists who come here."[46]

Complaints came from other directions as well. The most glaring problem was that drag had a long and storied history on the Strip. Comedians had appeared in drag for decades, with no qualms from Branson audiences, and this new ordinance would affect their livelihoods. Alderman Marshall Howden proposed a modification of language: no drag performances *that included sexual content* outside the adult entertainment zone. The distinction was muddy because all drag involves gender play and thus highlights humans as sexual beings. The "family-friendly" drag of the 1990s variety shows on the Strip loved to mock Dolly Parton's giant breasts. But the belief that nonsexual drag was possible was accepted, and the modified ordinance passed 4–2. Alderman Chuck Rodriguez explained his "no" vote in the name of individual freedom and the free market: "I think we shouldn't discriminate. I don't think we should put them in a corner. . . . We shouldn't pick winners and losers. . . . We should let the market dictate what happens."[47] He claimed that outside agitators had forced the issue on Branson and did not reflect the town's ethos. The following spring, however, Rodriguez lost his reelection campaign.[48]

Rodriguez's successor, Glenn Schulz, emphasized the unique promise of Branson, stating, "Where else can you have small town values of Faith, Family and Flag while entertaining more than 10 million visitors annually? We are truly blessed."[49] For many of those who fill the ranks of the nation's entertainment industry, Branson has also been a blessing. In March 2020, Minnesota native Alexis Solheid was pursuing a degree in musical theater at Viterbo University in La Crosse, Wisconsin, when COVID-19 shut down the university. She moved back in with her parents and seven siblings. "So I'm in my garage, doing clowning class, filming it for my professors, doing all the weird stuff that you do with online theater school," she said. She tried to find a job, but nobody was hiring. One day her mom mentioned that she saw on Facebook that Branson was opening. Alexis sent her résumé and cover letter to every Branson theater manager she could find on Google. Chris Newsom at the Americana Theatre responded immediately and invited her to join them. Within two weeks, Solheid had packed her bags and driven down, arriving on May 19, 2020.[50]

Solheid spent the summer as a Jill-of-all-trades at the Americana: stage manager, spotlight operator, box-office worker, concessionaire, gift shop attendant. She even cleaned sticky spilled soda and popcorn out of the aisles. When she got the email that Viterbo would again be online in the fall, she decided to stay. The first season felt surreal, as "it was weird to be in a place that was open and functioning kind of normal and then seeing all my friends all around the world being shut in their homes not even open at all."[51] The Americana hired her to perform in the *Rock 'n' Roll Royalty* show as a tribute artist for the following season, and then asked her to choreograph a new tribute show, *Awesome 80's*, even though she had relatively little dance training. "If I had gone somewhere like New York or Chicago, I would've never been a choreographer," she stated. But she loved it and soon got hired for more gigs. For another show, *British Invasion*, she taught herself electric bass.

Alexis loved that Branson has remained a land of opportunity. "There are a lot of really amazing professionals here but there's also a lot of room for growth here," she said. If you worked hard, people would give you a chance. With no union or industry rules, she had to be self-regulating about those chances. In the 2021 season, she performed in fifteen to twenty shows a week: 10 a.m., 2 p.m., 5 p.m., and 8 p.m., getting home at 11 p.m. and waking up at 7 a.m. to start over again. She started working with a vocal coach online to not wreck her voice and eventually decided to balance out performance with backstage work.[52] For every attendee at a Reawaken America rally who sees Branson as a fortress in the culture war, there is an Alexis who sees it as a place of decent employment for theater professionals.

Despite gloomy predictions of Branson's demise — whether because it has abandoned its conservative values or conversely, because it has become too right wing — people like John Baltes of Ozark Mountain Legacy believe in the city's future. He embraces the three F's worldview with the intention to heal and provide hope. As Branson should know better than anyplace else, however, history bleeds into the present. Given its ideological roots in the yearning to return to a white pioneer past, "faith, family, and flag" seems questionable as a blueprint for an America that is racially, ethnically, and religiously diverse. But the theater is a place of creative renewal, where pasts can transform into new futures. If anyone can generate new meanings for the three F's that are truly inclusive, it is the performers who make and remake the world anew onstage night after night. What path Branson will follow remains to be seen.

EPILOGUE

On the Ground in the Culture War

In July 2018, I emerged from a Branson theater at intermission to a sky that had turned an ominous purplish green. The humid air pressed against my skin, and the wind whipped litter across the parking lot; I wondered if a tornado was coming. I felt a strong urge to run to my car and start the four-hour drive home to St. Louis. As a rule, I do not leave shows early. If performers are putting themselves out there, I believe they deserve my attention until the very end. But the whole atmosphere that night felt oppressive, with the weather only compounding the emotional toll that had been building up all week.

It was my first summer of in-person research in Branson. It was also the middle of the first Trump presidency, which had polarized the nation to an extent not seen in recent memory. My personal and professional circles were overwhelmingly dismayed. The president's latest affront had been a joint press conference with Russian president Vladimir Putin. Trump had praised the authoritarian leader and criticized US intelligence agencies. Even members of his own party voiced concern. An anchor on the pro-Trump Fox News Network tweeted, "No negotiation is worth throwing your own people and country under the bus."[1] While such news alerts were blowing up on my phone, giving me a sense of panic about the state of the country, my physical self was having a different experience. Days earlier, at this same theater, I had attended a different show where I sat in front of two military veterans. One wore a hat that said Make

America Great Again, the slogan of Donald Trump's 2016 presidential campaign. I chatted with them and learned that they had been coming to Branson for twenty-five years, drawn by the "clean," family-friendly atmosphere. They were kind and gracious, more than willing to answer questions from a stranger. After two hours of variety entertainment, during which the headliner charmingly bantered with audience members, sang country songs, and danced with his wife, the evening concluded with the crowd rising to sing the National Anthem. Inside this auditorium, all was right and good in the United States.

The dissonance weighed on me as I stood outside the theater that stormy July evening, deciding whether to stay or leave. Ultimately, I ignored the ominous skies and my own sense of foreboding. Duty to research called, as did my underlying respect for performers. I re-entered the theater to watch the second half of the show. Energetic siblings performed cover songs of popular hits from country to rock to R&B to top forty. They came down on wires; they tap-danced on platforms; they dazzled with rapid bow work on the violin and fast lips buzzing on the harmonica. The audience clapped appreciatively. Rumors flitted through my head as I watched. Off the record, many Branson residents had whispered to me that this group used tracked music and faked their instrumental virtuosity. Others claimed that they worked hand-in-glove with timeshare companies and filled their auditoriums with below-cost ticketholders to give the appearance of popularity.

As had happened so many times over the course of that first summer in Branson, I was uncertain about what I had actually witnessed. Were they talented, or not? Were they original, or not? Did their odes to rural living, tight-knit nuclear families, Christian faith, and the flag construct a perfectly viable, even enviable, worldview? Or were such ideas harmful and built upon a shaky foundation of capitalist exploitation and exclusionary definitions of what it meant to be a real American?

When I woke up the next morning, I discovered that my gut sense of foreboding had, in fact, divined a real tragedy. At 6:32 p.m.

the night before, the National Weather Service had issued a storm warning and measured winds up to 60 miles per hour at the nearby Branson Airport. At 7 p.m., as I had settled into my seat at the show, a Duck Boat operator had ignored the warning and set out with a group of tourists onto Table Rock Lake. A Duck Boat is a heavy, ungainly amphibious vehicle dating from the World War II era. The operator lowered canopies to prevent rain from lashing in; those canopies also prevented egress. None of the passengers wore life jackets. Nine minutes later, facing hurricane-like conditions as the winds reached 73 miles per hour, the boat sank, and seventeen out of the thirty-one people aboard died. Decades of anti-government sentiment in the area meant that the Duck Boat operators and the parent company, Ripley Entertainment, ignored National Transportation Safety Board recommendations about buoyancy, canopies, and securing the bow hatch that had been issued in 1999 after a Duck Boat sank in Arkansas and killed thirteen passengers. The Branson Duck Boat captain was not required to cancel outings when weather conditions worsened; he was not required to make passengers wear life jackets.[2] Personal freedom and profit had been elevated above the collective good. I could not help but extrapolate to see a fundamental flaw in Branson's version of the American Dream.

Four years later, I had a different experience. Over Christmas 2022, I took my family to the *Great American Chuckwagon Dinner Show* at the Shepherd of the Hills. The emcee in a bushy beard and overalls rang a triangle to call the performers and audience to attention. We gathered both physically and spiritually. Randy Plummer, bassist, stepped up to a microphone and doffed his hat. He led all of us in a simple Lord's Prayer. Plummer has been performing in Branson for fifty years. Throughout that time, he has seen his mission as bringing "goodness, love, and light to people." "I don't want to sound cliché," he later told me, "but this is how I really feel. . . . You'll never know, this side of heaven, the good you're doing. So, we keep putting out the good."[3] After watching Plummer and the four other singer-musicians perform cowboy Christmas songs for about an hour, the emcee asked all veterans to stand and be honored. Then we all rose to sing

"God Bless America" together, performers and audience members alike. Even though the state of our country had arguably gotten even worse and the political divisions even sharper over the past four years, this time I felt no qualms in standing. Years of research and face-to-face engagement with people in Branson had changed me. In my head, I still rehearsed my critiques of the cowboy trope, of the absence of Native Americans in this rendering of the American West, and of the Christian emphasis of the songs, but those seemed less important than the palpable grace I felt from Randy Plummer.

It was a grace that was lacking elsewhere in a nation emerging out of the COVID-19 pandemic. My kids loved our trip. As I witnessed them experience Branson performances, a quote from Sight & Sound Theatre's Chief Creative Officer came to my mind: "Whoever tells the best story wins our children."[4] Granted, I had carefully preselected what they would see; not every production would have elicited the same warm responses. But many Branson shows over the decades have fulfilled theater's best promise: to create more love, connection, empathy, and happiness in the world. That alchemy generates tremendous persuasive power.

It is an irony not lost on me that I have written a book about the culture wars at a time when academics (such as myself) have been drafted into the culture wars and accused of irredeemable leftist bias. I share my personal experiences here in the epilogue to acknowledge that I am a human being who inevitably has thoughts and emotions, but I argue that such feelings do not invalidate the analysis in the rest of this book. Instead, the opposite is true. My training as a historian with a deep expertise in performance enables me to articulate how Branson shows have operated to have an emotional effect on me and millions of others.

Michael S. Roth, the president of Wesleyan University, published an op-ed in the New York Times in November 2021 in which he argued that right-wing attacks on higher education were misguided, given that liberal arts institutions "cultivate the robust exchange of ideas across differences." He rejected the stereotype of college students and faculty as one-dimensionally leftist and narrow-minded.

Instead, he suggested that curiosity and empathy were still at the root of scholarly inquiry. He concluded, "Whatever your political position, embracing intellectual diversity means being brave enough to consider ideas and practices that might challenge your own beliefs or cause you to change your views, or even your life."[5]

When I decided to write a book about Branson, I implicitly accepted Roth's challenge (though I hadn't yet read his articulation of it) to be brave enough to change my views, even perhaps my life. But I was also scared to write it for precisely that reason. I had considered writing my dissertation about Branson as a graduate student at New York University in 2006, but I had abandoned the idea. I was not yet secure enough in my identity to risk such transformation. Eleven years later, I was ready. The words of anthropologist Anna Lowenhaupt Tsing rang in my head: "We are contaminated by our encounters; they change who we are as we make way for others."[6] Cult leaders know this intuitively, which is why they prohibit contact with the outside world. So do segregationists, nativists, and anyone else who pulls up the ramparts to exclude those deemed Others. Roth asserts that the "woke stereotype" promulgated by right-wing media stars like Ann Coulter is "wildly misleading." But in my nearly two decades in higher education, I have never talked to a professor who engaged with a conservative student and admitted that their perspective had changed as a result. When scholar Jill Stevenson told colleagues about her research on evangelical performance, many said they hoped she "wouldn't be 'converted' or 'won over' by these encounters."[7] Contaminated, one might say. In bursting my leftist bubble, I opened myself up to potential exclusion from the circles to which I had previously belonged.

That risk was worth the reward. I knew that I could not build a bridge to Branson if I didn't at least consider that my perspective might be changed by who and what I encountered. I could not hope to change those I met there — hope they might rethink their approach to American history or stereotypes of liberal academics after talking to me — if I didn't offer the reciprocal possibility that they might cause me to rethink things as well. Roth's promise of liberal arts education would then be dead in the water. The bridge would be built, but we would wave at each other from either end, perhaps straining to hear and squinting to see, but not moving one step closer.

Many would argue that this distance is okay. If one end of the bridge represents white supremacy, patriarchy, and Christian nationalism, then meeting in the middle is a nonstarter. At a certain point, empathy tips over into endorsement. This tipping point has become especially fraught in the moment that I write this epilogue in April 2025, four months into Donald J. Trump's second term as president. His brand of conservative populism has hardened into an authoritarian approach to governance. But the perspective that the tens of millions of people who voted for that government are damned from the beginning as irrevocably racist, sexist, homophobic, xenophobic, and antidemocratic seems equally a nonstarter. Who are the people along the broad middle expanse of the bridge? How, when, and why do they move in the directions they do? Something was missing from the picture. I tried to lead with curiosity to find out what it was.

My approach often felt like a lonely road. Advocacy overwhelmingly guides current scholarship in the performing arts. There is a valid reason why: the arts continuously face existential threats in the United States. They are written out of government budgets, dismissed as unimportant compared to STEM fields, and demonized because marginalized racial or sexual identity groups have historically used the arts to challenge oppression. At the same time, advocacy can lead to an intellectual dead end. When conclusions are preordained, what is there to learn? In the case of this book, my goal was not to advocate for Branson performers or their political positions. Instead, I wanted to discover how and why this unlikely place has helped shape American cultural and political discourse for the past one hundred years. I cannot predict what happens next. What I do know: whatever the future holds, Branson and its live entertainers will be along for the ride.

ACKNOWLEDGMENTS

Many people made this book possible. I would first like to thank my former dissertation advisor, Eric Foner, for believing that a book about Branson could have a life outside of academia and putting me in touch with the Sandra Dijkstra Literary Agency. I thank my agent, Jill Marr, for finding me the perfect press, University of Chicago, and the perfect editor, Tim Mennel. Tim, I couldn't imagine this book without you. Thank you for your enthusiasm about the subject and your push to make the writing as clear as possible.

In Branson, my first thanks go to Jean and Jim Babcock, the stalwart volunteer archivists at the Centennial Museum. They helped me with research in the archives, put me in touch with people to interview, and invited me to their home for meals and conversation. I will always treasure our time together. I also thank Trish Trimble at the White River Valley Historical Society, who was an invaluable resource and patiently answered my many email queries. I am grateful to everyone who was willing to do an interview with me: John Baltes, Jim Barber, Lynn Berry, Melissa Calasanz, Heather Castillo, Joshua Clark, Shannon Cody, Harvey Day, Kimberly Fletcher, Madison Foreman, John Fullerton, Wayne Glenn, Larry Hoover, Marty Hughes, Bob Mabe, Jody Madaras, Jae McFerron, Lara Menard, Larry Musgrave, Darren Myers, Nicholas Naioti, Patrick Needham, Steve Plaster, Randy Plummer, Rick and Michi Porter, Gary Presley, Jerry Presley, Lisa Rau, Isabelle Roig, Terry Wayne Sanders, Alexis Solheid, Eddie Stovall, Joy Thomas, Ryan Thomas, Trajana Thomas, Keith Thurman, Earl Vaughn, June Ward, and Tam Warner. Others spoke with me off the record and in casual conversations, including dozens of Branson performers, tourists, hotel workers, and restaurant staff. Not everyone is directly quoted in this book, but collectively your perspectives helped me understand Branson and its history.

I thank my colleagues at Washington University, particularly Pannill Camp, Ellie Harrison, Rob Henke, Elizabeth Hunter, David Marchant, and Paige McGinley, for listening to me present on this work, reading drafts of chapters, and giving me feedback. Marie Griffiths offered me an opportunity to present at the Washington University John C. Danforth Religion and Politics Colloquium, where I also received valuable feedback. This book would also not be possible without funding. I was fortunate to get a Washington University Center for the Humanities Summer Seed Grant, a junior research leave, and a one-year ACLS Fellowship to support this project.

I had just gotten my Branson research off the ground when the COVID-19 pandemic hit. In that dark and lonely first year, Elizabeth Craft provided a much-needed lifeline to keep going. Writing over Zoom with her, from my attic, was a blessing. Soon we added others, and the #Ready2Write Crew has been a rock for the past several years. In addition to Elizabeth, it includes Rachel Carrico, Dasha Chapman, Saroya Corbett, Adanna Kai Jones, and Esther Kurtz. I had a second Zoom crew support system — Colleen Hooper, Ariel Nereson, and Katelyn Hale Wood — with whom I navigated not only research, but also school shootings, parenthood, and academic life. This was the first book I have written with a small army of student research assistants. Eli Bradley, Jay Buchanan, Natasha Cole, Maddie House-Tuck, Ryan Hung, Oliver Parsons, and Ella Urton: thank you. From thought partners to fact checkers, you collectively shaped and contributed to this research in myriad ways. Along the way, I published two essays related to the book, one coauthored with Jay Buchanan and the other with Maddie House-Tuck. I thank Victoria Fortuna and Angie Ahlgren, guest editors of the journal *Theatre History Studies,* and Jake Johnson, editor of *The Possibility Machine: Music and Myth in Las Vegas* (University of Illinois Press, 2023), for their comments on those essays, which helped sharpen my analysis of Branson entertainment and its cultural meanings.

During the course of researching and writing about Branson, I joined the Musical Theatre Forum. This group has become my foundational intellectual community; I write this book, in many ways, for them. Thank you to Ryan Donovan, Liza Gennaro, Ray Knapp, Jeff Magee, Doug Reside, David Savran, Jessica Sternfeld, Dominic Symonds, Stacy Wolf, Tamsin Wolff, and Liz Wollman for reading my work and encouraging me to have the courage of my convictions. Finally, at the last stage, Brooks Blevins corrected crucial errors. I'm grateful for his expertise and scholarship.

Last but not least, I would like to thank my family. My parents, Jeff and Susan Dee, have always been my biggest cheerleaders and my role models. My spouse, Koushik Das, has been my rock. When I needed to calm down, he was a voice of moderation; when I felt lost or uncertain, he was a devil's advocate who sharpened my thinking. He also cooked, took care of the kids, and provided support in countless other ways. Finally, I would like to dedicate this book to my children, Keerthan and Jaya, both of whom were born during the years I spent researching and writing about Branson. Through this book, I hope to model for you how to engage in the world with both compassion and integrity.

APPENDIX

Branson Shows, 1959 to 2024

No comprehensive database exists for Branson shows. This appendix is a start, culled from multiple sources: Branson/ Tri-Lakes Convention and Visitors Bureau publications, ticketing websites, tourism websites, a 1996 dissertation by Jessica Howard, the *Springfield News-Leader*, and the *Branson Tri-Lakes News*. When possible, I cross-referenced listings from at least two sources and from two different times of the tourist season (which generally runs March to December). This table only includes shows that were in residence in Branson for at least a few weeks of the tourist season, not one-weekend-only performances. Therefore, it does not list the Oak Ridge Boys' onetime performance at Ozark Mountain Amphitheater on May 25, 1991, but does list their show at the Grand Palace in 1993, which they performed several times over the course of six months. Opening acts are not included, nor are performances at Silver Dollar City, Mutton Hollow, or Kimberling City. I list shows in chronological order of when they opened, and within each year, alphabetically. I try to account for name changes as well as venue changes. Sometimes a show did not change venue, but the name of the venue itself changed. When dates of those changes are known, they are indicated.

Spellings often varied. The Owen Theatre was also listed as Owen's Theater and Owens' Theatre, for example. Many venues were listed as both a *theater* and a *theatre*. I have gone with the spelling on the physical building or with what appeared the first time in print.

Show name	First year	Last year	Venue
Baldknobbers Hillbilly Jamboree (1959–1995) — Baldknobbers Jamboree (1996–2016) — Branson's Famous Baldknobbers (2017–2024)	1959	2024	Branson Municipal Building (1959–1961) Sammy Lane Pavilion (1962–1965) Branson Skating Rink (1966–1967) Hillbilly Jamboree Theatre (1968–1995) Baldknobbers Theatre (1996–2016) Branson Famous Theatre (2017–2023) Hughes Brothers Theatre (2024)
Shepherd of the Hills Pageant — Shepherd of the Hills Outdoor Drama	1960	2024	Old Mill Theatre
Mountain Music Jubilee (1967–1995) — Presleys' Country Jubilee (1996–2024)	1967	2024	Mountain Music Theatre (1967–1995) Presleys' Country Jubilee Theatre (1996–2024)
Hills-a-Poppin' (A Toby Show) — Toby Show	1969	1986	Corn Crib Theatre
Jim Nash	1972	1972	Country-Style Opry Theater
Plummer Family — Plummer Family Country Music Show	1973	1990	Plummer Family Theater
Foggy River Boys Music Show — New Foggy River Boys	1974	1993	Foggy River Boys Theater
Bob-O-Link's Country Hoe-Down	1977	1986	Bob-O-Link's Country Hoedown
Ozarks Mountain Hayride Show	1977	1979	Ozarks Mountain Hayride Theater
Stan Hitchcock Show — Old Sawmill Opry	1979	1980	Old Sawmill Theatre
Ozark Mountain Country Music Show (1980–1981) — Lowe's Country Music Show — Lowe Sisters — The Lowes	1980	1990	Lowe's Theater at Indian Point (1980–1982) Lowe's Country Music Theatre/Lowes Theatre (1982–1990)
The Terrys/Great American Musical Review	1980	1980	Owen Theatre
Guinn Brothers, Nashville Extension, and We Three	1981	1981	Starlite Theatre
Hee Haw Show (1981–1983) — Ozark Hee Haw Show (1984) — Roy Clark's Ozark Hee Haw Show (1984)	1981	1984	Hee Haw Theatre
Opryland USA on the Road	1981	1984	Kirkwood Center
Ozarks Country Jubilee — Campbell's Ozark Country Jubilee — Ozark Jubilee Show	1981	1995	Ozarks Country Jubilee Theatre (1981–1985) Campbell's Ozark Country Jubilee Theater/Ozark Jubilee Theater (1985–1995)
Wilkinson Brothers Country Music Show — The Wilkinsons	1981	1989	Wilkinson Brothers Theatre (1981–1986) Starlite Theatre (1986) Jerry Foster's Show Palace (1989)
Banjo's Dinner Music Show (1982–1983) — Banjo's Country Music Show (1984)	1982	1984	Banjo's Music Theater
Collins Family Gospel Music Show	1982	1985	Red Barn Theater (1982–1983) Branson Inn (1984) 76 Center (1985)

Show name	First year	Last year	Venue
Grapevine Opry (1982–1985) — Starlite Grand Opry (1986) — Opry Show (1987)	1982	1987	Starlite Theatre
Roy Clark Show	1983	1999	Roy Clark Celebrity Theatre (1983–1998) BransonTown U.S.A. Theatre (1999)
The Texans (1983–1990) — The Texans/"Stars on Revue" (1991–1993)	1983	1993	Plummer Family Theater (1983–1986) The Texans Bob-O-Link Theater (1987–1991) Kirkwood Inn (1992) Memory Lane Theatre (1993)
The Braschlers Quartet Country Music Show — The Braschler Music Show — The Braschlers	1984	2006	Lowe's Theater at Indian Point (1984) Musicland, USA Theater (1985–1990) Braschler Theater (1990–2001) Sons of the Pioneers Theater (2002–2004) Victorian Theater (2004) Hamner Barber Theater (2005–2006)
The Buddy Green Show	1984	1987	Branson Opry House/Kirkwood Center
Lester Family	1984	1984	Musicland, USA Theater
Love's Greatest Story: A Passion Play	1984	1986	Love's Greatest Story Arena
Ozark Mountain Gospel Opry	1984	1984	Owen Theatre
Puppet Palace Show	1984	1985	Puppet Palace Theater
Sons of the Pioneers — Sons of the Pioneers Chuckwagon Dinner Show (2007–2011)	1984	2018	Lowe's Country Music Theatre (1984–1985) Foggy River Boys' Theatre (1986–1992) Braschler Theater (1993–1998, 2001) Moe Bandy Americana Theatre (1999–2001) Sons of the Pioneers Theater (2003) Pavilion Theatre at Shepherd of the Hills (2004, 2007–2011) Baldknobbers Jamboree/Branson Famous Theatre (2014–2016, 2018)
All American Music Revue featuring the Noblemen	1985	1985	Old Sawmill Opry Theatre
Blake Family	1985	1987	Branson City Limits
Country Music World Show	1985	1988	Country Music World
Top O' the Strip Show	1985	1985	Top O' the Strip Dinner Theater
A Tribute to Elvis	1985	1985	The King's Mansion
76 Music Hall Show	1987	1989	76 Music Hall
Boxcar Willie — Boxcar Willie Country Music Show	1987	1998	Boxcar Willie Theatre
Buck Trent (1987) — Buck Trent Morning Show (1991–2018)	1987	2018	Starlite Theatre (1987) Buck Trent Theatre (1991–1993) Pump Boys and Dinettes Theatre (1994) Jim Stafford Theatre (1996) Anita Bryant Theatre (1997) Dinner Bell Restaurant (1998–2004) Grand Country Music Hall (2005–2009) Clay Cooper Theatre (2010–2011) RFD-TV Theatre (2012–2013) Baldknobbers Theatre (2014–2018)

Show name	First year	Last year	Venue
Country Castle Music Show	1987	1987	Country Castle Theater
Jumping Jacks Show	1987	1988	Jumping Jacks Variety Theater
Tennessee Country Show	1987	1987	Branson City Limits Theater
Texas Gold Miners —Texas Goldminors —Texas Goldminers	1987	1997	Ozarks Country Jubilee Theater (1987–1989) 76 Music Hall (1991–1997)
Barbara Fairchild Show	1988	2016	Lowe's Country Music Theatre (1988–1991) Mel Tillis Theater (1992) Jim Stafford Theatre (1993) Charley Pride Theatre (1994) Barbara Fairchild Theatre (1996–1998) Braschler Theater (1999–2001) Majestic Theatre (2002) Baldknobbers Theatre (2007) Barbara Fairchild Diner (2011, 2015–2016)
Branson Brothers —Jim Ed Brown and the Branson Brothers —Sunday Morning Gospel Show with the Branson Brothers	1988	2009	Jerry Foster's Show Palace (1988) Echo Hollow Amphitheater (1990) Ozark Theater (1994) Bart Rockett Theatre (2006–2007) God and Country Theatre (2009)
Cody Brothers —John and Paul Cody —The Codys	1988	1993	Cody Country Theater (1988–1989) Stars of the Ozarks Theater (1990) Waltzing Waters (1991–1993)
Jerry Foster	1988	1988	Jerry Foster's Show Palace
Ray Price	1988	1995	Starlite Theatre (1988) Roy Clark Celebrity Theatre (1990) Cristy Lane Theatre (1991–1992) Gettysburg Theatre (1993–1995)
Al Brumley Show —Brumley Music Show —The Brumley Family Show	1989	2004	Cody Country Theater (1989) Ozark Country Jubilee Theater (1990–1991) 76 Music Hall (1991–2003) Branson Mall Music Theatre (2004)
Cristy Lane Show	1989	1996	Starlite Theatre (1989) Cristy Lane Theatre (1990–1996)
Danny Davis and the Nashville Brass	1989	1999	Country Music World (1989) Danny Davis Theater (1990–1991) Cristy Lane Theatre (1992) Branson Variety Theater (1992) New Foggy River Boys Theater (1993) Dockers Restaurant (1998–1999)
Freddy Fender Tex-Mex Show	1989	1989	Kirkwood Motor Inn
The Memory Makers	1989	1996	76 Music Hall
Ozark Comedy Show	1989	1989	76 Music Hall
Ozark Mountain Boys	1989	1989	Lowe's Country Music Theatre
Ozark Mountain Daredevils	1989	1989	Cadillac Theatre
Ozark Mountain Opry Show	1989	1991	Plummer Family Theater (1989–1990) Stars of the Ozarks Theater (1991)

Show name	First year	Last year	Venue
Shoji Tabuchi Show (1989–2019) — An Evening with Shoji (2022)	1989	2022	Shoji Tabuchi Theatre at the Auto Show (1989) Shoji Tabuchi Theatre (1990–2017) Clay Cooper Theatre (2019) IMAX Little Opry Theatre (2022)
Aaron Patrick (as Elvis Presley)	1990	1990	Legends Theater
The Blackwood Singers — The Blackwood Quartet — The Blackwood Family — The Blackwoods — Blackwood Morning Show — Blackwood Singers Gospel Show	1990	2022	Legends Theater (1990) Ozark Country Jubilee Theater (1991–1992) Memory Lane Theatre (1992) Ozark Theater (1993) Thunderbird Theatre (1994–1997) Starlite Theatre (2016) Dutton Family Theater (2017–2018) Branson Famous Theatre (2019) Americana Theatre (2021–2022)
Jim Stafford Show	1990	2019	Wildwood Flower Lounge (1990) Stars of the Ozarks Theater (1990–1991) Jim Stafford Theatre (1992–2013, 2016–2019)
Mel Tillis Show — Mel Tillis and the Statesiders — Mel Tillis and Family — Mel and Pam Tillis — Mel Tillis and "How the West Was Sung" (1995) — Mel Tillis and Brenda Lee (1997) — Mel Tillis and Connie Smith (2007)	1990	2016	Mel Tillis Ozark Theater (1990–1991) Mel Tillis Theater (1992–2002) Tri-Lakes Center (2004–2006) Welk Resort Theatre (2007) Clay Cooper Theatre (2012–2016)
Mickey Gilley Show	1990	2015	Mickey Gilley's Family Theatre/Mickey Gilley Theatre
Steve Hall and Shotgun Red	1990	1990	Stars of the Ozarks Theater
Sunday Gospel Jubilee with the Bacon Family	1990	2016	Plummer Family Theater (1990) 76 Music Hall (1992–2002) Grand Country Music Hall (2003–2016)
Bob Nichols Ozark Morning Show — Bob Nichols Show	1991	1997	Ozark Country Jubilee Theater (1991–1994) Branson Mall Music Theatre (1995–1997) Wild West Theatre (1997)
Dino Kartsonakis — Dino's Piano Extravaganza — Dino's Christmas Pinorama — Dino's Christmas Show — Dino Kartsonakis Somewhere in Christmastime — Dino Morning Show — Christmas with Dino and Cheryl Kartsonakis	1991	2019	Mel Tillis Ozark Theater (1991) Dino's Theatre (1992) Loretta Lynn Ozark Theater (1993) Will Rogers Theater (1994–1995) Glen Campbell Goodtime Theatre (1996) Grand Palace (1997–1998) Grand Mansion (1999–2000, 2002) Remington Theatre (2001) Tri-Lakes Center (2003–2008) Shepherd of the Hills Playhouse (2019)
Down Home Country Music Show — Down Home Country Show	1991	2024	76 Music Hall (1991–2003) Grand Country Music Hall (2010–2024)
Jeanne Pruett	1991	1991	Buck Trent Theatre

Show name	First year	Last year	Venue
Moe Bandy Show	1991	2011	Moe Bandy Americana Theatre (1991–1995, 1998–2002, 2004–2006) Mickey Gilley Theatre (1996–1997) Majestic Theatre (2003) Starlite Theatre (2007–2008) Jim Stafford Theatre (2009–2011)
Ozark Country Opry	1991	1991	Kirkwood Inn
Ray Stevens	1991	2004	Ray Stevens Theatre (1991–1993, 2004) Wayne Newton Theatre (1996)
Andy Williams — Andy Williams Christmas Show — Andy Williams with Glen Campbell (2000) — Andy Williams and Ann-Margret (2004) — Andy Williams and Petula Clark (2005)	1992	2012	Moon River Theatre
Barbara Mandrell	1992	1997	Grand Palace (1992–1995, 1997) Glen Campbell Goodtime Theatre (1996)
Branson's Second Generation	1992	1992	Branson Variety Theater
Celebration Singers	1992	1992	Celebration Theater
Charley Pride	1992	1997	Mel Tillis Theater (1992) Loretta Lynn Ozark Theater (1993) Charley Pride Theatre (1994–1997)
Eddie Cash	1992	1995	Memory Lane Theatre (1992) Owen Theatre (1993, 1995) Thunderbird Theatre (1994)
Elvis-a-Rama	1992	1992	Memory Lane Theatre
Ferlin Husky — Ferlin Husky Breakfast Show	1992	1998	Cristy Lane Theatre (1992–1994) Funny Bone Theatre (1993) Boxcar Willie Theatre (1996–1998)
Glen Campbell	1992	1995	Grand Palace (1992–1993) Glen Campbell Goodtime Theatre (1994–1995)
Jennifer Wilson — Jennifer in the Morning — Jennifer's Americana	1992	2002	Roy Clark Celebrity Theatre (1992–1994) U.S.O. Americana Theatre (1995) Americana Theatre (1996) Jennifer's Americana Theatre (1997–2002)
Jim Owen Show — Jim Owen Morning Show	1992	2014	Memory Lane Theatre (1992) Pump Boys and Dinettes Theatre (1993) Mickey Gilley Theatre (1994–2001) Dutton Family Theater (2002, 2007) Starlite Theatre (2003–2004) Country Tonite Theatre (2005) Clay Cooper Theatre (2008–2009) Branson Mall Music Theatre (2011) Doug Gabriel Theater (2014)
Jimmie Rodgers	1992	1992	Jimmie Rodgers Honeycomb Theatre
John Davidson	1992	2002	Jim Stafford Theatre (1992) John Davidson Theatre (1993–1994) Will Rogers Theater (1995, 2002)

Show name	First year	Last year	Venue
Loretta Lynn	1992	1993	Lowe's Country Music Theatre (1992) Loretta Lynn Ozark Theater (1993)
Louise Mandrell	1992	1994	Grand Palace
Merle Haggard	1992	1992	Willie Nelson Ozark Theater
The Osmonds — The Osmond Brothers — Osmonds Celebrating 40 Years of Entertainment (1998) — The Osmonds' An American Dream (2004) — Osmonds Family Jukebox	1992	2014	Osmond Family Theater (1992–2009) Country Tonite Theatre (2002) Branson Music Mall Theatre (2004) Music City Centre (2010) Caravelle Theatre (2011) Moon River Theatre (2014)
Sounds of Time	1992	1992	76 Music Hall
Willie Nelson	1992	1993	Willie Nelson Ozark Theater
All American Music Show	1993	1993	All American Music Show Theater
Anita Bryant	1993	1997	Ozark Theater (1993) Shenandoah South Theatre (1994) Anita Bryant Theatre (1994–1997)
Arizona	1993	1993	Rex Allen Jr. Theater
Blondes, Blondes, Blondes	1993	1994	Cristy Lane Theatre (1993) Ozark Jubilee Theater (1994)
Bobby Berosini and Kirby Van Burch	1993	1994	Five Star Theatre
Bobby Vinton and the Glenn Miller Orchestra — Bobby Vinton Show	1993	2008	Bobby Vinton's Blue Velvet Theatre (1993–2002) Branson Variety Theater (2005) The Mansion (2008)
Branson Gospel Hour	1993	1993	Ozark Country Jubilee Theater
Conway Twitty	1993	1993	Gilley's Family Theatre/Jim Stafford Theatre
David Frizzell	1993	1993	Loretta Lynn Ozark Theater
Dondino	1993	1994	Dondino Theatre
Forget Me Not Tribute Show	1993	1993	Owen Theatre
Frontier Show	1993	1995	76 Music Hall
Gospel Hour	1993	1993	Cristy Lane Theatre
Gospel Music Showcase	1993	1993	Thunderbird Theatre
Johnny Cash	1993	1994	Wayne Newton Theatre (1993) Shenandoah South Theatre (1994)
Memories of Elvis	1993	1993	Memory Lane Theatre
Norris Twins	1993	1993	All American Music Show Theater
Oak Ridge Boys	1993	2023	Grand Palace (1993, 1998–2007) Glen Campbell Goodtime Theatre (1994) Charley Pride Theatre (1995–1997) The Mansion (2008) Oak Ridge Boys Theatre (2008–2015) The Mansion Theatre for the Performing Arts (2016–2019)

Show name	First year	Last year	Venue
Oklahoma!	1993	1993	Thunderbird Theatre
Pump Boys and Dinettes	1993	1998	Pump Boys and Dinettes Theatre
Rudy Gatlin and "A Broadway Branson Christmas"	1993	1993	Loretta Lynn Ozark Theater
That's Showbiz	1993	1993	Memory Lane Theatre
Tony Orlando — Tony Orlando and the Lennon Sisters (2008, 2010) — Tony Orlando's Great American Christmas (2011–2013)	1993	2013	Tony Orlando Yellow Ribbon Music Theater (1993–1997) Talk of the Town Theatre (1998) Osmond Family Theater (2000) Mansion America Theatre (2004) Welk Resort Theatre (2008, 2010–2013)
Wayne Newton	1993	1999	Wayne Newton Theatre (1993–1996, 1999) Tony Orlando Yellow Ribbon Music Theater (1997) Talk of the Town Theatre (1998)
Yakov Smirnoff Show — Yakov Smirnoff Morning Show (1995) — Yakov's Moscow Circus (2009–2010) — Yakov Smirnoff Dinner Show (2015) — Yakov Smirnoff: Make America Laugh Again (2021)	1993	2024	Cristy Lane Theatre (1993) Osmond Family Theater (1994) Grand Palace (1995–1996) Yakov's American Pavilion (1997–1998) Yakov's What a Country Theater (1999–2000) Yakov Smirnoff Theater (2001–2015, 2019, 2021–2024) Caravelle Theatre (2020)
The $25,000 Game Show	1994	1996	Moe Bandy Americana Theatre (1994) Branson Magical Mansion (1995–1996)
Boots Randolph	1994	1994	Roy Clark Celebrity Theatre
Country Tonite — New Country Tonite Show (2004)	1994	2010	Country Tonite Theatre (1994–2004) Americana Theatre (2005–2006) Oak Ridge Boys Theatre (2008–2010)
David Brenner Super Summer Spectacular	1994	1994	Ozark Theater
Don Williams	1994	1995	Charley Pride Theatre
Doug Gabriel Morning Show — Doug Gabriel's Branson Spotlight (2005) — Doug Gabriel's #1 Hits Tribute Show — Doug Gabriel Show	1994	2024	Jim Stafford Theatre (1994–1995, 2005–2010) Roy Clark Celebrity Theatre (1996–1998) Starlite Theatre (1999–2000) Osmond Family Theater (2001) Legends Family Theater (2002–2004) Music City Centre (2011) Doug Gabriel Theater (2013–2017) Pierce Arrow Theatre (2018–2019) Branson Famous Theatre (2020–2023) Reza Live Theatre (2024)
Early Bird Morning Show	1994	1995	76 Music Hall
Eddie Rabbitt	1994	1994	Roy Clark Celebrity Theatre
Frederick's Variety Show — Pianist Fredrick — Frederick in Concert — The Amazing Frederick — Frederick and His Twin Pianos	1994	2006	Ozark Theater (1994) Waltzing Waters (1997–2006)
Hot Lava (Polynesian Revue)	1994	1994	Owen Theatre

Show name	First year	Last year	Venue
Jimmy Travis Morning Mania (1994) — Jimmy Travis Morning Show (1995) — Janie Fricke and Jimmy Travis Show (1996) — Jerry Reed with Jimmy Travis (1997)	1994	1997	Mel Tillis Theater (1994) Charley Pride Theatre (1995–1997)
The Kendalls	1994	1994	Owen Theatre
Kirby Van Burch and Phillip Wellford Show	1994	1997	Five Star Theatre (1994) Shenandoah South Theatre (1995) Magical Mansion (1995–1997)
Lennon Brothers Breakfast Show — Lennon Brothers Swing Music Show (2001) — Lennon Brothers Show	1994	2003	Welk's Champagne Theatre and Stage Door Canteen (1994–2002) Jim Stafford Theatre (2003)
Lennon Sisters — Tony Orlando and the Lennon Sisters — Christmas with the Lennon Sisters — Andy Williams Christmas Variety Show Starring the Osmonds and the Lennon Sisters	1994	2019	Welk Champagne Theatre Moon River Theatre/Andy Williams Performing Arts Center
Mr. Banjo	1994	1994	Buck Trent Theatre
Opry Show	1994	1994	Owen Theatre
Ozark Mountain Jubilee	1994	2016	76 Music Hall (1994–2002) Grand Country Music Hall (2003–2016)
Radio City Christmas Spectacular with the Rockettes	1994	2003	Grand Palace
Ragtime Lil and Banjo-Banjo	1994	1997	Thunderbird Theatre (1994–1996) Branson on Stage Theater (1997)
Showboat Branson Belle Revues	1994	2024	Showboat Branson Belle
The Thunderbird Band: 50s Rock and Roll	1994	1997	Thunderbird Theatre
Welk Show — Lawrence Welk Show	1994	2004	Welk Resort Champagne Theatre and Stage Door Canteen
Will Rogers Follies — with Pat Boone	1994	1994	Will Rogers Theater
1940s Radio Show Musical	1995	1995	Branson Mall Music Theatre
At the Hop Show — '50s at the Hop	1995	2010	50s Variety Theater (1995–1997) Branson Mall Music Theatre (1997–2003) Jim Stafford Theatre (2004–2006) 50s at the Hop Theatre (2007–2009) Legacy Theater (2010)
Branson Solid Gold Morning Show starring Kenton Wayne	1995	1995	Owen Theatre Ozark Jubilee Theater
Cannon and Ball	1995	1995	Will Rogers Theater
Chisai Childs and the Starliters	1995	1995	Ozark Jubilee Theater
Dolly Parton's Dixie Stampede (1995–2017) — Dolly Parton's Stampede (2018–2024) — Dolly Parton's Christmas Show	1995	2024	Dolly Parton's Dixie Stampede (1995–2017) Dolly Parton's Stampede (2018–2024)

Show name	First year	Last year	Venue
Elvis and the Superstars	1995	2011	Owen Theatre (1995–2008) Hot Hits Theatre (2010–2011)
Gettysburg	1995	1995	Gettysburg Theatre
Gospel Jubilee	1995	1995	50s Variety Theater
Hangzou Acrobatic Troupe	1995	1995	Will Rogers Theater
Hot Winter Fun Big Show	1995	2024	Jim Stafford Theatre (1995–2009) Dick Clark's American Bandstand Theater (2010–2023) Pepsi Legends Theater (2024)
Incredible Acrobats of China — Acrobats of China — Acrobats of China featuring the New Shanghai Circus	1995	2018	White River Theatre (1995) Wayne Newton Theatre (1999–2000) MGH Performing Arts Center (2000–2004) New Shanghai Theatre (2005–2013) RFD-TV Theatre (2014) Yakov Smirnoff Theater (2015–2017) Acrobats Theatre (2018)
Legends in Concert	1995	2024	Legends Family Theater (1998–2008) Dick Clark's American Bandstand Theater (2009–2023) Pepsi Legends Theater (2024)
Masci Family	1995	1995	Ozark Jubilee Theater
Mirror Images	1995	1995	Cristy Lane Theatre
Patsy!	1995	1995	Grand Palace
Peter Lemongello	1995	1998	Cristy Lane Theatre (1995) 50s Variety Theater (1996–1997) Branson Mall Music Theatre (1997–1998)
Peter Maxwell	1995	1995	Cristy Lane Theatre
Rick West Show	1995	1995	White River Theater
76 Country USA	1996	2000	76 Music Hall
Allen Edwards Show	1996	2001	Branson Mall Music Theatre (1996) Golden Corral (2000–2001)
Always . . . Patsy Cline	1996	1996	Tony Orlando Yellow Ribbon Music Theater
Doug Kershaw	1996	1997	Branson Mall Music Theatre
Hot Country Revue on Ice	1996	1997	Osmond Family Theater
The Hughes Brothers — Hughes Brothers Morning Show — Hughes Brothers Christmas Show — Hughes Brothers Family Show — Hughes Brothers Music Show	1996	2024	Wild West Theatre (1996) Branson on Stage Theater (1997) Legends Family Theater (1998–1999) Hughes Brothers Celebrity Theatre/ Hughes Brothers Theatre (2000–2024)
Johnny Lee — Johnny Lee and the Urban Cowboy Band (2008)	1996	2023	Barbara Fairchild Theater (1996) Branson Mall Music Theatre (1997) Gene Williams Theatre (2008) Mickey Gilley Grand Shanghai Theatre (2023)
Larry Musgrave — "The Great Pretender"/Larry Musgrave	1996	1997	Club Celebrity Dinner Mutton Hollow Revue

Show name	First year	Last year	Venue
Pat Paulsen	1996	1996	Funny Bone Theatre
The Promise	1996	2008	Will Rogers Theater (1996–1998) Promise Theatre (1999–2002) Mansion America Theatre (2006–2008)
Red, Hot and Blue — Red Hot and Blue! — Red, Hot . . . and Blue!	1996	2016	Engler Block Shopping Mall (1996–1997) Scherling's Cowboy Café (1997) Planet Branson (1998) Ain't Misbehavin' Theatre (1999–2001) Branson Mall Music Theatre (2002) Grand Country Music Hall (2003–2006) Music City Centre (2007–2008) Americana Theatre (2009–2011) Clay Cooper Theatre (2012–2016)
Remember When Show (1996–1997) — Mike Radford's Remember When Show (1998–2003)	1996	2003	Aunt Mollie's Parlor at Shepherd of the Hills (1996–1997) IMAX Remember When Theatre (1998–2002) Music City Centre (2003)
Shari Lewis and Lamb Chop	1996	1996	Moon River Theatre
Wild Wild West Show (1996–1998) — Great American Wild West Show (1999)	1996	1999	Wild West Theatre
World Famous Platters — Platters — Golden Sounds of the Platters	1996	2024	Roy Clark Celebrity Theatre (1998–1999) Hughes Brothers Celebrity Theatre (2000–2001) ShowTown Theatre (2002–2003) Americana Theatre (2004–2005) Starlite Theatre (2006, 2008–2010) Icon Theatre (2013) Branson Tribute Theatre (2014–2015, 2017–2019) Crystal Theatre (2016) Hot Hits Theatre (2020–2024)
Branson City Lights — Branson City All Star Revue	1997	1999	Remington Theatre
Golden Girls	1997	1998	Country Tonite Theatre
Masters of Illusion	1997	1997	Yakov's American Pavilion
Positive Country Express — Positive Country Show	1997	1999	Positive Country Theater
Positive Country Gospel Hour	1997	1999	Positive Country Theater
Positive Country Variety Show	1997	1997	Positive Country Theater
Ronnie Prophet Show — Ronnie Prophet's Grand Ole Country (2002)	1997	2004	Boxcar Willie Theatre (1997) Pickin' Parlor Theatre (at Shepherd of the Hills) (1998–2001) Moe Bandy Americana Theatre (2002) Branson Music Mall Theatre (2004)
Sagebrush	1997	1997	Branson On Stage Theater
What a World Show Club	1997	1997	Yakov's American Pavilion
All-Gospel Show	1998	1998	Braschler Theater
Ava Barber Country Music Show	1998	1999	Welk Champagne Theatre

Show name	First year	Last year	Venue
Breakfast with the Classics	1998	2002	Branson Mall Music Theatre
Broadway for Breakfast Show	1998	1999	Osmond Family Theater
The Duttons	1998	2024	Barbara Fairchild Theater (1998) Boxcar Willie Theatre (1999) Dutton Family Theater (2000–2022, 2023–2024) Yakov Smirnoff Theater (2022)
Grand Old Gospel Hour	1998	2007	Braschler Theater (1998–2001) Grand Palace (2002, 2004–2006) Remington Theatre (2003) New Shanghai Theatre (2007)
Kirby Van Burch Prince of Magic Show — Kirby Van Burch Show — Kirby Van Burch — Kirby and Bambi Van Burch Magic Show	1998	2014	Kirby Van Burch's Palace of Mystery (1998–2000) Remington Theatre (2002–2003) Kirby Van Burch Theater (2004–2014)
Kitty Kelley Show	1998	1998	Thunderbird Theatre
Melinda's Magical Mansion Show	1998	1998	Melinda's Magical Mansion
The Mystery Comedy Dinner	1998	1998	Settle Inn
Phillip Wellford — Phillip Wellford Comedy Show	1998	2000	Melinda's Magical Mansion (1998) Celebrity Theater (1999) Osmond Family Theater (2000)
Top Dog Show	1998	1998	Thunderbird Theatre
American Kids	1999	1999	Starlite Theatre
Bill Brooks Family and Friends	1999	1999	IMAX Entertainment Complex
The Delene Show	1999	2005	Engler Block (1999) Planet Branson (2000–2002) Hughes Brothers Celebrity Theatre (2003–2005)
Dinner with Di	1999	1999	Planet Branson
Jimmie Rodgers Remembers	1999	2001	IMAX Remember When Theater
Late Night Show with the McFadden Brothers	1999	1999	Branson Mall Music Theatre
Lost in the 50s — Lost in the Fifties — Lost in the 50s with the Platters	1999	2007	Starlite Theatre
Tony Melendez Morning Show (1999–2000) — Tony Melendez Show: A Gift of Hope (2001–2002)	1999	2002	Remington Theatre (1999) Braschler Theater (2000) IMAX Remember When Theatre (2001–2002)
Two from Galilee	1999	2001	Promise Theatre
Bart Rockett Show — Bart Rockett and Taylor Reed (2009)	2000	2009	Magical Palace (2000–2001) Bart Rockett Theater (2005–2008) 50s at the Hop Theatre (2009)

Show name	First year	Last year	Venue
Brett Family Singers (2000–2017) — Bob Nichols and Brett Family Morning Show (2000) — A Brett Family Christmas (2017–2022)	2000	2022	Legends Family Theater (2000–2001, 2005–2008) Jimmy Osmond's American Jukebox Theater (2002–2003) Country Tonite Theatre (2004) Dick Clark's American Bandstand Theater (2009–2022)
Broadway on Ice	2000	2000	Moon River Theatre
Changin' Up	2000	2000	Wild West Theatre
Cowboy Ain't Dead Yet	2000	2002	Moe Bandy Americana Theatre
Daniel O'Donnell	2000	2001	Jennifer's Americana Theatre
Flashback	2000	2000	Osmond Family Theater
Grand Ladies of Country Music (2000–2002) — Us Girls! (2003) — The Grand Ladies (2007–2008)	2000	2008	76 Music Hall (2000–2002) Jim Stafford Theatre (2003) God and Country Theatre (2007–2008)
The Hortons	2000	2000	Dutton Family Theater
Lowe Family of Utah — Lowe Family	2000	2006	Wayne Newton Theatre (2000) MGH Performing Arts Center (2001–2002) Welk Resort Theatre (2003–2006)
Magic of the Night	2000	2000	Remington Theatre
Pierce Arrow Show — Pierce Arrow and Paul Harris Show (2001) — Pierce Arrow Comedy Show and Jarrett Dougherty (2011)	2000	2017	Pierce Arrow Theater
Rodney and Beverly Dillard and the Boys from Mayberry	2000	2000	76 Music Hall
Smoke on the Mountain	2000	2024	Dogwood Theatre (2000) Mel Tillis Theater (2001–2002) God and Country Theatre (2007) IMAX Little Opry Theatre (2003, 2006, 2009–2011, 2015–2024)
Spirit of the Dance	2000	2015	Bobby Vinton's Blue Velvet Theatre (2000–2002) Branson Variety Theater (2003–2012) King's Castle Theatre (2013–2015)
Starlite Kids Revue	2000	2000	Starlite Theatre
Wild West Musical Trails	2000	2000	Wild West Theatre
Breakfast with Norman Rockwell — A Visit with Norman Rockwell	2001	2003	Owen Theatre
A Closer Walk with Patsy Cline	2001	2001	ShowTown Theatre
Cracklin' Rose	2001	2003	Grand Palace Remington Theatre (2001)
Gregory Popovich's Comedy Pet Theatre	2001	2006	Majestic Theatre (2001) Magical Palace (2002) Grand Country Music Hall (2003–2006)

Show name	First year	Last year	Venue
John Tweed Show — The Tweed Show — Reelin' in the Years Starring John Tweed	2001	2013	Planet Branson (2001–2002) Caravelle Theatre (2003) Moe Bandy Americana Theatre (2005–2006) Clay Cooper Theatre (2007–2008) God and Country Theatre (2011–2012) Americana Theatre (2013)
Mississippi Love	2001	2002	Mark Twain Playhouse
Nunsense	2001	2001	Ain't Misbehavin' Theatre
Sue Ann O'Neal — Celebrate Sunday with Sue Ann O'Neal	2001	2003	IMAX Little Opry Theatre
Tall Timber Lumberjack Show	2001	2008	Long Lonesome Trail (2001) Tall Timber Lumberjack Theatre (2004–2008)
Zhivago Show	2001	2001	Jennifer's Americana Theatre
Country Tradition with Tim Hadler	2002	2002	IMAX Remember When Theatre
The Dalena Show (2002) — The Dalena Show with Johnny Lee (2003) — Dalena Ditto (2004–2011) — Dalena Ditto Country Variety Show (2013) — Dalena Ditto's "Come Sail Away" (2014) — Dalena Ditto's Country Evolution (2021–2024)	2002	2024	Starlite Theatre (2002) Americana Theatre (2003) Mickey Gilley Theatre (2004–2006) Clay Cooper Theatre (2007) Oak Ridge Boys Theatre (2008–2009) Tri Lakes Center (2010) Hamner Barber Theater (2011) God and Country Theatre (2013–2014) IMAX Little Opry Theatre (2021–2022) Hughes Brothers Theatre (2023–2024)
The Haygoods	2002	2024	Music City Centre (2002–2008) Americana Theatre (2009–2013) Clay Cooper Theatre (2014–2024)
Jimmy Osmond's American Jukebox Show	2002	2018	Osmond Family Theater (2002) Jimmy Osmond's American Jukebox Theater (2003) Andy Williams Performing Arts Center (2018)
The John Wayne Story	2002	2005	Owen Theatre (2002–2003) IMAX Little Opry Theatre (2004) Wildwood Flower Theater (2005)
Larry Gatlin and the Gatlin Brothers — Larry Gatlin and the Gatlin Brothers costarring Pam Tillis — Larry Gatlin and the Gatlin Brothers and the Lennon Sisters — The Gatlin Brothers — The Gatlin Brothers and Debby Boone Christmas Show	2002	2016	Will Rogers Theater (2002–2003) Welk Resort Theatre (2004–2007) The Mansion (2009, 2011–2012) Oak Ridge Boys Theatre (2013) Starlite Theatre (2014–2016)
The Magnificent 7 — The Magnificent 7 Variety Show — Magnificent Variety Show — Magnificent Seven Decades of Music Variety Show	2002	2021	White House Theatre (2002–2008) Osmond Family Theater (2009) Branson Star Theatre /Superstars Live (2010) God and Country Theatre (2011–2013) Hamners' Variety Theater (2014–2021)

Show name	First year	Last year	Venue
Magnificent Country	2002	2003	White House Theatre
Magnificent Morning	2002	2002	White House Theatre
Raising America	2002	2003	Majestic Theatre
Saturday Night Jubilee	2002	2003	White House Theatre
World of Magic	2002	2002	Magical Palace
Broadway! The Star-Spangled Celebration	2003	2010	Branson Variety Theater
Fred Travalena	2003	2003	Ain't Misbehavin' Theatre
From Patsy to Present	2003	2008	Owen Theatre (2003) Music City Centre (2004) Branson Mall Music Theatre (2005) Nova Theatre (2006) IMAX Little Opry Theatre (2008)
Goldwing Express — Goldwing Express Bluegrass and BBQ — Goldwing Express Morning Show	2003	2024	IMAX Little Opry Theatre (2003–2004) Hughes Brothers Celebrity Theatre (2006) God and Country Theatre (2009) Shepherd of the Hills Playhouse (2024)
Grand Country Saturday Night	2003	2003	Grand Country Music Hall
Grand Jubilee	2003	2024	Grand Country Music Hall
Jim Bakker Live TV Show	2003	2003	Studio City Cafe
Joseph and the Amazing Technicolor Dreamcoat	2003	2005	Mansion America Theatre
Keepin' It Country — Rick Langston's Keepin' It Country	2003	2006	IMAX Little Opry Theatre
Magnificent America	2003	2003	White House Theatre
Motown Downtown — Hot Hits of Motown — Motown Experience	2003	2024	Owen Theatre (2003–2004) Bart Rockett Theater (2006) Branson Showcase Theater (2007) Hot Hits Theatre (2009–2024)
New's Country starring Leroy New	2003	2006	IMAX Little Opry Theatre
Pam Tillis	2003	2006	Yakov Smirnoff Theater (2003) Welk Resort Theatre (2006)
Paul Harris Show — Paul Harris and the Cleverlys	2003	2016	Caravelle Theatre (2003–2005) Clay Cooper Theatre (2008–2009) Music City Centre (2010–2011) Oak Ridge Boys Theatre (2011, 2013) White House Theatre (2012) Starlite Theatre (2014–2016)
Remembering Hank Williams — Hank Williams Remembered	2003	2003	Owen Theatre
Roy "Dusty" Rogers Jr. and the Highriders — Roy Rogers Jr.	2003	2016	Happy Trails Theater in the Roy Rogers and Dale Evans Museum (2003–2009) Mickey Gilley Theatre (2010–2011) RFD-TV Theatre (2012–2016)
Stuck on the '70s	2003	2005	Americana Theatre (2003–2004) Starlite Theatre (2005)

Show name	First year	Last year	Venue
The Yearys with the Branson Valley Boys — The Yeary's Music Show	2003	2009	ShowTown Theatre (2003) Gaslighter Showtown Theatre (2004) Musical Palace (2005) Branson Mall Hall of Fame Theatre (2009)
#1 Hits of the 60's — No. 1 Hits of the 60's — Hits of the 60's and 50's Too!	2004	2024	Musical Palace (2004–2005) Branson Showcase Theater (2006) Jim Stafford Theatre (2007–2008) Caravelle Theatre (2009–2015) Americana Theatre (2016) Clay Cooper Theatre (2017–2024)
Adam and Eve Live Radio Show	2004	2004	Club Vegas at the Lodge of the Ozarks
Bob Anderson Dinner Show — Bob Anderson Show — Bob Anderson, a Musical Tribute to Sinatra and Friends	2004	2008	Club Vegas at the Lodge of the Ozarks (2004–2006) Club 57 at Dick Clark's American Bandstand Theater (2007–2008)
Branson Idol	2004	2004	Legends Family Theater
Breakfast with Mark Twain and Norman Rockwell	2004	2008	Owen Theatre
Brett Daniels — Magic and Beyond	2004	2005	Grand Palace
Celebrate! America — Celebrate America	2004	2009	Mansion America Theatre
Christmas Dreams	2004	2005	Grand Palace
Cirque	2004	2006	Remington Theatre
Comedy Jamboree	2004	2024	Grand Country Music Hall
Cowboy Church with Norma Jean — Norma Jean and the Cowboys — Cowboy Church with Norma Jean and the Warnocks (2010)	2004	2010	IMAX Little Opry Theatre (2004) Branson Mall Music Theatre (2005) Circle B Chuckwagon (2006) God and Country Theatre (2010)
Darren Romeo, the Voice of Magic — Siegfried and Roy Present . . . Darren Romeo	2004	2007	Welk Resort Theatre
Gary Gleason Magic	2004	2004	Branson Music Mall Theatre
Hamner Barber Variety Show	2004	2014	Victorian Theater (2004) Hamner Barber Theater (2005–2014)
Hank and My Honky Tonk Heroes	2004	2004	Moe Bandy Americana Theatre
Hank Williams Revisited	2004	2020	IMAX Little Opry Theatre (2004–2013, 2020) Music City Centre (2014–2016)
Hector Olivera	2004	2004	Hughes Brothers Celebrity Theatre
John Denver Lives	2004	2004	Engler Block Mall
Les Brown and the Band of Renown	2004	2007	Mickey Gilley Theatre
Lunch with Hank Williams	2004	2004	Owen Theatre
Patsy and Friends	2004	2004	Owen Theatre
Rat Pack	2004	2005	Branson Variety Theater (2004) Branson Mall Music Theatre (2005)

Show name	First year	Last year	Venue
Red Skelton, a Tribute by Tom Mullica — Red Skelton Tribute	2004	2014	Music City Centre (2004–2007) The Mansion (2008–2012) Hamner Barber Theater (2013) Hamners' Variety Theater (2014)
Swing Swing Swing	2004	2004	Gaslighter Showtown Theatre
Tony Roi's Elvis Experience — The Elvis Experience with Tony Roi — Tony Roi Elvis and More	2004	2015	Branson Music Mall Theatre (2004) Music City Centre (2005–2008) Americana Theatre (2009–2010, 2015) Moon River Theatre (2011) Jim Stafford Theatre (2013)
Travelin' Freedom's Road	2004	2004	Moe Bandy Americana Theatre
14 Karat Country Music Show —14 Karat Gold Country	2005	2008	Wildwood Flower Theater (2005) Clay Cooper Theatre (2007–2008)
Act of God	2005	2006	Musical Palace (2005) Circle B Chuckwagon (2006)
Bounce, the All-American Basketball Show	2005	2005	Legends Family Theater
Branson Follies	2005	2005	Follies Theatre
Branson Late Night Comedy Show	2005	2005	Branson Music Mall Theatre
Broadway! Spirit of Christmas	2005	2006	Branson Variety Theater
Circle B Chuckwagon Cowboy Music Show	2005	2011	Circle B Chuckwagon
Clay Cooper's Country Express — Clay Cooper's Country Express Christmas	2005	2024	Caravelle Theatre (2005–2006) Clay Cooper Theatre (2007–2024)
Exploring Life in Heaven with Rose Martin	2005	2006	Nova Theatre
Friday Night Live Cabaret	2005	2006	Nova Theatre
Gene Williams Country Music Television Show	2005	2007	Branson Mall Music Theatre (2005) Branson Showcase Theater (2007)
Great American Songbook	2005	2005	Follies Theatre
Hank and Patsy Together Again	2005	2011	Owen Theatre (2005–2008) Hot Hits Theatre (2011)
Hot Seat Game Show (2005) — Hot Seat Comedy Improv (2006)	2005	2006	Hughes Brothers Celebrity Theatre
Joey Riley Comedy and Music Revue — Joey Riley — Joe Riley	2005	2011	Branson Mall Music Theatre (2005) Caravelle Theatre (2006) Mickey Gilley Theatre (2007–2011)
Justin Flom Live — Justin Flom: Experience Illusion	2005	2008	Branson Mall Music Theatre (2005) Majestic Steakhouse (2006–2007) Magic Parlor and Imaginary Theatre (2008)
Ladies of Motown	2005	2007	Owen Theatre
Legendary Tops and Temps Show	2005	2006	Nova Theatre
Lit'l Nashville Opry Show	2005	2005	Moe Bandy Americana Theatre

Show name	First year	Last year	Venue
Liverpool Legends — Liverpool Legends — Beatles Tribute	2005	2022	Branson Mall Music Theatre (2005) Caravelle Theatre (2006–2007) Starlite Theatre (2008–2009) The Mansion (2011) Moon River Theatre (2013) Caravelle Theatre (2014–2019) Andy Williams Performing Arts Center (2022)
Magic of Taylor Reed — The Magic and Comedy of Taylor Reed — Taylor Reed, Master Illusionist	2005	2019	Branson Mall Music Theatre (2005) Branson Showcase Theater (2007) Clay Cooper Theatre (2009) Kirby Van Burch Theater (2013) Jim Stafford Theatre (2016–2018) Dutton Family Theater (2019)
Murder in the Ozarks	2005	2005	American Jukebox Theater
Peter the Adequate	2005	2005	Owen Theatre
Rico J and the Hot Hit Show	2005	2005	Wildwood Flower Theater
Road to Rock	2005	2007	Gaslighter ShowTown Theatre (2005) House of Rock Theater (2006) Branson Showcase Theater (2007)
Rock N Country Christmas	2005	2005	Gaslighter ShowTown Theatre
Showcase Jubilee	2005	2006	White House Theatre
Splinter Middleton	2005	2005	Grand Country Music Hall
StarMania	2005	2005	Branson Mall Music Theatre
Two Fluffy Women	2005	2006	Owen Theatre
Adventures of a Performing Family starring the Warnocks — Warnock's Christmas	2006	2009	Hughes Brothers Celebrity Theatre (2006) God and Country Theatre (2009)
Amazing Pets	2006	2024	Grand Country Music Hall
Bill Medley of the Righteous Brothers with Paul Revere and the Raiders — Righteous Brothers' Bill Medley	2006	2011	Dick Clark's American Bandstand Theater (2006–2008) Moon River Theatre (2009) Starlite Theatre (2010–2011)
Chris Roberts Live	2006	2006	House of Rock Theater
The Christmas Music of Mannheim Steamroller	2006	2007	Grand Palace
The Comets	2006	2009	Dick Clark's American Bandstand Theater (2006–2007) Moon River Theatre (2009)
Cruisin' 57 Show	2006	2006	Dick Clark's American Bandstand Theater
Dean Church Variety Music Show	2006	2006	IMAX Little Opry Theatre
Gary Lewis and the Playboys	2006	2007	Dick Clark's American Bandstand Theater
Grand Country Friday Night	2006	2007	Grand Country Music Hall
Hank Williams Country Gospel Hour	2006	2006	IMAX Little Opry Theatre
Jim Reeves Tribute Show	2006	2009	Nova Theatre (2006) God and Country Theatre (2007–2009)

Show name	First year	Last year	Venue
Mike Nichols and Friends	2006	2006	Moe Bandy Americana Theatre
Oksana Pavilonis' Classical Christmas Show	2006	2006	House of Rock Theater
The Original Stars at American Bandstand	2006	2006	Dick Clark's American Bandstand Theater
Ozarks Jamboree	2006	2006	Nova Theatre
Ricky Boen and Texas Mud	2006	2010	Moe Bandy Americana Theatre (2006) Hamner Barber Theater (2007–2010)
Take the Twain Ride!	2006	2006	Owen Theatre
A Tribute to Rod Stewart featuring Rob Caudill	2006	2006	Nova Theatre
The Best of Motown	2007	2007	Hughes Brothers Celebrity Theatre
Blues Daddy	2007	2007	Bart Rockett Theater
Bob Nelson	2007	2009	Majestic Steakhouse (2007) Magic Parlor and Imaginary Theatre (2008) Clay Cooper Theatre (2009)
Branson Blues, Late Night	2007	2008	Owen Theatre
Branson Country USA — Branson Country USA Late Show	2007	2024	Grand Country Music Hall
Branson Divas	2007	2008	Bart Rockett Theater (2007) Magic Parlor and Imaginary Theatre (2008)
Christmas with the Standards	2007	2007	Welk Resort Theatre
Danny and the Juniors with Little Peggy March	2007	2007	Dick Clark's American Bandstand Theater
Dixieland Breakfast Show	2007	2008	White House Theatre
Elvis Gospel	2007	2007	Majestic Steakhouse
Elvis Sings Country	2007	2007	Owen Theatre
Fabian, Bobby Vee, the Chiffons, Brian Hyland, and Chris Montez	2007	2008	Dick Clark's American Bandstand Theater
Good Morning Branson	2007	2007	Branson Mall Hall of Fame Theatre
Hot Flash!	2007	2008	50's at the Hop Theater
The Isle of Dreams	2007	2007	Branson Showcase Theater
Jackson Cash: A Tribute to the Man in Black	2007	2007	Caravelle Theatre
Jammin' Country Morning with Cal Smith	2007	2007	Caravelle Theatre
John Wayne and America's Yodeling Sweetheart	2007	2008	Owen Theatre
Music Makes the World Go Round	2007	2009	Tower Theater
RFD-TV Revue	2007	2007	RFD-TV Theatre
Rocky Mountain High: A Tribute to John Denver — John Denver Tribute Morning Show	2007	2019	IMAX Little Opry Theatre

Show name	First year	Last year	Venue
Shirley Alston Reeves of the Shirelles and Johnny Preston	2007	2007	Dick Clark's American Bandstand Theater
SIX — SIX Christmas Show	2007	2024	Hughes Brothers Celebrity Theatre (2007–2011) Mickey Gilley Theatre (2012–2016) Hughes Brothers Theatre (2017–2019) Dick Clark's American Bandstand Theater (2020–2023) Pepsi Legends Theater (2024)
Spirit of Christmas with the Osmonds	2007	2008	Branson Variety Theater
Take It to the Limit: Eagles Tribute	2007	2019	Branson Showcase Theater (2007–2008) God and Country Theatre (2009–2012) Branson Tribute Theatre (2013–2019)
Tillis Family Reunion	2007	2008	Welk Resort Theatre
The Twelve Irish Tenors	2007	2016	Branson Variety Theater
Welk Stars Reunion 2007	2007	2007	Welk Resort Theatre
Wings of Christmas	2007	2008	Hamner Barber Theater
Xtreme Winter	2007	2007	Grand Palace
2 O'Clock Rocks	2008	2008	Dick Clark's American Bandstand Theater
Dueling Elvises	2008	2008	Owen Theatre
Elvis in the Morning	2008	2008	Owen Theatre
An Evening with Elvis	2008	2008	Gene Williams Theater
Freddy Hamilton	2008	2008	Mickey Gilley Theatre
Island Fire	2008	2011	Dutton Family Theater
Jeff Sallee's Classic Country Revue and Salute to Buck Owen Theatres	2008	2008	Gene Williams Theater
Joe Diffie	2008	2008	Yakov Smirnoff Theater
Jon England	2008	2008	Caravelle Theatre
Lisa Layne Country Show	2008	2008	God and Country Theatre
Loretta Lynn Tribute with JoDee Marie	2008	2008	Owen Theatre
Mike Walker — Mike Walker and Friends — Mike Walker Lasting Impressions	2008	2024	Mickey Gilley Theatre (2008) God and Country Theatre (2009–2016) Hamners' Variety Theater (2017–2024)
Noah: The Musical	2008	2011	Sight & Sound Theatre
Ol' Time Gospel Hour — Old Time Gospel Hour	2008	2022	IMAX Little Opry Theatre
Penny Gilley with Jeff Brandt — Penny Gilley	2008	2009	RFD-TV Theatre (2008) Branson Star Theatre (2009)
Ralph Kuster Breakfast Show	2008	2009	Majestic Steakhouse (2008) God and Country Theatre (2009)

Show name	First year	Last year	Venue
Rankin Brothers Classic Music Revue — Rankin Brothers	2008	2014	Welk Resort Theatre (2008) Starlite Theatre (2009) Caravelle Theatre (2010) Mickey Gilley Theatre (2011) Clay Cooper Theatre (2012–2013) Yakov Smirnoff Theater (2014)
Redhead Express	2008	2009	Circle B Chuckwagon (2008) Dutton Family Theater (2009)
Redneckers with Keith Red Allen	2008	2010	Branson Star Theatre
Scott Riley's Jammin' Country	2008	2008	Majestic Steakhouse
Shake, Rattle, and Stroll with Bill Haley's Original Comets, Dave Somerville of the Diamonds, and McKenna Medley	2008	2008	Club 57 in Dick Clark's American Bandstand Theater (2008)
Allen Family Simply Christmas	2009	2011	Circle B Chuckwagon
Branson Blast	2009	2009	Branson Star Theatre
Brulé — A Native American Experience	2009	2011	RFD-TV Theatre
Buckets 'N Boards	2009	2024	Clay Cooper Theatre (2009–2015) Starlite Theatre (2016–2018) Dick Clark's American Bandstand Theater (2019–2023) Reza Live Theatre (2024)
Cassandré — The Voice of an Angel — Cassandré Haygood and Friends — Cassandré — The Voice of an Angel Christmas Spectacular	2009	2024	Americana Theatre (2009–2019) Hughes Brothers Theatre (2024)
George Dyer — From Broadway to Bublé: George Dyer	2009	2024	Dutton Family Theater (2009–2016) Americana Theatre (2017–2024)
Good News Country	2009	2009	IMAX Little Opry Theatre
Good News Gospel	2009	2017	IMAX Little Opry Theatre
Jim Greeninger	2009	2009	Hughes Brothers Theatre
The Keatings	2009	2010	Branson Star Theatre (2009) Hamner Barber Theater (2010)
Lee Greenwood — Lee Greenwood and the Bellamy Brothers — Lee Greenwood and Louise Mandrell	2009	2011	Welk Resort Theatre
Miracle of Christmas	2009	2024	Sight & Sound Theatre
A Neil Diamond Tribute — Keith Allyn's A Neil Diamond Tribute	2009	2024	Branson Mall Hall of Fame Theatre (2009–2011) Jim Stafford Theatre (2012–2014) Historic Owen Theatre (2015–2017) Jerry Presley's God and Country Theaters (2021–2024)
Peter Pan	2009	2009	The Mansion
Rock 'n Roll Is Here to Stay with Don Solice	2009	2010	Branson Star Theatre
Rock U Mentally	2009	2011	Dick Clark's American Bandstand Theater

Show name	First year	Last year	Venue
Strait Country Show — George Strait: A Tribute Starring James Garrett — George Strait Tribute Dinner Show	2009	2021	IMAX Little Opry Theatre (2009–2019) Jackie B. Goode's Uptown Café (2021)
Top 10 Rock and Roll Revue	2009	2012	Branson Mall Music Theatre
Wade Landry — Wade Benson Landry's Swingin' Cajun Style — Wade Landry's Cajun Fiddle, Country, and Comedy	2009	2014	God and Country Theatre
Absolutely Patsy with Tracy Lynn DeMille — Absolutely . . . Patsy	2010	2016	Branson Mall Music Theatre (2010–2012) Hot Hits Theatre (2013–2015)
Always Patsy — Always Patsy Cline: A Musical Production	2010	2015	God and Country Theatre
Angels of Country Music	2010	2015	God and Country Theatre
Bill Chrastil	2010	2012	Historic Owen Theatre (2010–2011) Branson Central Theatre (2012)
Bill Haley's Original Comets	2010	2010	Moon River Theatre
Branson Radio Live	2010	2010	IMAX Little Opry Theatre
Cat's Pajamas	2010	2014	Dutton Family Theater (2010–2011) Moon River Theatre (2013–2014)
Country Reunion	2010	2010	RFD-TV Theatre
Dennis Yeary, Ralph Kuster, and John Sager	2010	2010	Branson Mall Music Theatre
Hank Williams Show with Tim Hadler	2010	2010	IMAX Little Opry Theatre
JEERK	2010	2013	Hughes Brothers Theatre (2010–2011) RFD-TV Theatre (2013)
Joseph Hall's Elvis Rock 'n Remember Tribute	2010	2015	Owen Theatre (2010) Americana Theatre (2011–2013) Clay Cooper Theatre (2014–2015)
New South Gospel	2010	2024	Grand Country Music Hall
Paul Revere and the Raiders	2010	2011	Starlite Theatre Moon River Theatre (2011)
Roddie McDowell	2010	2010	God and Country Theatre
Sanders Family Christmas	2010	2023	IMAX Little Opry Theatre
Shake Rattle and Roll	2010	2011	Branson Variety Theater
Superstars of Country	2010	2010	Superstars Live Theatre
The Texas Tenors — Texas Tenors "Deep in the Heart of Christmas"	2010	2024	Starlite Theatre (2010–2017) Andy Williams Performing Arts Center (2019–2020) Mickey Gilley Grand Shanghai Theatre (2021–2024)
Thomas Brothers	2010	2010	Music City Centre

Show name	First year	Last year	Venue
Til Death Do We Part — Ozark Murder Mysteries — Almost Famous Murder Mystery Dinner — Branson's Murder Mystery Dinner Show — Branson Murder Mystery	2010	2024	Circle B Chuckwagon (2010–2011) Branson Central Theatre (2013–2017) Majestic Theatre (2018–2024)
A Tribute to George Strait Show	2010	2011	Branson Mall Center Stage (2010) Jackie B. Goode's Uptown Café (2011)
Wissman Family Christmas	2010	2014	Music City Centre (2010–2013) Doug Gabriel Theatre (2014) Branson Star Theatre (2014)
3 Redneck Tenors — Three Redneck Tenors	2011	2015	The Mansion (2011) Americana Theatre (2013) Moon River Theatre (2014–2015)
Alabama Revival — Alabama Tribute Show — Alabama Rolls On	2011	2019	God and Country Theatre/Jerry Presley's God and Country Theaters
Breakfast with Mark Twain	2011	2011	Hot Hits Theatre
Cirque Montage	2011	2013	Starlite Theatre
Country Legends	2011	2011	Hot Hits Theatre
Dennis Alm — Magic Champion	2011	2011	Hot Hits Theatre
Hollywood's Christmas Spectacular — Christmas in Hollywood — Christmas in Hollywood presents Christmas Wonderland	2011	2024	Branson Variety Theater (2011) King's Castle Theatre (2013–2024)
Hooray for Hollywood	2011	2013	Branson Variety Theater (2011) King's Castle Theatre (2013)
John Sager	2011	2013	Branson Mall Music Theatre
Legend of Kung Fu	2011	2013	White House Theatre
Marty Haggard	2011	2011	Clay Cooper Theatre
Missouri Hayride	2011	2011	Branson Mall Music Theatre
Neal McCoy	2011	2022	Clay Cooper Theatre (2011) Oak Ridge Boys Theatre (2012–2015) The Mansion (2016–2019) Clay Cooper Theatre (2022)
Roger Miller Tribute Show	2011	2011	Branson Mall Center Stage
Todd Oliver and Friends	2011	2020	Jim Stafford Theatre (2011) Americana Theatre (2012–2013) Shepherd of the Hills Playhouse (2019–2020)
A Tribute to Marty Robbins — A Tribute to Marty Robbins and Classic Country Stars	2011	2019	IMAX Little Opry Theatre (2011–2018) Dutton Family Theater (2019)
24 Karat Country	2012	2014	God and Country Theatre (2012) Tower Theater (2014)
Bill Anderson — A Night with a Legend	2012	2012	RFD-TV Theatre
Brady Lunch	2012	2012	Yakov Smirnoff Theater

Show name	First year	Last year	Venue
Christmas on the Trail Chuckwagon Dinner Show — Round Up on the Trail Chuckwagon Dinner Show	2012	2016	Shepherd of the Hills Homestead
A Christmas Snow	2012	2012	Starlite Theatre
Joseph	2012	2013	Sight & Sound Theatre
Marty Stuart	2012	2013	RFD-TV Theatre
Mollie B Polka Party Christmas Show	2012	2016	RFD-TV Theatre
Oh What a Night!	2012	2013	Moon River Theatre
The Price Is Right Live!	2012	2013	Welk Resort Theatre
Statler Brothers Revisited	2012	2019	God and Country Theatre
70's Music Explosion — 70's Music Celebration! Starring Barry Williams	2013	2016	RFD-TV Theatre (2013) Hughes Brothers Theatre (2014–2016)
ABBA Tribute: Thank You for the Music	2013	2024	God and Country Theatre (2013–2016) Hamners' Variety Theater (2017–2024)
Adventures of Marco Polo	2013	2015	White House Theatre
All American Gospel	2013	2015	God and Country Theatre
Ayo Starring Voices of Glory	2013	2018	Hughes Brothers Theatre (2013–2016) Starlite Theatre (2017) Andy Williams Performing Arts Center (2018)
Billy Dean Branson	2013	2017	Starlite Theatre (2013–2016) Jim Stafford Theatre (2017)
California Dreamin': A Walk Down Memory Lane — Beach Boys: California Dreamin'	2013	2024	God and Country Theatre (2013–2016) Hamners' Variety Theater (2017–2024)
Conway Remembered	2013	2019	God and Country Theatre (2013–2016) Hamners' Variety Theater (2017–2019)
Dancing Queen: ABBA's Greatest Hits — Dancing Queen: The Ultimate 70s Show	2013	2024	The King's Castle Theatre
Don't Stop Believin' — Journey Tribute	2013	2019	Branson Tribute Theatre
Doo Wop and Chico Vegas Drifters — Doo Wop and the Drifters	2013	2022	Hot Hits Theatre (2013–2019) Ruby Room at the Majestic (2020–2022)
Fair Family	2013	2014	Hamner Barber Theater
Good Ole Boys	2013	2017	God and Country Theatre
A Heapin' Spoonful	2013	2014	God and Country Theatre
It	2013	2017	Hughes Brothers Theatre
Larry's Country Diner	2013	2023	Starlite Theatre (2013–2017) Clay Cooper Theatre (2019–2023)
Linda Ronstadt and Jackson Browne Tribute	2013	2016	Branson Tribute Theatre
Michael J and Friends	2013	2014	Hot Hits Theatre
Never Say Never: Justin Bieber Tribute	2013	2013	Branson Tribute Theatre

Show name	First year	Last year	Venue
New Jersey Nights: A Frankie Valli and the Four Seasons Celebration	2013	2024	King's Castle Theatre
Petersen Family Bluegrass Band —The Petersens	2013	2024	IMAX Little Opry Theatre
Pure Comedy Starring Joey I.L.O. — Pure Comedy Feud	2013	2016	Jim Stafford Theatre (2013–2014) Historic Owen Theatre (2015–2016)
Reelin' in the Years: Best of the '70s and More	2013	2013	Americana Theatre
Rock, Roll, and Reminisce: The Fabulous Fifties	2013	2017	God and Country Theatre
Toy Shoppe Broadway Show Presented by Kenny Rogers	2013	2013	Starlite Theatre
Twice Adopted Gospel Show	2013	2016	Historic Owen Theatre (2013–2015) Hamners' Variety Theater (2016)
A Yee Haw Celebration to Music	2013	2013	Branson Star Theatre
2 Kings	2014	2014	Music City Centre
8 O'Clock Rock	2014	2015	God and Country Theatre
80's Ladies Show	2014	2014	God and Country Theatre
Amazing Acrobats of Shanghai — Shanghai Circus — Grand Shanghai Circus — Amazing Acrobats	2014	2024	New Shanghai Theatre (2014–2016) Mickey Gilley Grand Shanghai Theatre (2017–2024)
Barney Fife . . . Fully Loaded	2014	2016	Hot Hits Theatre (2014) Branson Central Theatre (2015) Caravelle Theatre (2016)
Bee Gees and Beyond	2014	2016	God and Country Theatre
Chris Perondi's Stunt Dog Experience	2014	2014	Clay Cooper Theatre
Dancin' Through the Years — Dancin' Through the Ages	2014	2015	God and Country Theatre
Dublin's Irish Tenors and the Celtic Ladies	2014	2024	King's Castle Theatre
Hamners' Unbelievable Variety Show	2014	2024	Hamners' Variety Theater
Jerry Presley Elvis Tribute — Presley Sings Elvis — Elvis Live! Aloha from Hawaii — Elvis Live! Madison Square Garden — Elvis Live! Christmas	2014	2024	Branson Tribute Theatre (2014) God and Country Theatre (2014) Jim Stafford Theatre (2015) Baldknobbers Theatre (2016) Jerry Presley's God and Country Theaters (2017–2024)
Jonah	2014	2015	Sight & Sound Theatre
Lennon/Cathcart Trio	2014	2014	Branson Tribute Theatre
The Lettermen	2014	2016	Moon River Theatre
Patsy Cline Remembered	2014	2016	Hamners' Variety Theater
Revollusionists Magic and Illusionist Show	2014	2015	Music City Centre

Show name	First year	Last year	Venue
Rick Thomas Illusionist and Magic Show — Illusionist Rick Thomas: Mansion of Dreams	2014	2024	Moon River Theatre/Andy Williams PAC (2014–2019, 2022) Mickey Gilley Grand Shanghai Theatre (2021, 2023–2024)
Smokin' Hot Ladies of Classic Rock	2014	2015	God and Country Theatre
Sons of Britches	2014	2024	IMAX Little Opry Theatre
Three Men and a Lady	2014	2014	God and Country Theatre
50's La Bamba Tribute Show	2015	2016	Historic Owen Theatre
Andy Williams Moon River and Me	2015	2016	Moon River Theatre (2015) Andy Williams Performing Arts Center (2016)
Bad Moon Risin' Creedence Clearwater Revival Tribute Show	2015	2022	Branson Tribute Theatre (2015–2019) Branson Star Theatre (2020–2022)
Beautiful Noise starring Denny Diamond and the Jewels	2015	2015	Doug Gabriel Theatre
Bon Jovi Livin' on a Prayer Tribute Show	2015	2015	Branson Tribute Theatre
California Cruizin'	2015	2015	Hamners' Variety Theater
The Carpenters — Best of Neil Sedaka — Neil Sedaka, the Carpenters, and Captain and Tennille Tribute Show	2015	2021	God and Country Theatre
Carpenters Once More	2015	2024	Historic Owen Theatre (2015–2017) Jerry Presley's God and Country Theaters (2023–2024)
Forever Young	2015	2017	Music City Centre (2015) Hughes Brothers Theatre (2016) Americana Theatre (2017)
Hits Starring Collin Raye and the Comedy of Chipper Lowell	2015	2015	Moon River Theatre
Puttin' on the Ritz — The Song and Dance Extravaganza	2015	2016	King's Castle Theatre
Woodstock Folk Rock	2015	2015	Branson Tribute Theatre
All Hands on Deck!	2016	2022	Dutton Family Theater (2016–2022) Copeland Theater (2022)
The Big Show	2016	2016	Branson Central Theatre
British Invasion	2016	2016	God and Country Theatre
Comedy Hypnosis Dinner Show	2016	2017	Branson Central Theatre (2016) Majestic Steakhouse (2017)
Dailey and Vincent	2016	2018	Starlite Theatre (2016) Mansion Theatre (2018)
Dreams: A Classic Rock Fantasy	2016	2017	Branson's Dream Theatre
Eric Hinson and the Hinson Revival	2016	2016	Branson Star Theatre
Jerusalem	2016	2016	Hughes Brothers Theatre
Kenny Parrott — Kenny Parrott's Country Classics	2016	2016	God and Country Theatre
LegZZ — A ZZ Top/Tina Turner Tribute	2016	2017	Branson's Dream Theatre

Show name	First year	Last year	Venue
Lynyrd Skynyrd and Suthyrn Fryd Frynds	2016	2017	Branson Tribute Theatre
A Maxine Christmas	2016	2016	Andy Williams Performing Arts Center
Mickey Gilley and Johnny Lee: Urban Cowboy Reunion Show — Mickey Gilley and Johnny Lee: Urban Cowboys Ride Again!	2016	2021	Clay Cooper Theatre (2016) Mickey Gilley Grand Shanghai Theatre (2017–2021)
Million Dollar Quartet — Million Dollar Quartet Dinner Show	2016	2024	Welk Resort Theatre (2016–2019) Shepherd of the Hills Playhouse (2023–2024)
Moses	2016	2017	Sight & Sound Theatre
Pure Presley Gospel Show	2016	2016	Baldknobbers Theatre
Raiding the Country Vault	2016	2021	Mansion Theatre (2016) Starlite Theatre (2017–2018) Americana Theatre (2019–2021)
Ray Charles and Company	2016	2016	God and Country Theatre
Reza: Edge of Illusion	2016	2024	Starlite Theatre (2016) Branson Famous Theatre (2018–2023) Reza Live Theatre (2024)
Rock and Roll Revival	2016	2017	Jim Stafford Theatre
Tellin' Tales	2016	2016	Crystal Theatre at Lodge of the Ozarks
50 Years of Kenny Rogers	2017	2021	Jerry Presley's God and Country Theaters
Cash Alive! The Legend	2017	2019	Jerry Presley's God and Country Theaters
Country Rock 'N Blues Review	2017	2017	Branson's Dream Theatre
George Jones and Friends Remembered	2017	2024	IMAX Little Opry Theatre
Janice Martin Aerial and Musical Variety Show — A Janice Martin Cirque Show	2017	2019	Americana Theatre (2017) Starlite Theatre (2018) Americana Theatre (2019)
Ozark Bluegrass Jubilee	2017	2018	Jerry Presley's God and Country Theaters
Ozarks Country	2017	2024	Grand Country
Ozarks Gospel	2017	2024	Grand Country
Raiding the Rock Vault	2017	2018	Starlite Theatre
Rockabilly Rave — Buddy and More	2017	2017	Jerry Presley's God and Country Theaters
The Temptations Motown Legends	2017	2021	Jerry Presley's God and Country Theaters
Three Dog Night Road to Shambala — 3 Dog Night Shambala	2017	2021	Jerry Presley's God and Country Theaters
Billy Yates' Hit Songwriters in the Round	2018	2020	Americana Theatre (2018) Choices Concert Hall (2019) Shepherd of the Hills Playhouse (2020)
Bluegrass Remedy	2018	2018	Jim Stafford Theatre
Broadway — The Greatest Hits	2018	2019	King's Castle Theatre
CJ Newsom's Classic Country and Comedy	2018	2024	Americana Theatre
Crazy 'Bout Patsy	2018	2019	Hot Hits Theatre

Show name	First year	Last year	Venue
Dolly Parton and Friends — Dolly and Friends — A Tribute	2018	2019	Americana Theatre
Everly Brothers Tribute	2018	2018	Jerry Presley's God and Country Theaters
Glen Campbell Songbook	2018	2019	IMAX Little Opry Theatre
Heartland Country	2018	2018	Jim Stafford Theatre
Hot Rods and High Heels — Hot Rods and High Heels 1950s Christmas	2018	2024	Clay Cooper Theatre
Oh Happy Day! Goin' Back to Gospel	2018	2023	Hughes Brothers Theatre (2018–2021) Hamners' Variety Theater (2023)
Pierce Arrow Decades	2018	2024	Pierce Arrow Theater
Raiding the Country Vault Christmas	2018	2018	Starlite Theatre
Samson	2018	2019	Sight & Sound Theatre
A Shepherd's Christmas Carol Dinner Show	2018	2024	Shepherd of the Hills Playhouse
Sinatra and Friends	2018	2019	King's Castle Theatre
Waylon, Willie, and the Good Ol' Boys	2018	2021	Jerry Presley's God and Country Theaters
Acrobats on Ice	2019	2019	White House Theatre
Adele and Joe Cocker Tribute	2019	2019	Branson Tribute Theatre
Fleetwood Mac Dreams — Fleetwood Mac Tribute	2019	2021	IMAX Little Opry Theatre (2019) Jerry Presley's God and Country Theaters (2021)
Johnson Strings Family Music and Vocal Show	2019	2021	Majestic Theatre (2019) Americana Theatre (2020–2021)
Marvin Gaye Tribute — Marvin Gaye and the Masters of Soul	2019	2021	Hot Hits Theatre
Music from Across the Tracks	2019	2019	Hot Hits Theatre
Nashville Nights	2019	2019	Choices Concert Hall
Parrotville — Jimmy Buffett Tribute Show	2019	2020	Jim Stafford Theatre
Pierce Arrow: Gold	2019	2020	Pierce Arrow Theater
Shad and Mollie Heller's Original Toby Show	2019	2022	Shepherd of the Hills
Southern Rock Tribute	2019	2019	Branson Tribute Theatre
A Tribute to Aretha Franklin	2019	2019	Branson Tribute Theatre
Anthems of Rock	2020	2024	King's Castle Theatre
Comedy and Music of Steve Moris Lunch Show — The Music, Humor, and Stories of a Baby Boomer	2020	2021	Branson Central Theatre
Dancing in the Streets — A Motown Revue	2020	2022	Ruby Room at the Majestic Theatre
Dean Z — The Ultimate Elvis	2020	2024	Clay Cooper Theatre
Dean Z's Rockin' Christmas Show	2020	2024	Clay Cooper Theatre

Show name	First year	Last year	Venue
Doo Wop and More	2020	2024	Hot Hits Theatre
Escape Reality Dinner and Magic Show — Escape Reality: Magic and Illusions	2020	2024	Branson Central Theatre (2020–2021) Hughes Brothers Theatre (2022–2024)
Famous Impressions	2020	2021	Hughes Brothers Theatre
From Broadway to Hollywood to Branson	2020	2021	Hot Hits Theatre
Fusion: Where Metal Meets Classical	2020	2020	Branson Star Theatre
HardRock Nite	2020	2020	Branson Star Theatre
Hughes Brothers Country Show	2020	2024	Hughes Brothers Theatre
Kenny Rogers Experience featuring Rick McEwen	2020	2020	Branson Star Theatre
Matt Gumm and Company — Matt Gumm LIVE	2020	2024	Clay Cooper Theatre
Nashville Roadhouse Live	2020	2023	Nashville Roadhouse Theater at Branson Star
Rick McEwen's Big Show — Rick McEwen Presents the Gambler	2020	2024	IMAX Little Opry Theatre
Rock 'N' Roll Royalty	2020	2021	Americana Theatre
Shepherd of the Hills Chuckwagon Show featuring the Riders of the Circle B — The Great American Chuckwagon Dinner Show	2020	2024	Shepherd of the Hills Playhouse
That 80's Rock Show (with Love)	2020	2020	Branson Star Theatre
WhoDunnit Hoedown Murder Mystery Dinner Show	2020	2024	Shepherd of the Hills Playhouse
Women of Country Music	2020	2020	Branson Star Theatre
Awesome 80's	2021	2024	Americana Theatre
Back to the Bee Gees	2021	2024	Hamners' Variety Theater
British Invasion	2021	2024	Americana Theatre
Chris Stanley's Comedy Magic Hour	2021	2021	IMAX Little Opry Theatre
Comic Book Heroz	2021	2021	Jerry Presley's God and Country Theaters
Country Legends Lunch Show	2021	2021	Jackie B. Goode's Uptown Cafe
Dean Martin and Friends — Dean Martin and More — Best of Dean Martin	2021	2023	Hot Hits Theatre
Elvis Sunday Gospel — Elvis and Blackwoods Gospel — Elvis Live! Gospel Concert with the Blackwood Singers	2021	2024	Jerry Presley's God and Country Theaters
Funny Farm Dinner Feud	2021	2023	Shepherd of the Hills Playhouse
James Taylor and Soft Rock of the 70s and 80s Tribute	2021	2024	Hot Hits Theatre
Jesus	2021	2022	Sight & Sound Theatre
Jim Barber and Friends	2021	2021	Shepherd of the Hills Playhouse

Show name	First year	Last year	Venue
Legends of Country	2021	2023	Dick Clark's American Bandstand Theater
Majestic Crooners	2021	2021	Majestic Theatre
Melody Hart Family and Friends	2021	2021	IMAX Little Opry Theatre
Patsy to Patsy	2021	2024	Hot Hits Theatre
Pierce Arrow Country	2021	2024	Pierce Arrow Theater
Re-Vibe	2021	2024	Hughes Brothers Theatre
The Sons Music Celebration	2021	2024	IMAX Little Opry Theatre (2021) Majestic Theatre (2022) Jerry Presley's God and Country Theaters (2023–2024)
America's Top Country Hits	2022	2024	Americana Theatre
Best of Motown and More	2022	2024	Nashville Roadhouse Theater at Branson Star (2022) Americana Theatre (2023–2024)
Chicago: Color My World — A Chicago Tribute	2022	2024	Jerry Presley's God and Country Theaters
Dean Martin and Friends Trey Dees	2022	2023	Nashville Roadhouse Theater at Branson Star
Elvis: Story of a King	2022	2024	Americana Theatre
Freedom Journey Show	2022	2024	Freedom Encounter Theater
Milsap Tribute	2022	2022	Majestic Theatre
Outlaw Eagles	2022	2022	Nashville Roadhouse Theater at Branson Star
Phil Dalton: Theater of Illusion	2022	2023	Nashville Roadhouse Theater at Branson Star
Sedaka Songbook	2022	2022	Majestic Theatre
Terry Bradshaw Show	2022	2024	Clay Cooper Theatre
Classic Rock Icons	2023	2024	Americana Theatre
Elvis: The Last Concert	2023	2023	Jerry Presley's God and Country Theaters
The Hits	2023	2023	Copeland Theater
Listen to the Music	2023	2023	Nashville Roadhouse Theater at Branson Star
On Fire: The Jerry Lee Lewis Story	2023	2023	Copeland Theater
Once Upon a Fairytale	2023	2024	Americana Theatre
Queen Esther	2023	2024	Sight & Sound Theatre
Rocketman: Elton John Tribute	2023	2024	Jerry Presley's God and Country Theaters
Strait to Branson — George Strait and Friends Tribute	2023	2024	Jerry Presley's God and Country Theaters
Matthew Boyce's Retro Christmas Spectacular	2024	2024	Americana Theatre
Murder by Eggnog	2024	2024	Majestic Theatre
Wild West Murder Mystery	2024	2024	Shepherd of the Hills Playhouse

NOTES

INTRODUCTION

1. TripAdvisor reviews of *The Shoji Tabuchi Show*, 2015–2022, https://www.tripadvisor.com/; Jessica Howard, "America's Hometown: Performance and Entertainment in Branson, Missouri" (PhD diss., New York University, 1997), 195–98; Jeanne Marie Laskas, "Branson in My Rearview Mirror," *GQ* 64 (May 1994): 172.

2. Numbers are for 1999. Kathryn Buckstaff, "Thriving Amid Change," *Springfield News-Leader*, September 17, 2006.

3. Branson Convention & Visitors Bureau, 2024 Marketing Report, https://www.explorebranson.com/industry-portal/research-reports; Steven Conn, *The Lies of the Land: Seeing Rural America For What It Is — and Isn't* (University of Chicago Press, 2023).

4. Otto Ernest Rayburn, *Ozark Country* (University of Arkansas Press, 2021 [1941]), 20; Vance Randolph, *The Ozarks: An American Survival of Primitive Society* (University of Arkansas Press, 2017 [1931]).

5. Lynn Berry, interview by Joanna Dee Das, Branson, Missouri, July 19, 2018.

6. Christ Casteel, "Campaign Slogan Is Well-Traveled," *The Oklahoman*, September 3, 2006; Adam Meyerson, "Family. Faith. Freedom. A Manifesto for Cultural Renewal," Hoover Institution, May 1, 1997, https://www.hoover.org/research/family-faith-freedom; Natasha Cole, "Faith, Family, Freedom Usage," unpublished research notes, June 28, 2023.

7. Laskas, "Branson in My Rearview Mirror."

8. There is one scholarly monograph about Branson entertainment: Aaron Ketchell's *Holy Hills of the Ozarks: Religion and Tourism in Branson, Missouri* (Johns Hopkins University Press, 2007). There are two PhD dissertations from theater departments, but neither has resulted in publication. See Howard, "America's Hometown"; and Jennifer Worth, "Real American Entertainment: Performance and Nationalism in Branson, Missouri" (PhD diss., City University of New York, 2011).

CHAPTER ONE

1. Ronald Reagan, *The Reagan Diaries*, ed. Douglas Brinkley (HarperCollins, 2007), 210–25; "The Daily Diary of President Ronald Reagan," March 4–8, 1984, Ronald Reagan Presidential Library & Museum, https://www.reaganlibrary.gov/archives/reagans-daily-diary; Ronald Reagan, *An American Life* (Simon & Schuster, 1990), 324–25.

2. Jean B. Wright to White House Press Secretary Larry Speakes, February 28, 1984, Ronald Reagan Presidential Library Digital Library Collections, Case File Number 187447.

3. Ronald Reagan to Mrs. Jean B. Wright, undated handwritten letter; date of March 9 is gleaned from a note from Kathy Osborne, personal secretary to the president, to Biff Henley, dated March 9, 1984, that says, "The press office has a copy and is typing the letter." Typed version of the letter is dated March 13, 1984. All in Ronald Reagan Presidential Library Digital Library Collections, Case File Number 187447; Ronald Reagan, letter to Mrs. Wright, March 13, 1984, Branson Centennial Museum.

4. "God's Country" was a phrase that emerged in the late 1800s to boost tourism in locations nationwide. Wright was not the first to use it in reference to the Ozarks, but he "led the way in transforming the term" from a marketing one to "one that was rooted in a Christian view of the world." Brooks Blevins, email, January 15, 2025; see also Erin Smith, "Melodrama, Popular Religion, and Literary Value: The Case of Harold Bell Wright," *American Literary History* 17, no. 2 (2005): 229.

5. The Harold Bell Wright Museum is now a part of the World's Largest Toy Museum in Branson. The letter is now housed at the Branson Centennial Museum.

6. Harold Bell Wright, *To My Sons* (Harper, 1934), 21.

7. Lawrence Tagg, *Harold Bell Wright: Storyteller to America* (Westernlore Press, 1986), 20.

8. Wright, *To My Sons*, 81, 86.

9. Wright, *To My Sons*, 113–15.

10. Tagg, *Harold Bell Wright*, 87.

11. Wright, *To My Sons*, 252.

12. Wright, *To My Sons*, 197–218. The Shepherd of the Hills Historical Society, founded in 1967, told a more romantic story, one more commonly repeated in Branson. It didn't mention an uncle. Instead, it claimed that that in the summer of 1896 Wright was traveling by horseback in the Ozarks and reached the flooded White River. He had to turn around, unable to ford the river. As the sun was setting, he felt despondent about spending the night in a wet tent when suddenly he happened upon the homestead of John and Anna Ross. They invited him to spend the night, and instead he ended up spending the whole summer. See "Shepherd of the Hills" Souvenir Program, 1969, White River Valley Historical Society (hereafter WRVHS).

13. Brooks Blevins, *A History of the Ozarks, Volume 1: The Old Ozarks* (University of Illinois Press, 2018), 60–67.

14. Blevins, *A History of the Ozarks, Volume 1*, 238.

15. Michael Fellman, *Inside War: The Guerrilla Conflict in Missouri During the Civil War* (Oxford University Press, 1989), 3, 22; Elmo Ingenthron and Mary Hartman, *Bald Knobbers: Vigilantes on the Ozarks Frontier* (Pelican Publishing Company, 1988), 15; Thomas Spencer, ed., *The Other Missouri History: Populists, Prostitutes, and Regular Folk* (University of Missouri Press, 2004), 34; Matthew J. Hernando, *Faces Like Devils: The Bald Knobber Vigilantes in the Ozarks* (University of Missouri Press, 2015), 39–40; Vickie Hooper, "Who the Heck Was Alf Bolin? Forsyth Remembers an Outlaw," *Bittersweet* 10, no. 3 (1983, orig. pub. 1981), uploaded by Springfield-Greene County Library, https://thelibrary.org/lochist/periodicals/bittersweet/sp83b.htm.

16. Ingenthron and Hartman, *Bald Knobbers*, 16; Spencer, *The Other Missouri History*, 34, 36.

17. Hernando, *Faces Like Devils*, 80.

18. For more on Bald Knobber origins, see Lucile Morris Upton, *Bald Knobbers* (Caxton Publishers, 1939); and Hernando, *Faces Like Devils*.

19. Hernando, *Faces Like Devils*, 68, 77, 116, 130–35, 142, 175.

20. Wright, *The Shepherd of the Hills*, 48, 52, 54, 72.

21. Wright, *The Shepherd of the Hills*, 63.

22. Wright, *The Shepherd of the Hills*, 122.

23. Wright, *The Shepherd of the Hills*, 127.

24. Wright, *The Shepherd of the Hills*, 130.

25. Wright, *The Shepherd of the Hills*, 184.

26. "A Million from Novels," *Literary Digest* 56 (March 2, 1918): 32; Fred Lewis Pattee, "The Later Flood of Fiction," in *The New American Literature: 1890–1930*, 460–77 (The Century Co., 1930), reprinted in "Harold Bell Wright," *Twentieth Century American Criticism*, vol. 183 (Gale, 2007), 349. Joshua Clark, "A Homestead's History," *Branson Tri-Lakes News*, October 19–22, 2013, Branson Centennial Museum. Some sources say it was the first book in US history to sell a million copies, but others say that Harriet Beecher Stowe's *Uncle Tom's Cabin* (published in 1852) already held that honor.

27. Smith, "Melodrama, Popular Religion, and Literary Value," 221.

28. Jack Shafer, "Scourge of the Booboisie," *Reason*, February 2013, https://reason.com/2003/02/01/scourge-of-the-booboisie-2/; Smith, "Melodrama, Popular Religion, and Literary Value," 217.

29. H. L. Mencken, "The National Letters," in *Prejudices: Second Series* (Alfred A. Knopf, 1920), reprinted in "Harold Wright," *Twentieth-Century Literary Criticism*, vol. 183, 348.

30. Tagg, *Harold Bell Wright*, 75–77; H. L. Mencken, *Prejudices: Second Series* (London: Jonathan Cape, 1921), 32–33; quoted in Smith, "Melodrama, Popular Religion, and Literary Value," 225.

31. Quoted in Smith, "Melodrama, Popular Religion, and Literary Value," 226; Tagg, *Harold Bell Wright*, 74.

32. For more on the legacy of Buffalo Bill's Wild West Show, see Richard White, "Frederick Jackson Turner and Buffalo Bill," in *The Frontier in American Culture: An Exhibition at the Newberry Library*, ed. James R Grossman (University of California Press, 1994); Joy S. Kasson, *Buffalo Bill's Wild West: Celebrity, Memory, and Popular History* (Hill and Wang, 2000).

33. White, "Frederick Jackson Turner and Buffalo Bill." See also Allan G. Bogue, "Frederick Jackson Turner Reconsidered," *The History Teacher* 27, no. 2 (1994); William Cronon, "Revisiting the Vanishing Frontier: The Legacy of Frederick Jackson Turner," *The Western Historical Quarterly* 18, no. 2 (1987): 157–76.

34. Smith, "Melodrama, Popular Religion, and Literary Value," 229.

35. Lynn Morrow and Linda Myers-Phinney, *The Shepherd of the Hills Country: Tourism Transforms the Ozarks, 1880s–1930s* (University of Arkansas Press, 1999), 7.

36. bell hooks called this "eating the other." See bell hooks, *Black Looks: Race and Representation* (South End Press, 1992), 21–39.

37. James N. Gregory, *The Southern Diaspora: How the Great Migrations of Black and White Southerners Transformed America* (University of North Carolina Press, 2005); Dawn Larsen, "The Canvas Cathedral: Toby Shows as Nativistic Social Movements," *Theatre History Studies* 21 (2001): 95.

38. The Toby Show, Corn Crib Theatre, Branson, 1985, www.youtube.com.

39. Larry Dale Clark, "Toby Shows: A Form of American Popular Theatre" (PhD diss., University of Illinois, 1963), 2, 9–12, 24, 68, 71, 100, 102; William Slout, *Theatre in a Tent: The Development of Provincial Entertainment* (Bowling Green State University Press, 1972), 83; Jere C. Mickel, "The Genesis of Toby: A Folk Hero of the American Theater," *Journal of American Folklore* 80, no. 318 (1967): 334–40; Arthur Cash, "A Memoir of the Toby Shows," *The North American Review* 279, no. 5 (1994): 52–56.

40. Dickson Terry, "There's Gold in Those Ozark Hills," *St. Louis Post-Dispatch*, August 29, 1965; National Register of Historic Places Inventory, Nomination Form, "Old Matt's Cabin," June 21, 1983, https://catalog.archives.gov/id/63821169; Michael Lewis Frizell, "A History of the *Shepherd of the Hills* Dramatizations: The Branson Productions" (MA thesis, Missouri State University, 1996), 20.

41. Terry, "There's Gold in Those Ozark Hills."

42. Morrow and Myers-Phinney, *The Shepherd of the Hills Country*, 32; "Find a Grave: Susie B. Johnson," https://www.findagrave.com/memorial/20718841/susie -b-johnston.

43. Tombstone of John Keever "Old Matt" Ross and Anna "Aunt Molly" Ross, Evergreen Cemetery, Notch, Stone County, Missouri, photo by Debbie Lee, https:// www.findagrave.com/memorial/5037732/john-keever-ross.

44. Jae McFerron, interview by Joanna Dee Das, Branson, Missouri, March 1, 2022; Bob McGill, *Branson's Entertainment Pioneers: A Success Story for Our Times* (White Oak Publishing, 2011), 15.

45. "Driver Buys Famous Farm," *Columbia Missourian*, December 28, 1910; Lynn Morrow, "Old Matt's Cabin," *OzarksWatch* 3, no. 4 (1090), published online by Springfield-Greene County Library, https://thelibrary.org/lochist/periodicals /ozarkswatch/ow304k.htm; National Register of Historic Places Inventory, Nomination Form, "Old Matt's Cabin."

46. Morrow and Myers-Finney, *The Shepherd of the Hills Country*, 34; Townsend Godsey, "'Shepherd' Legend Still Grows," *Springfield Leader and Press*, August 4, 1957.

47. Brooks Blevins, "Wretched and Innocent: Two Mountain Regions in the National Consciousness," *Journal of Appalachian Studies* 7, no. 2 (2001): 259.

48. Anthony Harkins, *Hillbilly: A Cultural History of an American Icon* (Oxford University Press, 2005), 4, 6, 49; Marion Hughes, *Three Years in Arkansaw* (M. A. Donahue Co., 1904), 35; Hathi Trust Digital Library, https://catalog.hathitrust.org /Record/009590564.

49. Randolph, *The Ozarks*, 15, 20; Rayburn, *Ozark Country*, 27.

50. Blevins, "Wretched and Innocent," 261.

51. Frizell, "A History of the *Shepherd of the Hills* Dramatizations," 26, 44.

52. *Shepherd of the Hills* souvenir booklet. Ownership of Shepherd of the Hills Farm was slightly complicated. When Lizzie McDaniel died, she willed the property to the Branson Civic League. The Trimbles purchased the 161 acres of land, but the Civic League initially maintained ownership of Old Matt's Cabin, which they leased to the Trimbles to operate as a tourist destination. See Frizell, "A History of the *Shepherd of the Hills* Dramatizations."

53. Frizell, "A History of the *Shepherd of the Hills* Dramatizations," 42.

54. Frizell, "A History of the *Shepherd of the Hills* Dramatizations," 47.

CHAPTER TWO

1. Margaret Newton, *"Shad": A Biography of Lloyd "Shad" Heller* (Pin Oak Publishing Company, 1982), 33.

2. 16th Annual Smoki Ceremonials and Snake Dance Brochure, 1936, Grace M. Sparkes Collection, Arizona Historical Foundation.

3. Newton, *"Shad,"* 56.

4. Philip Joseph Deloria, *Playing Indian* (Yale University Press, 1998).

5. Newton, *"Shad,"* 69.

6. Randolph, *The Ozarks*.

7. Newton, *"Shad,"* 88–107.

8. Newton, *"Shad,"* 140.

9. Brooks Blevins, *A History of the Ozarks, Volume 3: The Ozarkers* (University of Illinois Press, 2021), 153; McGill, *Branson's Entertainment Pioneers*, 9.

10. For more on the folk music movement, see Dick Weissman, *Which Side Are You On? An Inside History of the Folk Music Revival in America* (Continuum, 2006); and Daniel Gonczy, "The Folk Music Movement of the 1960s: Its Rise and Fall," *Popular Music and Society* 10, no. 1 (1985): 15–31.

11. Zachary J. Lechner, *The South of the Mind: American Imaginings of White Southernness, 1960–1980* (University of Georgia Press, 2018), 40; Jack Gould, "Hillbillies' Lead in Nielsen Study; Ratings Say TV Program Still Holds First Place," *New York Times*, October 29, 1963.

12. Andrew Patrick Nelson, "Hollywood Westerns: 1930s to the Present," in *A History of Western American Literature*, ed. Susan Kollin (Cambridge University Press, 2015), 337.

13. Joan Didion, "John Wayne: A Love Song," in *Slouching Toward Bethlehem* (Farrar, Straus & Giroux, 1968).

14. Blevins, "Wretched and Innocent," 266.

15. Clayborne Carlson, ed., "Chapter 31: The Poor People's Campaign," *The Autobiography of Martin Luther King, Jr.*, The Martin Luther King, Jr. Research and Education Institute, Stanford University, https://kinginstitute.stanford.edu /publications/autobiography-martin-luther-king-jr/chapter-31-poor-peoples -campaign.

16. Elmo Ingenthron, "The Ozarkian Heritage," Shepherd of the Hills Souvenir Program, 1969, WRVHS.

17. Randolph, *The Ozarks*, 1931, 15, 20; Rayburn, *Ozark Country*, 31; Blevins, "Wretched and Innocent," 266.

18. Crystal Payton, *The Story of Silver Dollar City: A Pictorial History of Branson's Famous Ozark Mountain Theme Park*, 2nd ed. (Lens & Lens Publishing, 2007), 18.

19. "Plumb Nelly Parade to Assemble at Anchor Village," *White River Leader*, April 15, 1960; "Plumb Nelly Means Gaiety in Hills," *Kansas City Times*, April 28, 1960; Frizell, "The Shepherd of the Hills," 48, 56–57; Newton, *"Shad,"* 153, 159; "The Shepherd Walks the Hills Again," *Stone County Republican*, August 4, 1960. Some sources erroneously list the name of the corporation as Shepherd of the Hills Players, Inc. The official filing with the State of Missouri was Old Mill Theatre Players, Inc., under the name Ruth Heller, on August 22, 1960. See https://bsd.sos .mo.gov/BusinessEntity/BusinessEntityDetail.aspx?page=beSearch&ID=97665. The *Stone County Republican* says Shepherd of the Hills Players. See "Plan to Open Theater by August 1st," *Stone County Republican*, June 30, 1960.

20. "Shepherd Story at Home," *White River Leader*, June 10, 1960.

21. Newton, *"Shad,"* 165–66.

22. Frizell, "A History of the *Shepherd of the Hills* Dramatizations," 57.

23. Newton, *"Shad,"* 167.

24. George Whittington, "Come Back With Us to 'Shepherd of the Hills,'" *Springfield News-Leader*, July 1, 1963.

25. Newton, *"Shad,"* 166.

26. "Panning and Scanning," *Springfield Leader and Press*, February 13, 1966.

27. "Shepherd of the Hills" Souvenir Program; National Register of Historical Places.

28. "Shepherd of the Hills" Souvenir Program, 5.

29. Mark Trimble, quoted in Frizell, "A History of the *Shepherd of the Hills* Dramatizations," 60–61.

30. McGill, *Branson's Entertainment Pioneers*, 17.

31. "Shepherd of the Hills" Souvenir Program.

32. Keith Thurman, interview by Joanna Dee Das, Branson, Missouri, July 17, 2018.

33. William Glover, "Outdoor Dramas of Local Origin Bloom in U.S.," *St. Joseph News-Press*, August 20, 1972.

34. "Shepherd of the Hills" Souvenir Program.

35. Glover, "Outdoor Dramas of Local Origin Bloom in U.S."

36. Quoted in Frizell, "A History of the *Shepherd of the Hills* Dramatizations," 82.

37. Thurman, interview.

38. For a recent diagnosis of these ills, see Robert Putnam, *Bowling Alone: The Collapse and Revival of American Community, Revised and Updated* (Simon and Schuster, 2020).

39. Kermit Hunter, "The Outdoor Historical Drama," *The North Carolina Historical Review* 30, no. 2 (1953): 218–20.

40. Hunter, "The Outdoor Historical Drama," 220.

41. Frances Shemanski, "Drama-Pageants: The Heartland's Answer to Broadway," *New York Times*, June 21, 1970.

42. William Glover, "Outdoor Drama Festivals Look to Record Season," *Hartford Courant*, April 27, 1975.

43. Ted Cramer to Mark Summer, October 3, 1977, Institute of Outdoor Drama Archives, Box 307, Folder G, Eastern Carolina University.

44. Cramer to Summer.

45. "'Shepherd of the Hills' Pageant Set for Opening," *Springfield Leader and Press*, May 14, 1961; "Third Annual Performance: 'Shepherd of Hills' Play Tryouts at Branson Today," *Springfield News-Leader*, March 31, 1962; "It's Out of Print: 'Shepherd' over Hill as Novel?," *Springfield Leader and Press*, August 9, 1962; "Doubled," *Springfield Leader and Press*, July 17, 1966; "Old Mill Theatre Among Nation's Top," *Douglas County Herald* (Ava, MO), November 23, 1967; "Old Mill Theater 3rd in Nation," *Springfield News-Leader*, October 12, 1968; "'Shepherd of the Hills' Plans Expanded Schedule," *Springfield Leader and Press*, February 3, 1973; Institute for Outdoor Drama, Outdoor Drama Attendance Reports, 1982–1985, Institute of Outdoor Drama Archives, Box 307, Folder G, Eastern Carolina University; Frizell, "A History of the *Shepherd of the Hills* Dramatizations," 63.

46. Payton, *The Story of Silver Dollar City*, 34–36.

47. Payton, *The Story of Silver Dollar City*, 41.

48. McGill, *Entertainment Pioneers*, 24.

49. Payton, *The Story of Silver Dollar City*, 26.

50. Eric Avila, *Popular Culture in the Age of White Flight: Fear and Fantasy in Suburban Los Angeles* (University of California Press, 2004), 106–19; Jill Anne Morris, "Disney's Influence on the Modern Theme Park and the Codification of Colorblind Racism in the American Amusement Industry," in *Performance and the Disney Theme Park Experience: The Tourist as Actor*, ed. Jennifer A. Kokai and Tom Robson (Palgrave Macmillan, 2019), 220.

51. Michael Barrier, *The Animated Man: A Life of Walt Disney* (University of California Press, 2007), 18.

52. Bethanee Bemis, *Disney Theme Parks and America's National Narratives: Mirror, Mirror, for Us All* (Routledge, 2023), 38. For more, see Richard Francaviglia, "History after Disney: The Significance of 'Imagineered' Historical Places," *The Public Historian* 17, no. 4 (1995): 69–74.

53. "Jefferson City," *St. Louis Post-Dispatch*, June 3, 1884; "A Marble Cave," *Springfield News-Leader*, May 25, 1884.

54. The myth persists that the Bald Knobbers burned down the town, but no evidence exists of that. Instead, it burned due to a forest fire. Rick J. Gunter, personal communication, May 8, 2022.

55. Payton, *The Story of Silver Dollar City*, 51.

56. In 2020, Plimouth Plantation was renamed Plimouth Patuxet Museums.

57. Disney scaled down the buildings on Disneyland's Main Street, constructed in 1955. While there is not a good scholarly resource to explain why, some sources allude to Walt Disney wanting the buildings to be "pony-sized," presumably meaning quainter and more accessible. See Francaviglia, "History after Disney."

58. Payton, *The Story of Silver Dollar City*, 59; McGill, *Branson's Entertainment Pioneers*, 24–25; Newton, "Shad," 200.

59. Payton, *The Story of Silver Dollar City*, 53; "Silver Dollar City Opens This Sunday," *White River Leader*, April 29, 1960.

60. Newton, "Shad," 194.

61. Newton, "Shad," 187.

62. "Silver Dollar City Opening May 1," *White River Leader*, April 22, 1960. Courtesy of Lisa Rau.

63. "Ozark Playgrounds to Get Help from Vacation Book," *Webb City Sentinel*, April 19, 1960.

64. "Silver Dollar City Opens This Sunday."

65. "Silver Dollar City Opening May 1"; "SDC Opens to Crowd of 18,000," *Branson Beacon*, May 5, 1960.

66. Forrest Bradley, "250,000 Visitors Expected This Year," *Springfield Leader and Press*, June 25, 1961; Terry, "There's Gold in Those Ozark Hills."

67. *The Beverly Hillbillies*, season 8, episodes 1–5, available on www .youtube.com.

68. Mary Kimbrough, "She Built Her Own City," *St. Louis Globe-Democrat*, reprinted in the US Congressional Record, Extension of Remarks, September 23, 1969, 26753, https://www.congress.gov/bound-congressional-record/1969/09 /23/extensions-of-remarks-section; Paul Stubblefield, "Ozarks Sprucing Up for Tourism Season," *Kansas City Star*, April 23, 1971.

69. June Ward, interviewed by Joanna Dee Das, Silver Dollar City, May 11, 2022.

70. McFerron, interview.

71. Ella Mae Tucker, "Out Our Way," *Springfield Leader and Press*, September 9, 1962.

72. Quoted in Payton, *The Story of Silver Dollar City*, 65. JoDee Remien would go on to marry Pete Herschend.

73. McFerron, interview.

74. Art Gorlick, "Reporter from Chicago Praises Ozarks Area and Finds Branson Gives Strangers Real Welcome," *White River Leader*, August 24–25, 1968.

75. Silver Dollar City Brochure, 1970s, courtesy Lisa Rau.

76. Descriptions come from interviews with various SDC employees who have performed the skit, as well as from historic photographs of the skit, courtesy of Lisa Rau.

77. "Talking Things Over," *Springfield Leader and Press*, April 29, 1962; Larry Klinger, "Area Has a New Railroad Line," *Springfield Daily News*, May 28, 1962.

78. See chapter one.

79. Leader and Press Staff, "Off Beat," *Springfield Leader and Press*, October 31, 1963.

80. McGill, *Branson's Entertainment Pioneers*, 26; Payton, *The Story of Silver Dollar City*, 57–68; Ward, interview.

81. I rode Flooded Mine on May 11, 2022, and shot my laser gun at the animatronic figures.

82. Descriptions taken from my visit in May 2022 and Patricia Morris and Tammi Arford, "'Sweat a Little Water, Sweat a Little Blood': A Spectacle of Convict Labor at an American Amusement Park," *Crime Media Culture* (2018): 8, 12. The ride was not much updated between its opening in 1968 and our visits.

83. "Talking Things Over," *Springfield Leader and Press*, February 11, 1968. That area would later be named as part of the Tar Creek Superfund Site for its toxic waste. See US Environmental Protection Agency, "Superfund Site: TAR CREEK (OTTOWA COUNTY), OTTAWA COUNTY, OK," https://cumulis.epa.gov/supercpad/SiteProfiles/index.cfm?fuseaction=second.Cleanup&id=0601269#bkground.

84. For more on "dark tourism," see Alana Barton and Alyson Brown, "Dark Tourism and the Modern Prison," *Prison Service Journal* 199 (2012): 44–49. Missouri State Penitentiary tours have varying age restrictions — some tours ages five and up, others seventeen and up; see https://www.missouripentours.com/tours/. The Auschwitz-Birkenau Museum is recommended for ages fourteen and up. See https://www.auschwitz.org/gfx/auschwitz/userfiles/_public/visit/30_en.pdf.

85. Payton, *The Story of Silver Dollar City*, 75.

86. McGill, *Branson's Entertainment Pioneers*, 28.

87. Tammy Hayes, "Mary Herschend Is Honored in Congressional Record," *Branson Beacon*, October 16, 1969; Hon. Durward G. Hall, "She Built Her Own City," Tuesday, September 23, 1969, Extensions of Remarks, Congressional Record, 26752, https://www.congress.gov/bound-congressional-record/1969/09/23/extensions-of-remarks-section.

88. Joseph E. Lowndes, *From the New Deal to the New Right: Race and the Southern Origins of Modern Conservatism* (Yale University Press, 2008), 117.

89. Lowndes, *From the New Deal to the New Right*, 113–15.

90. "Mrs. Herschend Picked to Help Greet Nixon," *Branson Beacon*, September 19, 1968, WRVHS.

91. Hayes, "Mary Herschend Is Honored in Congressional Record."

92. Ella Mae Tucker, "Out Our Way," *Springfield Leader and Press*, December 10, 1961.

93. Lisa Rau stated this in multiple conversations and in emails between March and May 2022.

CHAPTER THREE

1. Arline Chandler, *The Heart of Branson: The Entertaining Families of America's Live Music Show Capital* (The History Press, 2010), 75, 84.

2. *Branson's Famous Baldknobbers*, 60th Anniversary Show, October 25, 2019, DVD.

3. Seth Dowland, *Family Values and the Rise of the Christian Right* (University of Pennsylvania Press, 2015), 3, 8; Matthew D. Lassiter, "Inventing Family Values," in *Rightward Bound: Making America Conservative in the 1970s*, ed. Bruce J. Schulman and Julian E. Zelizer (Harvard University Press, 2008), 13–28. For another important factor in how ideology became aligned with political party, see Sam Rosenfeld, *The Polarizers: Postwar Architects of Our Partisan Era* (University of Chicago Press, 2017).

4. US Census, 1940.

5. Bob Mabe, interview by Joanna Dee Das, Branson, Missouri, December 13, 2018.

6. Joe Newman, *Race and the Assemblies of God Church: The Journey from Azusa Street to the "Miracle of Memphis"* (Cambria Press, 2007), 2.

7. Newman, *Race and the Assemblies of God Church*, 8, 66–68.

8. Robert K. Gilmore, *Ozark Baptizings, Hangings, and Other Diversions: Theatrical Folkways of Rural Missouri, 1885–1910* (University of Oklahoma Press, 1984), 18; Ron Marr, *The Presley Family Story: The First 74 Years* (Missouri Life, Inc., 2008), 15; Mabe, interview.

9. Gilmore, *Ozark Baptizings, Hangings, and Other Diversions*, 9; "Blind Boone Coming," *The Republican Pilot* (Maysville, MO), May 11, 1905; Janet Schroeder, "Choreographing Appalachia as America: The Hazards of Nostalgia on the Concert Stage," *Dance Chronicle* 43, no. 3 (2020): 270–94.

10. Benjamin Filene, *Romancing the Folk: Public Memory & American Roots Music* (University of North Carolina Press, 2000); Karl Hagstrom Miller, *Segregating Sound: Inventing Folk and Pop Music in the Age of Jim Crow* (Duke University Press, 2010), 245; David Whisnant, *All That Is Native and Fine: The Politics of Culture in an American Region* (University of North Carolina Press, 2009 [1983]).

11. Miller, *Segregating Sound*, 4; Paige McGinley, *Staging the Blues: From Tent Shows to Tourism* (Duke University Press, 2014), 7, 11–12.

12. Richard A. Peterson, *Creating Country Music: Fabricating Authenticity* (University of Chicago Press, 1997), 60–64; Katherine Brucher, "Assembly Lines and Contra Dance Lines: The Ford Motor Company Music Department and Leisure Reform," *Journal of the Society for American Music* 10, no. 4 (2016): 471.

13. Heather Grimm, "Rank Strangers: Performing the Bluegrass Repertoire in the Contemporary Market" (PhD diss., Northwestern University, 2024), 56–57.

14. I. Michael Heyman, "The Festival: More Than a Song," Smithsonian Institution, 1997 Festival of American Folklife Program Booklet, https://folklife-media.si.edu/docs/festival/program-book-articles/FESTBK1997_01.pdf.

15. Bill C. Malone, *Country Music USA*, 50th anniversary ed. (University of Texas Press, 2018), 76–81.

16. Conn, *The Lies of the Land*, 2–3.

17. Clark, "Toby Shows," 126–29; Peterson, *Creating Country Music*, 70.

18. Marr, *The Presley Family Story*, 15.

19. McGill, *Branson's Entertainment Pioneers*, 32.

20. Mabe, interview.

21. Kitty Ledbetter and Scott Foster Siman, *Broadcasting the Ozarks: Si Siman and Country Music at the Crossroads* (University of Arkansas Press, 2024), 45–126; Howard, "America's Hometown," 35–36; Dickson Terry, "Hillbilly Music Center," *St. Louis Post-Dispatch*, February 5, 1956.

22. Diane Pecknold, *The Selling Sound: The Rise of the Country Music Industry* (Duke University Press, 2007), 5, 22–25.

23. Peterson, *Creating Country Music*; Malone, *Country Music USA*.

24. Mabe, interview; Chandler, *The Heart of Branson*, 85; Marr, *The Presley Family Story*, 19. Sources conflict on whether the show took place in the basement or on the second floor of the city hall. Some sources say it took place in the police station, but that the police station was within the municipal building.

25. Mabe, interview.

26. Chandler, *The Heart of Branson*, 77.

27. Mabe, interview; newspaper advertisements.

28. Told to Marr, *The Presley Family Story*, 22.

29. For more on how this theatrical norm developed in the mid-nineteenth century, see Lawrence W. Levine, *Highbrow/Lowbrow: The Emergence of Cultural Hierarchy in America* (Harvard University Press, 1988).

30. Jay Jones, "Out of the Cave and into the Limelight: A Branson Attraction's Success," *Los Angeles Times*, June 21, 2017, https://www.latimes.com/travel/deals/la-tr-branson-anniversary-20170620-story.html; Gary Groman, "Pursuit of a Dream Leads Presleys onto the Airwaves and into the Caves," Branson Tourism Center, July 6, 2017, https://www.bransontourismcenter.com/info/2017/07/06/pursuit-of-a-dream-leads-presleys-onto-the-airwaves-and-into-the-caves/.

31. "Baldknobbers in New Site, Building for Eighth Year," *Springfield Leader and Press*, April 20, 1969, 65; Marr, *The Presley Family Story*, 33–35.

32. *We Always Lie to Strangers*, directed by David Wilson and A. J. Schnack (Spacestation/Seed&Spark, 2013), DVD.

33. Stephanie R. Rolph, "Courting Conservatism: White Resistance and the Ideology of Race in the 1960s," in *The Right Side of the Sixties: Reexamining Conservatism's Decade of Transformation*, ed. Laura Jane Gifford and Daniel K. Williams (Palgrave Macmillan, 2012), 21–40; Rayburn, *Ozark Country*; Randolph, *The Ozarks*; Catherine S. Barker, *Yesterday Today: Life in the Ozarks* (University of Arkansas Press, 2020 [1941]).

34. *Baldknobbers Hillbilly Jamboree* Booklet, 1970, R1218, State Historical Society of Missouri.

35. "Baldknobbers: Commemorative Collectors Edition, 35 years, 1959–1994," 7, Branson Centennial Museum, Entertainment Archive; Kathy Maniaci, "Baldknobbers Mix Music and Comedy for Fun and Profit," *Springfield Leader and Press*, August 27, 1978; Marr, *The Presley Family Story*, 25.

36. "Baldknobbers: Commemorative Collectors Edition."

37. For more, see Robert McDowell, "Bones and the Man: Toward a History of Bones Playing," *Journal of American Culture* 5, no. 1 (1982): 38–43; Eileen Southern, *The Music of Black Americans* (Norton, 1971), 136; Randolph, *The Ozarks*, 183; Brian K. Smith, "African Influence in the Music of Mexico's Costa Chica Region," *McNair Scholars Research Journal* 15, California State University Long Beach, June 2011.

38. *The Beverly Hillbillies*, season 8, episode 3, 1969, available on www .youtube.com.

39. Bob Mabe stated that Allen had "about three-quarters Indian in him." Mabe, interview. Census data lists Allen and his parents as white.

40. https://secondhandsongs.com/performance/171564/all; https:// secondhandsongs.com/work/113622.

41. *The Baldknobbers Hillbilly Jamboree*, 1968 LP recording, personal collection.

42. Beverly D. Flaxington, "Distracted Living," *Psychology Today*, August 28, 2015, https://www.psychologytoday.com/us/blog/understand-other-people /201508/distracted-living.

43. In productions of the *Baldknobbers* and *Jubilee* I have viewed from 1996, 2004, 2005, 2006, 2016, 2017, 2018, 2019, and 2021, there has been a balanced mix of classic country, contemporary country, bluegrass, instrumental medleys, gospel, comedy bits, and interactive audience banter.

44. See, for example, TripAdvisor reviews of the Presleys and the Baldknobbers, www.tripadvisor.com. It was also something that came up in multiple conversations with audience members at dozens of shows in Branson.

45. All such claims should be taken with a grain of salt. It is among the most-recorded gospel songs in history. See W. K. McNeil, *Encyclopedia of American Gospel Music* (New York: Routledge, 2005), 54.

46. "Hillbilly Jamboree Show to Be in Belton Nov. 10," *The Star-Herald* (Belton, MO), October 13, 1977; "Music" Listings, *St. Louis Post-Dispatch*, December 1, 1977.

47. *Presleys' Mountain Music Jubilee*, uploaded to www.youtube.com as "The Basement Tapes: 1982 Full Show."

48. *Baldknobbers Jamboree*, 1996 show, VHS.

49. *Baldknobbers Jamboree*, 2004 show, DVD; *Presleys' Country Jubilee*, 2005 show, DVD.

50. *Presleys' Mountain Music Jubilee*, 1982.

51. *Baldknobbers Jamboree*, June 11, 2018.

52. Levine, *Highbrow/Lowbrow*, 103, 134.

53. David Savran, "Toward a Historiography of the Popular," *Theatre Survey* 45, no. 2 (2004): 211–17.

54. *Baldknobbers* Booklet, 1970.

55. It contracted to 1,500 seats in 2008, though this fact is not advertised in the performances I have witnessed between 2018 and 2022, or in the DVDs from earlier productions. See also Marr, *The Presley Family Story*, 9.

56. Stephanie Coontz, *The Way We Never Were: American Families and the Nostalgia Trap* (Basic Books, 2016); David Brooks, "The Nuclear Family Was a Mistake," *The Atlantic*, March 2020, https://www.theatlantic.com/magazine/archive/2020/03 /the-nuclear-family-was-a-mistake/605536/.

57. See the appendix for a database of Branson shows. For more on these mentioned families, see https://www.theduttons.com/about-the-duttons/; https://www.hughes-brothers.com/our-story/the-family/.

58. Gary Groman, "Branson Up-Close and Personal with the 'M&M' of the Hughes Brothers Family," *The Branson Blog by Branson Tourism Center*, August 2, 2016, accessed November 2, 2021, https://www.bransontourismcenter.com/info/2016/08/02/branson-up-close-and-personal-with-the-m-m-of-the-hughes-brothers-family/.

59. McGill, *Branson's Entertainment Pioneers*, 39, 41; Chandler, *The Heart of Branson*, 75–76; Ryan Thomas, discussion with Joanna Dee Das, January 17, 2020; Isabelle Roig, interview by Joanna Dee Das, Washington University in St. Louis, October 15, 2018.

60. In 1999, Walmart became the world's largest employer. In 2001, it surpassed Exxon Mobil as having the largest revenues, officially becoming the largest corporation in the world. Twenty years later, in 2021, it was still the largest company in the world, with Sinotec of China and Amazon of the United States running second and third. See https://www.britannica.com/topic/Walmart. Bethany Moreton, *To Serve God and Wal-Mart: The Making of Christian Free Enterprise* (Harvard University Press, 2009), 12; McGill, *Branson's Entertainment Pioneers*, 42; Marr, *Presley Family Story*.

61. Baldknobbers brochure and Presleys brochure, 1983, WRVHS.

62. Bruce J. Schulman and Julian E. Zelizer, "Introduction," in *Rightward Bound: Making America Conservative in the 1970s*, ed. Schulman and Zelizer (Harvard University Press, 2008), 7; Lassiter, "Inventing Family Values," 18; Dennis Lim, "Reality-TV Originals, in Drama's Lens," *New York Times*, April 15, 2011, https://www.nytimes.com/2011/04/17/arts/television/hbos-cinema-verite-looks-at-american-family.html. For more on the cohesion around the idea of "liberal media bias," see Nicole Hemmer, *Messengers of the Right: Conservative Media and the Transformation of American Politics* (University of Pennsylvania Press, 2018).

63. Malone, *Country Music USA*, 319.

64. Advertisement for Oakmont Shores Development, Branson, MO, in *The Wichita Eagle* (Wichita, KS), May 18, 1973, 10–11, accessed via newspapers.com, February 11, 2022.

65. Maniaci, "Baldknobbers Mix Music and Comedy for Fun and Profit."

66. "Want Country Music? Missouri Has It!," *Eldon Advertiser* (Eldon, MO), May 12, 1977, 30.

67. "Ring of Cash Registers Is Music to the Ears," *Springfield Leader and Press*, August 27, 1978.

68. Gary Presley, interview by Joanna Dee Das, Branson, Missouri, July 18, 2018.

69. Pecknold, *The Selling Sound*, 209–13.

70. Marr, *The Presley Family Story*, 11.

71. Adam Smith, "Branson Infamous," *Boston Herald*, December 28, 2014, https://www.bostonherald.com/2014/12/28/branson-infamous/.

CHAPTER FOUR

1. Morley Safer, "60 Minutes — $ound of Music — Part 1 and II (Branson, Missouri)," December 8, 1991, www.youtube.com.

2. See the epigraph that opens this chapter.

3. Katelynn Harris, "Forty Years of Falling Manufacturing Employment," US Bureau of Labor Statistics, November 2020, https://www.bls.gov/opub/btn /volume-9/forty-years-of-falling-manufacturing-employment.htm.

4. Tim Smart, "Big Mergers Get Bigger in the 1990s," *Washington Post*, October 27, 1997.

5. Marty Hughes, telephone interview by Joanna Dee Das, January 10, 2023.

6. Fountainhead Tours, List of Shows, 2000 season, Mary Ann Sharp Collection, Branson Centennial Museum.

7. B. Joseph Pine and James H. Gilmore, *The Experience Economy: Updated Edition* (Harvard Business Review Press, 2011 [1999]), xxv–xxvi, 14, 17, 21.

8. Ron Sylvester and Sara B. Hansen, "Field of Dreams: Branson Built It and They Came," *Springfield News-Leader*, April 8, 1990, 1.

9. *Field of Dreams* (Universal Pictures, Carolco Pictures, 1989).

10. "Ring of Cash Registers Is Music to the Ears," 31–32.

11. Payton, *Story of Silver Dollar City*, 80–81.

12. Gary Sifford, "Herschend: Tourism Dollars Aid Real Estate," *Springfield News-Leader*, May 14, 1981.

13. Kevin Madden, "Ozarks Tourism Push Launched," *Springfield News-Leader*, May 16, 1980.

14. Sara B. Hansen, "Developers Lure More Affluent to Relax, Invest," *Springfield News-Leader*, April 8, 1990; Lynn Berry, interview by Joanna Dee Das, Branson, Missouri, July 19, 2018.

15. Gary Sifford, "Ozarks Tourism Council Sets '81 Targets," *Springfield News-Leader*, June 8, 1980.

16. "Area Attractions Report Big Upswing in Ozarks Tourism," *Branson Beacon-Leader*, August 3, 1981; "Tourism Picture Reported Bright Here Despite National Trend," *Branson Beacon Leader*, August 20, 1981; "Marketing Council Investor Drive to Begin Soon," *Branson Beacon-Leader*, September 17, 1981; 1980 Census.

17. Jenell Wallace, "Ozarks Promoters Report Success," *Springfield News-Leader*, December 13, 1981. Revenues hit $925 billion, up from $849 billion.

18. Joy Thomas, telephone interview by Joanna Dee Das, February 13 and 14, 2020.

19. Thomas, interview.

20. Michael A. Urquhart and Marillyn A. Hewson, "Unemployment Continued to Rise in 1982 as Recession Deepened," *Monthly Labor Review*, February 1983, Bureau of Labor Statistics, https://www.bls.gov/opub/mlr/1983/02/art1full.pdf.

21. Thomas, interview.

22. Carlton S. Van Doren and Sam A. Lollar, "The Consequences of Forty Years of Tourism Growth," *Annals of Tourism Research* 12 (1985): 467–89; Harsha E. Chacko and Eddystone C. Nebel III, "The Group Tour Industry: An Analysis of Motorcoach Tour Operators," *Journal of Travel & Tourism Marketing* 2, no. 1 (1993): 69–83.

23. McFerron, interview.

24. Ad for Starlite Theatre and Shoji, *Branson Beacon-Leader*, April 16, 1985.

25. "Country Music World Plans Changes," *Branson Beacon-Leader*, April 10, 1986.

26. Joshua Clark, "Branson Bids Farewell to Its 'Belle,'" *Branson Tri-Lakes News*, March 3, 2017.

27. Louise Whall, "Survey Calls Quiet Hills Ozarks' Top Tourist Draw," *Spring-*

field News-Leader, August 5, 1984, 1; Laurie Glenn, "Branson Attractions Are Still Crowded but the Crowds Aren't Spending Much," *Springfield News-Leader*, August 5, 1984.

28. Whall, "Survey Calls Quiet Hills Ozarks' Top Tourist Draw"; Glenn, "Branson Attractions Are Still Crowded but the Crowds Aren't Spending Much."

29. Dawn Erickson, "Area Business Owners 'Eating Others Alive," *Branson Beacon-Leader*, September 23, 1986.

30. Erickson, "Area Business Owners 'Eating Others Alive.'"

31. "Ozark Mountain Country and you . . . A winning Combination!" Advertisement, *Branson Beacon-Leader*, January 9, 1986.

32. Josh Levin, *The Queen: The Forgotten Life Behind an American Myth* (Little, Brown and Company, 2019).

33. Louise Whall, "Ozark Marketing Council Sets '85 Tourism Strategy," *Springfield News-Leader*, and "Marketing Council Director Says Group Isn't Rejecting Springfield," *Springfield News-Leader*, November 14, 1984.

34. "Singer Compliments Branson," *Branson Beacon-Leader*, November 14, 1985.

35. Peterson, *Creating Country Music*, 14–15.

36. Lisa Walker, "Our Footloose Correspondents: Down Toward Arkansas," *New Yorker* 65, no. 31 (September 18, 1989): 105–12.

37. Walker, "Our Footloose Correspondents," 105–12.

38. Kathryn Buckstaff, "Boxcar Willie's Last Show," *Springfield News-Leader*, April 18, 1999.

39. Ron Sylvester, "Headliners Praise Heartland," *Springfield News-Leader*, April 9, 1990.

40. Ron Sylvester, "Country Stars Adjusting to Homes in Branson as Tourist Season Nears," *Springfield News-Leader*, April 9, 1990; Tillis Family, "The Marvelous and Memorable Mel Tillis," https://www.youtube.com/watch?v=w21BiVLdmkw&t =7s, February 21, 2023, Branson Centennial Museum, Branson.

41. "1991–1992 Ratings History," The TV Ratings Guide, http://www.thetvratingsguide.com/1991/08/1991-92-ratings-history.html. An estimated 20.1 million people watched *60 Minutes* every week. The numbers $7.2 million in advertising and 40 million viewers come from Jerry S. Madsen, "Branson: A Historical Timeline from 1860," *Ozark Trails Magazine* (Galena, MO), 1997, WRVHS; Associated Press, "4.6 Million People Visit Branson: Town Top Tour Bus Destination in the U.S.," *Columbia Daily Tribune* (Missouri), November 27, 1992.

42. Sylvester and Hansen, "Field of Dreams"; Kevin Zimmerman, "Battle Is Brewing Over Twang Turf," *Variety* 347, no. 4 (May 11, 1992); Rich Brown, "Cable Hears Strains of Another Country," *Broadcasting*, July 27, 1992, 122, 131.

43. Deborah Wilker, "Stars Regaining Control, But They Live in Branson," *South Florida Sun-Sentinel*, June 5, 1992.

44. Amy Smith, "Boxcar Blocks Smut at City Limits," *Knoxville News-Sentinel*, July 6, 1993.

45. Jim White, "A Boom Town Built on Broken Hearts: Branson," *The Independent*, July 30, 1993.

46. Kevin Bonham Knight-Ridder, "Branson, Mo. Is Becoming 'Nashville of the North,'" *The Spokesman-Review*, July 9, 1995.

47. Census Bureau, 1990 Census of Population, Tennessee: Table 6, Race and

Hispanic Origin, Nashville, p. 38; Missouri: Table 6, Race and Hispanic Origin, Branson, p. 30.

48. Martin Booe, "The Land That Nashville Forgot: Branson, MO, Builds a Following with Heaping of Corn," *Washington Post*, December 20, 1992.

49. Conversation with Jean Babcock, archivist at the Branson Centennial Museum.

50. Booe, "The Land That Nashville Forgot."

51. Patrick Doyle, "All Roads Lead to Willie," *Rolling Stone*, no. 1216 (August 28, 2014).

52. Daniel Durchholz, "When Merle Met Branson," *St. Louis Magazine*, March 8, 2011, https://www.stlmag.com/culture/When-Merle-Met-Branson/.

53. Mike Weatherford, "Postcards from Branson, MO," *Las Vegas Review-Journal*, December 1, 1996.

54. Opinion, Missouri Court of Appeals Southern District, Case Number 22124, *Cotner Productions, Inc., and Steve Litman Productions, Inc., v. Gary W. Snadon and Patsy Snadon*, handed down March 8, 1999, https://www.courts.mo.gov. Also available at https://caselaw.findlaw.com/court/mo-court-of-appeals/1342315.html.

55. Tamlya Kallaos, "Bankruptcies Show Branson Market Leveling," *Springfield News-Leader*, July 26, 1997; Kathryn Buckstaff, "Bank Only Bidder as Theater Sold at Auction," *Springfield News-Leader*, February 12, 1998.

56. Mike Weatherford, "Show Business Brings Different Kind of Feud," *Las Vegas Review-Journal*, December 1, 1996; Kathryn Buckstaff, "Orlando, Newton Move to New Theatre," *Springfield News-Leader*, October 23, 1997; Associated Press, "Newton Says He Locked Orlando Out over Debts," *Daily American Republic* (Poplar Bluff, MO), December 15, 1998; "Wayne Newton," https://en.wikipedia.org/wiki/Wayne_Newton; "Wayne Newton | Established on Television and in Movies as Actor," https://waynenewton.com/biography/.

57. Ron Sylvester, "Fiddler Enthralls Audience with Opening Show in Branson," *Springfield News-Leader*, April 8, 1989.

58. "Sound Off," Letters to the Editor, *Springfield News-Leader*, April 22, 1989, 6.

59. Amy Smith, "Showman Shoji, the Far-Eastern Fiddler," and "Stars," *Knoxville News-Sentinel*, July 5, 1993.

60. Performance descriptions in this and subsequent paragraphs come from viewing the 1993 VHS recording of a live performance of *The Shoji Tabuchi Show*. Additional context comes from viewing the 1989 and 2002 VHS recordings of live performances of *The Shoji Tabuchi Show*, as well as my own experience seeing the show in person in 2006 and 2018.

61. Telephone conversation with Heather Paul, Christian Tours, February 13, 2023.

62. Sara B. Hansen, "Attendees Target Traffic Congestion," *Springfield News-Leader*, May 20, 1992, 1.

63. Sylvester and Hansen, "Field of Dreams."

64. "1992: The Top Stories of the Year," *Branson Tri-Lakes Daily News*, January 2–4, 1993.

65. Howard, "America's Hometown," 136–37.

66. Kathryn Buckstaff, "One Last Audience for Boxcar," *Springfield News-Leader*, April 14, 1999.

67. Kathryn Buckstaff, "Newest Branson Attraction Opens," *Springfield News-*

Leader, June 16, 2003; James Payne, Readers' Letters, "Help for Roads Is Long Overdue," *Springfield News-Leader*, May 24, 2005.

68. "1992: The Top Stories of the Year."

69. Linda Putman, "Union Questions Four Ballots; Theater Election Results Delayed," *Branson Daily News*, September 11, 1993; Kathy Oechsle, "Union May Have No Place Backstage in Branson," *Springfield News-Leader*, September 18, 1993; Kathy Oechsle, "Tourist City's Building Boom Drives Growth of Unions," *Springfield News-Leader*, February 1, 1994.

70. Kathy Oechsle, "Branson City Workers to Vote on Union," *Springfield News-Leader*, March 4, 1994; "City Workers Decide to Put on Union Caps," *Springfield News-Leader*, March 5, 1994.

71. "Ex-Regulator: Branson Probes Led to Dismissal," *Springfield News-Leader*, October 19, 1995.

72. Ron Sylvester, "High-Stakes Marketing on a Down-Home Budget," *Springfield News-Leader*, February 27, 1995.

73. Kathy Oeschle, "Economic Mecca No 'Flash in the Pan,'" *Springfield News-Leader*, February 27, 1994.

74. Sylvester, "High-Stakes Marketing on a Down-Home Budget."

75. For more on Dollywood, see Graham Hoppe, *Gone Dollywood: Dolly Parton's Mountain Dream* (Ohio University Press, 2018).

76. Kathy Oechsle, "Parton Ponies Up for Arena and Show," *Springfield News-Leader*, April 8, 1994.

77. Ron Sylvester, "Chicken 'n' Grinnin': The Dixie Stampede in Branson Offers Fun, Real 'Finger' Food," *Springfield News-Leader*, July 1995.

78. *Dolly Parton's Dixie Stampede*, Branson, Missouri, VHS recording, 2003; personal viewing, 2006.

79. For more on the Lost Cause and its lingering effects, see David Blight, *Race and Reunion: The Civil War in American Memory* (Belknap Press, 2001).

80. Kathy Buckstaff, "Crowd Hopes Dolly's Stampede Spurs Branson Tourist Numbers," *Springfield News-Leader*, July 18, 1995.

81. Christian tours; "Branson Motorcoach Tour" advertisement, "Chuck Ehlert of Eventtours" advertisement, *St. Louis Post-Dispatch*, July 31, 1995.

82. "The Clipsheet: Your Free Guide to Branson's Best Deals!," vol. 2, no. 10, October 1993. For more on *Pump Boys & Dinettes*, see Stacy Bandelier, "Pump Boys & Dinettes Bring Broadway to Branson," *The Shepherd of the Hills Gazette*, ca. 1993, Branson Centennial Museum.

83. Jason Wert, "Rockettes in Branson Remembered at Centennial Museum," *Branson Tri-Lakes News*, July 22, 2022; Doug Johnson, "Branson Gets a Kick Out of Those 'Missouri Natives,' The Rockettes," *Seattle Times*, December 12, 1999, https://archive.seattletimes.com/archive/?date=19991212&slug=3001131.

CHAPTER FIVE

1. Randy Plummer, telephone interview by Joanna Dee Das, January 10, 2023.

2. Melissa Calasanz, telephone interview by Joanna Dee Das, May 15, 2023.

3. Calasanz, interview; Heather Castillo, telephone interview by Joanna Dee Das, May 11, 2023.

4. For a historical accounting of the rise of the Christian Right, see Daniel K.

Williams, *God's Own Party: The Making of the Christian Right* (Oxford University Press, 2010); Dowland, *Family Values and the Rise of the Christian Right*. For current critiques of the movement, coming especially in the wake of the 2017 "Unite the Right" white supremacist rally in Charlottesville, Virginia, see Samuel L. Perry and Andrew L. Whitehead, *Taking Back America for God: Christian Nationalism in the United States* (Oxford University Press, 2020); and Phillip Gorsky and Samuel L. Perry, *The Flag and the Cross: White Christian Nationalism and the Threat to American Democracy* (Oxford University Press, 2022).

5. Hughes, interview.

6. Christian Smith, *American Evangelicalism: Embattled and Thriving* (University of Chicago Press, 1998).

7. For more on the gap between the Right's economic gains and social failures, see Kim Phillips-Fein, *Invisible Hands: The Making of the Conservative Movement from the New Deal to Reagan* (W. W. Norton & Company, 2009).

8. Calasanz, interview.

9. Lisa Freeman, *Antitheatricality and the Body Public* (University of Pennsylvania Press, 2017); R. Laurence Moore, *Selling God: American Religion in the Marketplace of Culture* (New York: Oxford University Press, 1995).

10. For more, see Freeman, *Antitheatricality and the Body Public*; Moore, *Selling God*.

11. Moore, *Selling God*, 95, 120.

12. David W. Bebbington, "The Nature of Evangelical Religion," orig. pub. 1989, in *Evangelicals: Who They Have Been, Are Now, and Could Be*, ed. Mark A. Noll, David W. Bebbington, and George M. Marsden (William B. Eerdmans Publishing Company, 2019), 31–55.

13. Moore, *Selling God*, 41.

14. Moore, *Selling God*; Heather Hendershot, *Shaking the World for Jesus: Media and Conservative Evangelical Culture* (University of Chicago Press, 2004).

15. For more on Wright and Christianity in early Branson tourism, see Ketchell, *Holy Hills of the Ozarks*. See also note 4 from chapter 1.

16. Stacey Hamby, "Silver Dollar City: Owners Build Empire on Christian Principles," *Word & Way*, June 10, 1999, 9; quoted in Ketchell, *Holy Hills of the Ozarks*, 57.

17. Ketchell, *Holy Hills of the Ozarks*, 68. There have been other theme parks with churches, notably Jim and Tammy Faye Bakker's *Heritage USA*, but not these types of service offerings for employees.

18. "The Christ of the Ozarks," the Great Passion Play, https://www.greatpassionplay.org/christ-of-the-ozarks.html.

19. Christian Tours, 1982 "Ozark Mountain Holiday" brochure, courtesy of Heather Paul.

20. Ketchell, *Holy Hills of the Ozarks*, 51–53; Frizell, "A History of the *Shepherd of the Hills* Dramatizations," 72.

21. See, for example, "1982 Outdoor Drama Attendance," Institute for Outdoor Drama, Box 307, Folder G. *The Great Passion Play* had 243,652 people, and *Shepherd of the Hills* 241,969.

22. "SDC Hosts Young Christians' Weekends," *Branson Beacon-Leader*, February 28, 1985, WRVHS.

23. Elizabeth Barmeier, "Adoration Parade Slated for Sunday," *Branson Tri-Lakes News,* November 29, 2016; Chris Carlson, "A History of the Branson Adoration Scene," *Branson Tri-Lakes News,* November 29, 2022.

24. Don Mahnken, "Branson's Winter Tourist Season Pays Off," *Springfield News-Leader,* April 23, 1989.

25. Rick Brunson, "Behind the Boom in Branson Mo.," *Charisma,* July 1993, 46–48.

26. Brunson, "Behind the Boom."

27. Hughes, interview.

28. For more, see Megan Sanborn Jones, "Mormons Think They Should Dance," in *Play, Performance, and Identity: How Institutions Structure Ludic Spaces,* ed. Matt O'Masta and Drew Chappell (Routledge, 2015).

29. Moore, *Selling God,* 96–97; Jake Johnson, *Mormons, Musical Theater, and Belonging in America* (University of Illinois Press, 2019).

30. Peggy Fletcher Stack, "Mormons and Patriotism," *Salt Lake Tribune,* reprinted in Sojourners, courtesy of Religious News Service, July 2, 2012, https://sojo.net/articles/mormons-and-patriotism; Tim Townsend, Religion News Service, "Missouri Remains Land of Religious Promise for Mormons," *Washington Post,* September 20, 2012, https://www.washingtonpost.com/national/on-faith/missouri-remains-land-of-religious-promise-for-mormons/2012/09/20/d40cbbd4-0348-11e2-9132-f2750cd65f97_story.html; Kent Brown, "When Did Jesus Come to the Americas?," in *From Jerusalem to Zarahemla: Literary and Historical Studies of the Book of Mormon* (Religious Studies Center, Brigham Young University, 1998), 146–56, https://rsc.byu.edu/jerusalem-zarahemla/when-did-jesus-visit-americas.

31. Laskas, "Branson in My Rearview Mirror."

32. Hughes, interview.

33. Hughes, interview.

34. Hughes, interview.

35. Hughes, interview.

36. Hughes, interview.

37. Hughes, interview.

38. Stewart John Van Cleve, "Beyond the Yellow Brick Road: Queer Localization in the Age of Anita Bryant, 1974–1980" (MA thesis, Portland State University, 2013), 4.

39. Mary Ellen Snodgrass, "Anita Bryant," in *American Women Speak: An Encyclopedia and Document Collection of Women's Oratory,* vol. 1 (Bloomsbury, 2016); Thomas C. Tobin, "Bankruptcy, Ill Will Plague Bryant," *St. Petersburg Times,* April 28, 2002, https://web.archive.org/web/20110123001005/http://www.sptimes.com/2002/04/28/State/Bankruptcy_ill_will_.shtml.

40. Anthea Disney, "Folk Heroine with a Neat Sales Line," *London Daily Mail,* September 5, 1973.

41. NBCUniversal Archives, "Anita Bryant's Pie to the Face," 1977, available on www.youtube.com.

42. "Anita Bryant Biography," http://www.anitabmi.org/3.html, copyright 2006; Snodgrass, "Anita Bryant," 1.

43. Anita Bryant, *A New Day,* reprinted in "Anita Bryant Biography," http://www.anitabmi.org/3.html.

44. Gary Indiana, "Town of the Living Dead," *The Village Voice,* September 21,

1993; Jimmy Lancaster, "Anita Bryant," *Ozark Mountain Visitor*, Fall 1996, 14, Entertainment File, Centennial Museum.

45. Lancaster, "Anita Bryant."

46. Tobin, "Bankruptcy, Ill Will Plague Bryant."

47. Peter Applebome, "Judge Cuts Bakker's Prison Term, Making Parole Possible in 4 Years," *New York Times*, August 24, 1991, https://www.nytimes.com/1991/08/24/us/judge-cuts-bakker-s-prison-term-making-parole-possible-in-4-years.html.

48. Ronald Smothers, "Ex-Television Evangelist Bakker Ends Prison Sentence for Fraud," *New York Times*, December 2, 1994.

49. Kathryn Buckstaff, "Bilked Believers Forgiving of Jim Bakker," *Springfield News-Leader*, September 15, 2002; Todd C. Frankel, "A Resurrected Career," *St. Louis Post-Dispatch*, February 17, 2008; Galen Bacharier, "Jim Bakker Show Settles COVID-19 'Cure' Lawsuit with Missouri," *Springfield News-Leader*, June 23, 2021, https://www.news-leader.com/story/news/local/ozarks/2021/06/23/jim-bakker-show-tv-pastor-church-settle-missouri-false-covid-19-cure-lawsuit-mo/5324592001/.

50. Di Webster, "If It Ain't Another Honky-Tonk Town," *The Age* (Melbourne, Australia), October 2, 1993.

51. Webster, "If It Ain't Another Honky-Tonk Town."

52. Gary Indiana, "Town of the Living Dead," *The Village Voice*, September 21, 1993.

53. Laskas, "Branson in My Rearview Mirror."

54. Laskas, "Branson in My Rearview Mirror."

55. Laskas, "Branson in My Rearview Mirror."

56. Joe Queenan, *Red Lobster, White Trash, and the Blue Lagoon: Joe Queenan's America* (Hyperion, 1998), 166–67.

57. "In the Heart of Branson," *Life* 17 (April 1994): 88–89.

58. "In the Heart of Branson."

59. Doug Johnson, "Hillbilly Jokes Start Opinion War in Ozarks," *Springfield News-Leader*, January 14, 2001, 6B.

60. In 1995, newspapers listed the show as *Baldknobbers Hillbilly Jamboree*. In 1996, the show was listed as *Baldknobbers Jamboree — Branson's First Show!* Presley, interview; *Baldknobbers Jamboree — Branson's First Show*, VHS, 1996.

61. Leis Grossberger, "The Rush Hours," *New York Times*, December 16, 1990, 58.

62. Richard L. Berke, "The 1994 Election: The Voters: Religious-Right Candidates Gain as G.O.P. Turnout Rises," *New York Times*, November 12, 1994.

63. Pew Research Center, "America's Changing Religious Landscape," May 12, 2015.

64. Ada Louise Huxtable, "Living with the Fake, and Liking It," *New York Times*, March 30, 1997; John Seabrook, *Nobrow: The Culture of Marketing, the Marketing of Culture* (Knopf, 2000).

65. Malone, *Country Music USA*, 493.

66. Nadine Hubbs, *Rednecks, Queers, and Country Music* (University of California Press, 2014), 23.

67. Hubbs, *Rednecks, Queers, and Country Music*, 4.

68. Kathy O. Buckstaff and Ron Sylvester, "Easy Money? Think Again," *Springfield News-Leader*, February 26, 1995.

69. Sara J. Bennett, "Branson Bashing," *Springfield News-Leader*, October 7, 1998.

70. Ron Sylvester, "Headliner Bush Takes the Show," *Springfield News-Leader*, August 22, 1992.

71. "Ozarks Results in Statewide Elections," *Springfield News-Leader*, November 4, 1992.

72. Jim White, "A Boom Town Built on Broken Hearts: Branson," *The Independent*, July 30, 1993. Stafford kept this joke in his routine; another reporter mentioned it in 1996. See Bill Heavey, "If the Show Fits . . . ," *Washington Post*, November 10, 1996.

73. Laskas, "Branson in My Rearview Mirror"; personal observation, 2018.

74. "About the 700 Club," Christian Broadcasting Network, https://cbn.com/700club#pgf-113063.

75. Dawn Peterson, "Robertson Will Tape '700 Club' Shows at Silver Dollar City Today," *Springfield News-Leader*, June 12, 1998; Traci Shurley, "Pat Robertson Fans Turn Out for Taping," *Springfield News-Leader*, June 13, 1998; Ward, interview.

76. Mark Marymont, "The Baptist Bible College Graduate Will Speak at the Revival Fires Celebration," *Springfield News-Leader*, April 3, 1999.

77. Brandon Cone, "Branson Officials Also Say No Dice to Gambling," *Branson Tri-Lakes News*, November 17, 2007; "Rockaway Beach Delegation Visited Several Casino Towns," *Springfield News-Leader*, August 22, 2003; "Branson Gambling Opposed," *The Kansas City Star*, July 30, 2003.

78. White, "A Boom Town Built on Broken Hearts."

79. Howard, "America's Hometown," 219–20.

80. In 2020, the Dixie Chicks dropped "Dixie" from their name in solidarity with Black Lives Matter. *Baldknobbers Jamboree*, live performance, Branson, Missouri, June 2007.

CHAPTER SIX

1. Eddie Stovall, interview by Joanna Dee Das, Branson, Missouri, May 12, 2022. See also Doug Johnson, "Defying Conventional Wisdom, the Platters Make Branson Their Home," *The Manhattan Mercury* (Manhattan, KS), November 5, 2000.

2. Stovall, interview.

3. Jason Wert, "Milton to Declare Branson America's Most Patriotic City," *Branson Tri-Lakes News*, October 21, 2022, https://www.bransontrilakesnews.com/news/local/article_1062e938-515d-11ed-af66-1f79d87b1950.html.

4. "Tie A Yellow Ribbon Round the Ole Oak Tree," lyrics by Irwin Levine and L. Russell Brown.

5. "Stories of Diplomacy: 'Tie a Yellow Ribbon': The Origin of the National Response to the Iran Hostage Crisis," National Museum of American Diplomacy, January 19, 2021, https://diplomacy.state.gov/stories/yellow-ribbon-hostages/; Gerald E. Parsons, "How the Yellow Ribbon Became a National Folk Symbol," *Folklife Center News* (Library of Congress) 13, no. 3 (1991): 9–11.

6. Kathryn Buckstaff, "Veterans Events Find Fertile Ground," *Springfield News-Leader*, May 23, 1997.

7. Buckstaff, "Veterans Events Find Fertile Ground."

8. Branson Veterans Task Force Inc., Millennium Schedule 2000, 2001 Schedule of Events, Centennial Museum Entertainment Archives. For more on the museum, see Worth, "Real American Entertainment."

9. Quoted in Ketchell, *Holy Hills of the Ozarks*, 114–15.

10. Marr, *The Presley Family Story*, 7.

11. Yakov Smirnoff, Facebook post, February 7, 2020.

12. Ross Ufberg, "Yakov Smirnoff Brings Reagan-Era Optimism to the Age of Trump," *Tablet*, March 22, 2017, https://www.tabletmag.com/sections/arts-letters/articles/yakov-smirnoff-reagan-trump.

13. Avi Steinberg, "The Impossible Dream of Yakov Smirnoff," *The Guardian*, January 22, 2015, https://www.theguardian.com/news/2015/jan/22/-sp-can-king-cold-war-comedy-make-comeback-yakob-smirnoff.

14. Yakov Smirnoff, *I Bet You Never Looked at It That Way*, filmed live in Branson, Missouri, 1996, VHS.

15. Jason Wert, "Yakov Smirnoff Reveals the Full Story of His 9/11 Mural," *Branson Tri-Lakes News*, September 11, 2021, https://www.bransontrilakesnews.com/news/local/article_77602b9c-1260-11ec-a6ba-b7c18c2ab78e.html.

16. Wert, "Yakov Smirnoff Reveals the Full Story of His 9/11 Mural."

17. Wert, "Yakov Smirnoff Reveals the Full Story of His 9/11 Mural."

18. For an example of the nightly news coverage, see "ABC Nightly News with Peter Jennings," September 11, 2002, https://www.youtube.com/watch?v=y9ImFsmB-Z0, particularly minutes 8:33–9:15.

19. Kathryn Buckstaff, "20 New Choices Add Diversity to Branson's Mix," *Springfield News-Leader*, April 25, 2004.

20. Sony Hocklander, "America at Center Stage: Family-Friendly Production Highlights Our Freedom," *Springfield News-Leader*, July 18, 2004.

21. Worth, "Real American Entertainment," 131–41.

22. Frederick Douglass, "What to the Slave Is the Fourth of July?," July 5, 1852, National Constitution Center, https://constitutioncenter.org/the-constitution/historic-document-library/detail/frederick-douglass-what-to-the-slave-is-the-fourth-of-july-1852. For an important work that challenged existing interpretations of the Civil War and Reconstruction, see Eric Foner, *Reconstruction: America's Unfinished Revolution, 1863–1877* (Harper & Row, 1988). For critiques of how tourism sites like Branson portray American history, see Barbara Kirshenblatt-Gimblett, *Destination Culture: Tourism, Museums, and Heritage* (University of California Press, 1998).

23. Charles M. Blow, "The Horrible History of Thanksgiving," *New York Times*, November 27, 2019; President Joseph R. Biden, "A Proclamation on Indigenous People's Day, 2021," White House, October 8, 2021, https://www.whitehouse.gov/briefing-room/presidential-actions/2021/10/08/a-proclamation-indigenous-peoples-day-2021/.

24. One graduate student wrote a PhD dissertation about Branson that mentioned *Celebrate America*, but it was not published. See Worth, "Real American Entertainment."

25. Lauren Wilcox, "Big Time in Tune Town," *Washington Post*, March 25, 2007.

26. Roger Cohen, "Presley, Palin and True Republicanism," *New York Times*, October 15, 2008.

27. Branson CVB, 2011 Year-End Report and 2012 Marketing Plan. The Branson Chamber of Commerce registered Branson/Lakes Convention & Visitors Bureau as a "fictitious name" in 2006. See Missouri Secretary of State, Missouri Online Business Filings, https://bsd.sos.mo.gov/.

28. Amos Bridges, "3 Killed, Dozens Injured by Separate Lines of Storms," *Springfield News-Leader*, March 1, 2012; "One Month after Tornado, Branson Isn't Missing a Beat," *The Hopkins Journal* (Missouri), April 5, 2012.

29. Branson CVB, 2012 Marketing Plan.

30. "History of Branson Visitation," Branson CVB, 2019 Year-End Marketing Report, March 10, 2020.

31. Gogo Lidz, "Branson, Missouri, Reacts to Billionaire Branson's Prank," *Newsweek*, April 1, 2015, https://www.newsweek.com/branson-mo-reacts-billionaire-bransons-prank-318602.

32. Lidz, "Branson, Missouri, Reacts to Billionaire Branson's Prank."

33. "Income and Poverty in the United States: 2015," https://www.census.gov/library/publications/2016/demo/p60-256.html; "Percent of Population Below the Poverty Level in Taney County, MO," 2015, https://fred.stlouisfed.org/series/S1701ACS029213.

34. This has been true since the 1990s. See Calasanz, interview; Shannon Cody, telephone interview by Joanna Dee Das, July 1, 2019.

35. Gogo Lidz, "Richard Branson's April Fools' Prank May Have Sunk Branson's Mayor," *Newsweek*, April 10, 2015, https://www.newsweek.com/mo-pranks-mo-problems-april-fools-gag-sinks-towns-mayor-321299.

36. Trevor Mitchell, "Branson Mayor Unseated after 8 Years," *Springfield News-Leader*, April 9, 2015.

37. Lidz, "Richard Branson's April Fools' Prank May Have Sunk Branson's Mayor."

38. Gregory J. Holman, "In Branson, 'Record Growth' and Discontent," *Springfield News-Leader*, February 26, 2017, https://www.news-leader.com/story/news/local/ozarks/2017/02/26/branson-record-growth-and-discontent/96961970/; Berry, interview.

39. Holman, "In Branson, 'Record Growth' and Discontent."

40. Branson CVB, 2018 Marketing Plan.

41. TN News Service, "Timesharing Faces Ashcroft's Big Stick," *Branson Beacon-Leader*, March 29, 1984, WRVHS; Ed Wales, "Heavy Agenda Frustrates Branson Aldermen," *Branson Beacon-Leader*, March 29, 1984, WRVHS.

42. Three local business owners — Allen Zuercher, Robert McDowell, and Linda Sprague — founded the Branson/Lakes Area Convention & Visitors Bureau, Inc., as a not-for-profit corporation in 1994, but it dissolved in 1997. See Missouri Secretary of State, Missouri Online Business Filings, https://bsd.sos.mo.gov/. Branson's Chamber of Commerce has run the "Branson/Lakes Area Convention & Visitors Bureau" since 2006. See note 28 in this chapter.

43. More interviews than can be listed here.

44. See Appendix. For theater sizes, see Jessica Howard, "America's Hometown," Appendix A.

45. "Obituary: Gene Pitney," *The Economist* 379, no. 8473 (April 15, 2006).

46. Jackie Rehwald, "Ozarks Joins Debate: Heritage or Hate?," *Springfield News-Leader*, June 24, 2015.

47. Historic photographs of Silver Dollar City in author's possession; Calasanz, interview.

48. I accessed the Christian Identity Center's site on July 5, 2023. The "about"

tab, from which this quote comes, has since been deleted. See https://www
.christianidentitychurch.net/.

49. Jackie Rehwald, "Flag Defender Has Ties to KKK," *Springfield News-Leader*, June 27, 2015.

50. Aisha Harris, "Springtime for the Confederacy," *Slate*, August 24, 2017, https://slate.com/culture/2017/08/visiting-dolly-partons-dinner-show-dixie -stampede.html.

51. Gregory J. Holman, "Citing Changing Attitudes, Dolly Parton's Dixie Stampede Dropping 'Dixie' from Its Name," *Springfield News-Leader*, January 10, 2018, https://www.news-leader.com/story/news/local/ozarks/2018/01/10/citing -changing-attitudes-dolly-partons-dixie-stampede-drops-dixie-its-name /1020135001/; personal observations, *Dolly Parton's Stampede* show, June 2018; conversation with Jim Babcock, 2018; Joshua Clark, "Dolly Drops 'Dixie' from 'Stampede,'" https://www.bransontrilakesnews.com/news_free/article_105b9c90 -f7c2-11e7-83a1-4f63c61bff96.html, January 12, 2018. Every time I have gone to the Stampede in the past five years, it has been entirely full.

52. Quoted in Brett Carr, "Kaepernick's Kneel: Performance, Protest, and the National Football League," *Callaloo* 41, no. 3 (2018): 5.

53. "Ragged Old Flag," written by Johnny Cash, © 1974 (renewed) SONG OF CASH, INC. Available at "EDSITEment! The Best of the Humanities on the Web," National Endowment for the Humanities, https://edsitement.neh.gov/sites /default/files/2018-08/Ragged_Old_Flag.pdf.

54. This was true in three different iterations of the show that I witnessed between 2016 and 2018. *Presleys' Country Jubilee*, 2016 season DVD; live performance, July 17, 2018. See also "Mighty Proud of That Ragged Old Flag," posted to www .youtube.com on December 15, 2018.

55. Larry Buchanan, Quoctrung Bui, and Jugal K. Patel, "Black Lives Matter May Be the Largest Movement in U.S. History," *New York Times*, July 3, 2020, https:// www.nytimes.com/interactive/2020/07/03/us/george-floyd-protests-crowd-size .html.

56. Cliff Sain, "For Second Week, Protesters Target Branson Confederate-Themed Business," *Branson Tri-Lakes News*, June 21, 2020, https://www .bransontrilakesnews.com/news_free/article_6fa118d0-b429-11ea-87c0 -0b21210ea01f.html; Kevin Hardy, "It Has No Place.' Black Lives Matter Brings Protest to Branson's Dixie Outfitters," *The Kansas City Star*, June 23, 2020, https://www .kansascity.com/news/state/missouri/article243699687.html.

57. Associated Press, "Confederate Store in Branson, Missouri at Protests' Center," *AP News*, June 24, 2020, https://apnews.com/article/us-news-mo-state-wire -michael-brown-ar-state-wire-branson-13bb9ea2bee3e25c38eaa730b18e20a9; "Branson Woman Apologizes after Remarks at Black Lives Mater [sic] Protest," KMBC 9, posted June 28, 2020, www.youtube.com. The video has since been taken down.

58. Cliff Sain, "Branson Aldermen, Members of Public, Talk about Protests and Racism During City Meeting," *Branson Tri-Lakes News*, June 24, 2020, https:// www.bransontrilakesnews.com/news_free/article_a9b24924-b639-11ea-a146 -c3ad9802cf04.html; Sara Karnes, "Branson Woman Apologizes for Shouting Racist Remarks at Black Lives Matter Protesters," *Springfield News-Leader*,

June 24, 2020, https://www.news-leader.com/story/news/local/ozarks/2020/06/24/branson-woman-apologizes-racist-remarks-blm-protests-kkk-missouri/3252964001/.

59. Dixie Outfitters Store Facebook post, June 24, 2020, https://www.facebook.com/dixieoutfittersbranson.

60. Trump Depot, companion website to Trump Patriotic Superstore of Branson, Missouri, trumpdepot.com; "Dixie Outfitters, Branson, Mo.," accessed May 24, 2024, https://www.bransondixieoutfitters.com/index.cfm.

61. Jan Wolfe, "Four Officers Who Responded to U.S. Capitol Attack Have Died by Suicide," *Reuters*, August 2, 2021, https://www.reuters.com/world/us/officer-who-responded-us-capitol-attack-is-third-die-by-suicide-2021-08-02/; US Attorney's Office, District of Columbia, "40 Months since the Jan. 6 Attack on the Capitol," updated May 6, 2024, https://www.justice.gov/usao-dc/39-months-since-the-jan-6-attack-on-the-capitol.

62. 2016 United States Presidential Election in Missouri, https://en.wikipedia.org/wiki/2016_United_States_presidential_election_in_Missouri; 2020 Presidential Election in Missouri, https://en.wikipedia.org/wiki/2020_United_States_presidential_election_in_Missouri.

63. Unknown author, "Dear Red States; We're Leaving," attributed to John Vodonick, on *Medium*, September 21, 2020, https://suehirsch.medium.com/dear-red-states-were-leaving-by-john-vodonick-33895bb6ffb4. An earlier version of this letter was published on October 26, 2012, in *The Roanoke Times*, with "Opry-Land" instead of "Branson"; it has since disappeared from the newspaper's website. I suspect that the successful rebranding of Opryland's home city of Nashville as hip and attractive in the mid-2010s led to Branson as a replacement symbol of Red State undesirability.

64. Nikole Hannah-Jones, "Our Democracy's Founding Ideals Were False When They Were Written. Black Americans Have Fought to Make Them True," *The 1619 Project*, in *The New York Times Magazine*, August 14, 2019, https://www.nytimes.com/interactive/2019/08/14/magazine/black-history-american-democracy.html.

65. Hannah-Jones, "Our Democracy's Founding Ideals Were False When They Were Written."

66. Victoria Bynum, James M. McPherson, James Oakes, Sean Wilentz, and Gordon S. Wood, quoted in Jake Silverstein, "We Respond to the Historians Who Critiqued The 1619 Project," December 20, 2019, https://www.nytimes.com/2019/12/20/magazine/we-respond-to-the-historians-who-critiqued-the-1619-project.html.

67. Silverstein, "We Respond to the Historians Who Critiqued The 1619 Project."

68. Hannah-Jones, "Our Democracy's Founding Ideals Were False When They Were Written"; Jake Silverstein, "An Update to The 1619 Project," *New York Times*, March 11, 2020.

69. Claudette Riley, "College of the Ozarks Leader Named to White House's Advisory 1776 Commission," *Springfield News-Leader*, December 20, 2020, https://www.news-leader.com/story/news/education/2020/12/20/college-ozarks-president-jerry-davis-named-trump-1776-commission/3984804001/.

70. College of the Ozarks, News Release, "College of the Ozarks President Jerry Davis Appointed by White House to 1776 Commission," December 19, 2020,

https://www.cofo.edu/News/moduleId/4295/articleId/128/controller/Article
/action/View.

71. American Historical Association, "AHA Statement Condemning Report of
Advisory 1776 Commission," January 20, 2021, https://www.historians.org/news
/aha-statement-condemning-report-of-advisory-1776-commission/.

72. Pulitzer Center, "Curricular Resources," https://1619education.org
/curricular-resources.

73. The President's Advisory 1776 Commission, *The 1776 Report*, January
2021, https://trumpwhitehouse.archives.gov/wp-content/uploads/2021/01/The
-Presidents-Advisory-1776-Commission-Final-Report.pdf.

74. Richard Slotkin, *A Great Disorder: National Myth and the Battle for America*
(Belknap Press, 2024).

CHAPTER SEVEN

1. John Baltes, telephone interview by Joanna Dee Das, July 12, 2023.

2. Baltes, interview.

3. Baltes, interview.

4. John Winthrop, "City upon a Hill," 1630, Gilder Lehrman Institute of American History, https://www.gilderlehrman.org/sites/default/files/inline-pdfs
/Winthrop%27s%20City%20upon%20a%20Hill.pdf.

5. Alexandra Pierson et al., "Theatre in Crisis: What We're Losing, and What
Comes Next," *American Theatre*, July 24, 2023, https://www.americantheatre.org
/2023/07/24/theatre-in-crisis-what-were-losing-and-what-comes-next/; see also
Bill Kopp, "Touring in a Post-Pandemic World: How Costs, Personnel & Festival
Culture Have Affected 2023 Performances," https://www.grammy.com/news/2023
-post-pandemic-touring-changes-festivals-costs-personnel-backstage-behind
-the-scenes.

6. Joshua Clark, "Smirnoff Sets Sights on 'Strip' Spot," *Branson Tri-Lakes News*,
May 8, 2020, https://www.bransontrilakesnews.com/entertainment/article
-48a76e0e-9148-11ea-b5c4-0f2661f8dad3.html.

7. Harrison Keegan, "Comedian Yakov Smirnoff Says Mask Mandate Could
Make Branson Like Soviet Russia," *Springfield News-Leader*, July 28, 2020.

8. Austin Huguelet, "It's Like 'Game of Thrones.' COVID Backlash Purges
Branson City Hall," *St. Louis Post-Dispatch*, April 28, 2022, https://www.stltoday
.com/entertainment/arts-and-theatre/its-like-game-of-thrones-covid-backlash
-purges-branson-city-hall/.

9. Kevin Hardy, "Tourism Is Booming in Branson as City Nixes Its Mask Mandate," *Kansas City Star*, April 22, 2021; Huguelet, "It's Like 'Game of Thrones.'"

10. H2R Marketing Firm, "Key Performance Indicators Dashboard 2023 Q4,"
prepared for Branson Convention & Visitors Bureau, delivered March 2024; 2024
Branson Show Tickets & Schedules, www.branson.com/shows.

11. Brandon Cone, "Tourism-Related Businesses Show Growth in 2006," *Branson Tri-Lakes News*, February 9, 2007; Branson/Lakes Area Convention & Visitors
Bureau, "2024 Directory of Shows by Theater," https://www.explorebranson.com
/article/2024-directory-shows-theater.

12. Jerry Presley, interview by Joanna Dee Das, Branson, Missouri, May 10, 2022.

13. Stovall, interview. See also Kathryn Buckstaff, "Entertainers Join Car Parade," *Springfield News-Leader*, August 28, 1998, 69.

14. Stovall, interview.

15. Presley, interview.

16. For more on these definitional debates, see Whitehead and Perry, *Taking America Back for God*; Gorski and Perry, *The Flag and the Cross*.

17. Bob Smietana, "In Branson, God and Country Serve as Red, White and Blue Comfort Food," *Religion News Service*, October 19, 2022, https://religionnews.com/2022/10/19/in-branson-god-and-country-serve-as-red-white-and-blue-comfort-food/.

18. Darren Myers, interview on PlayBranson, May 27, 2022, https://www.facebook.com/watch/?v=527810708985559.

19. Myers, PlayBranson interview.

20. Myers, PlayBranson interview; Darren Myers, interview by Joanna Dee Das, Freedom Encounter Theater, Branson, Missouri, May 24, 2023.

21. Myers, interview by Joanna Dee Das.

22. Myers, PlayBranson interview.

23. Freedom Journey Show, live performance at Freedom Encounter Theater, Branson, Missouri, May 23, 2023.

24. Freedom Encounter, Form 990 tax return, 2023, available via ProPublica, https://projects.propublica.org/nonprofits/organizations/833572407; Articles of Organization, Freedom Encounter Properties, LLC, filed with Missouri Secretary of State, January 31, 2022, available via https://bsd.sos.mo.gov/; Taney County Tax receipt, 2023 Real Estate Paid, Freedom Encounter Properties, LLC, available via Taney County Collector, taneycountycollector.com.

25. Jason Wert, "Reawaken America Tour Stops in Branson," *Branson Tri-Lakes News*, November 4, 2022, https://www.bransontrilakesnews.com/news/local/article_3d0f2056-5cba-11ed-be33-07317c9a11de.html.

26. Kimberly Fletcher, telephone interview by Joanna Dee Das, June 14, 2022.

27. Donald J. Trump, "Save America" Rally speech, Washington Mall, January 6, 2021, reprinted in Brian Naylor, "Read Trump's Jan. 6 Speech, A Key Part of Impeachment Trial," *NPR*, February 10, 2021, https://www.npr.org/2021/02/10/966396848/read-trumps-jan-6-speech-a-key-part-of-impeachment-trial.

28. Fletcher, interview.

29. Fletcher, interview.

30. Fletcher, interview.

31. Glenn Eshelman, "The Birthing of Sight & Sound Theatres," Larry Kreider Leadership Podcast, September 7, 2022, https://larrykreiderpodcast.castos.com/episodes/glenn-shirley-eshelman-on-the-birthing-of-sight-sound-theatres; "Sight & Sound Theatres — Story of Faith," 2017, https://www.sight-sound.tv/videos/a-story-of-faith.

32. Matt Neff, "The Branson Story," produced by Sight & Sound Theatres, 2021, https://www.sight-sound.tv/history/videos/branson.

33. Kathryn Buckstaff, "Branson Venue Is Labor on Level of Noah's Ark," *Springfield News-Leader*, June 3, 2007; Shubert Organization, "Theatre Specs," Belasco Theatre, Shubert Theatre, Ambassador Theatre, Broadway Theatre, https://shubert.nyc/theatres/.

34. Buckstaff, "Branson Venue Is Labor on Level of Noah's Ark"; Diana Lambdin Meyer, "Behold the Ark: New Show Brings Bible Story to Life," *Kansas City Star*, June 15, 2008, 71.

35. Diana Lambdin Meyer, "Behold the Ark: New Show Brings Bible Story to Life," *Kansas City Star*, June 15, 2008, 71.

36. Buckstaff, "Branson Venue Is Labor on Level of Noah's Ark."

37. Josh Enck, interview by "Nashville Wife," April 1, 2016, https://www .youtube.com/watch?v=lqpDd5EveRo&t=3s.

38. Josh Enck, interview by Corey Pennypacker, "You CAN Tell the Children" podcast, episode 34, March 8, 2022, https://bible2school.podbean.com/e/bringing -the-bible-to-life-through-storytelling-with-josh-enck-episode-34/.

39. Josh Enck, interview by Dan Rupple of Mastermedia International, November 3, 2019, https://mastermedia.com/articles/josh-enck/.

40. Sony Hocklander, "'Noah – the Musical' at Sight & Sound Theatre," *Springfield News-Leader*, May 22, 2008, 3; Meyer, "Behold the Ark." Additional observations from my viewing of a digital film of a live performance of *Noah*, accessed February 21–23, 2023.

41. TripAdvisor reviews of Sight & Sound Theatres Branson, www .tripadvisor.com.

42. Thomas Turino, *Music as Social Life: The Politics of Participation* (University of Chicago Press, 2008), 12–15. *STOMP* ended its run at the Orpheum Theatre in New York on January 8, 2023, after twenty-nine years. The US national tour continues.

43. Leah MarieAnn Klett, "Sight & Sound's 'Queen Esther' Needed 'for Such a Time as This,' Say Creators," *Christian Post*, September 4, 2020, https://www .christianpost.com/news/sight-sounds-queen-esther-needed-for-such-a-time -as-this-say-creators.html.

44. Shawna Mizelle and Dave Alsup, "Tennessee Becomes First State in 2023 to Restrict Drag Performances," CNN, March 3, 2023, https://www.cnn.com/2023 /03/02/politics/tennessee-ban-drag-show-performances-governor/index.html; Noman Merchant, "Pentagon Stops US Military Bases from Hosting Drag Shows," *Associated Press/Military Times*, June 1, 2023, https://www.militarytimes.com /news/pentagon-congress/2023/06/02/pentagon-stops-us-military-bases-from -hosting-drag-shows/.

45. Josie Lenora, "Despite All the Talk, No States Have Active Laws Banning Drag in Front of Kids," National Public Radio, *All Things Considered*, July 29, 2023, https://www.npr.org/2023/07/29/1190306861/drag-bans-fail-lgbtq-first -amendment-prurient-arkansas-florida-tennessee-montana; Jason Wert, "Branson Aldermen Vote 3–2 for Drag Show Ordinance," *Branson Tri-Lakes News*, July 28, 2023, https://www.bransontrilakesnews.com/news/local/article_263747b2-2d54 -11ee-94e2-efd919d39712.html.

46. Wert, "Branson Aldermen Vote 3–2 for Drag Show Ordinance"; Jason Wert, "Branson Drag Show Ordinance Gains Final Passage," *Branson Tri-Lakes News*, August 11, 2023, https://www.bransontrilakesnews.com/news/local/article_b5c1975c -37b3-11ee-aece-47c38a0d8a2f.html.

47. Wert, "Branson Aldermen Vote 3–2 for Drag Show Ordinance."

48. Jason Wert, "Schulz Defeats Rodriguez for Branson Alderman," *Branson Tri-Lakes News*, April 5, 2024, https://www.bransontrilakesnews.com/news/local /article_af5ff942-f376-11ee-9e52-13cd3522080e.html.

49. "Glenn Schulz for Branson," https://schulzforbranson.com/.

50. Alexis Solheid, interview by Joanna Dee Das, Branson, Missouri, May 10, 2022.

51. Solheid, interview.

52. Solheid, interview.

EPILOGUE

1. Julie Hirschfeld Davis, "Trump, at Putin's Side, Questions U.S. Intelligence on 2016 Election," *New York Times*, July 16, 2018, https://www.nytimes.com/2018/07/16/world/europe/trump-putin-election-intelligence.html; Michael M. Grynbaum, "TV Anchors Agape after the Trump-Putin Appearance," *New York Times*, July 16, 2018, https://www.nytimes.com/2018/07/16/business/media/trump-putin-helsinki-cnn.html.

2. Cliff Sain, "NTSB Issues Findings on Fatal Duck Boat Incident," *Branson Tri-Lakes News*, April 28, 2020, https://www.bransontrilakesnews.com/news_free/article_5c9814ce-8999-11ea-8368-0b68d280b1cc.html.

3. Plummer, interview.

4. Enck, interview by Corey Pennypacker.

5. Michael S. Roth, "Anxiety about Wokeness is Intellectual Weakness," *New York Times*, November 18, 2021, https://www.nytimes.com/2021/11/18/opinion/woke-students-scapegoats.html.

6. Anna Lowenhaupt Tsing, *The Mushroom at the End of the World: On the Possibility of Life in Capitalist Ruins* (Princeton University Press, 2015), 27.

7. Jill Stevenson, *Sensational Devotion: Evangelical Performance in Twenty-First-Century America* (University of Michigan Press, 2013), 237.

BIBLIOGRAPHY

Primary Source Materials

ARCHIVAL COLLECTIONS
Branson Centennial Museum
Institute of Outdoor Drama Archives
Newspapers.com
Ronald Reagan Presidential Library & Museum
State Historical Society of Missouri
White River Valley Historical Society

NEWSPAPERS
Branson Beacon
Branson Beacon-Leader
Branson Tri-Lakes News
Springfield Leader & Press
Springfield News-Leader
White River Leader

VISUAL MEDIA
The All Hands on Deck! Show. "Classic 1940's American Song & Dance." Madaras
    Productions Group, 2018. CD.
The Andy Williams Christmas Show. Filmed live in Branson, MO. Kultur Films,
    n.d. DVD.
The Baldknobbers, *Hillbilly Jamboree Time*. Recorded live in Branson, MO. Dimen-
    sion Records, ca. 1968. LP.
Baldknobbers Jamboree. Filmed live in Branson, MO. Baldknobbers, 1996, 1999, 2004,
    2005. VHS and DVD.
Boxcar Willie Country Music Show. Filmed live in Branson, MO. Trainman Produc-
    tions, 1994. VHS.
Branson/Lakes Area Chamber of Commerce. *The Branson Effect*. Destination
    Marketing, 1997. VHS.
Branson/Lakes Area Chamber of Commerce & CVB. *Branson's Centennial Birthday
    Spectacular*. Recorded live at RFD-TV Theatre, Branson, MO, April 15, 2012. DVD.
Branson's Famous Baldknobbers: 60th Anniversary Celebration Show. Filmed live in
    Branson, MO. Baldknobbers Theatre, 2019. DVD.
The Bretts Christmas Show Live. Filmed live in Branson, MO. Brett Family Singers,
    2016. DVD.
The Bretts Live. Filmed live in Branson, MO. Brett Family Singers, 2016. DVD.

Comedy Jamboree. Filmed live in Branson, MO. Grand Country Entertainment Productions, 2022. DVD.

Dolly Parton's Dixie Stampede and Dinner Show. Filmed live in Branson, MO. 1990s. VHS.

Hamner Barber Variety Show. Filmed live in Branson, MO. Hamner Barber, 2005. DVD.

The Haygoods Ultimate DVD Collection: From 1988 to NOW! Filmed in Branson, MO. Haygood Family Enterprises, 2017. DVD.

Hughes Brothers Christmas Show. Filmed live in Branson, MO. Hughes Entertainment, n.d. DVD.

Jarrett Dougherty: He Ain't Right! Filmed live in Branson, MO. Pierce Arrow, 2004. DVD.

Jim Stafford: Live and Kickin'! Filmed live in Branson, MO. Jim Stafford Theatre/Strats, 1993. VHS.

The Lawrence Welk Show: Then & Now. Filmed live in Branson, MO. 1995. VHS.

Mel Tillis Live in Branson, Missouri. Mel Tillis Theater Production, 1994. VHS.

Mountain Music Jubilee. Filmed live in Branson, MO. Presleys' Country Jubilee, 1982. YouTube.

Presleys' Country Jubilee: Live from Branson. Presley Family, 2000, 2005, 2009, 2013, 2017, 2021. VHS and DVD.

The Promise. Filmed live in Branson, MO. Promise Entertainment Group, 1998. VHS.

Schnack, AJ, and David Wilson, dir. *We Always Lie to Strangers: The Incredible True Story of Branson, Missouri*. Virgil Films & Entertainment, 2014. DVD.

The Shepherd of the Hills. Filmed live in Branson, MO. ca. 1990s. VHS.

Shoji Tabuchi: Fiddlin' Around. Filmed live in Branson, MO. Shoji and Dorothy Tabuchi, 1989. VHS.

The Shoji Tabuchi Show! Filmed live in Branson, MO. Dorothy Tabuchi, 1993. VHS.

The Shoji Tabuchi Show! Filmed live in Branson, MO. Shoji Entertainments, Inc., 2002. VHS.

This is Branson, Missouri. American Vacation Videos, 1993. VHS.

Yakov: I Bet You Never Looked At It That Way! Filmed live in Branson, MO. Yakov Smirnoff, 1996. VHS and DVD.

Interviews

John Baltes
Jim Barber
Lynn Berry
Melissa Calasanz
Heather Castillo
Joshua Clark
Shannon Cody
Harvey Day
Kimberly Fletcher
Madison Foreman
John Fullerton
Wayne Glenn
Larry Hoover

Marty Hughes
Bob Mabe
Jody Madaras
Jae McFerron
Lara Menard
Larry Musgrave
Darren Myers
Nicholas Naioti
Patrick Needham
Steve Plaster
Randy Plummer
Rick and Michi Porter
Gary Presley

Jerry Presley
Lisa Rau
Isabelle Roig
Alexis Solheid
Eddie Stovall
Joy Thomas
Ryan Thomas
Trajana Thomas
Keith Thurman
Earl Vaughn
June Ward
Tam Warner

Select Books, Articles, and Dissertations

Avila, Eric. *Popular Culture in the Age of White Flight: Fear and Fantasy in Suburban Los Angeles*. University of California Press, 2004.

Barker, Catherine. *Yesterday Today: Life in the Ozarks*. University of Arkansas Press, 2020 [1941].

Barrier, Michael. *The Animated Man: A Life of Walt Disney*. University of California Press, 2007.

Barton, Alana, and Alyson Brown. "Dark Tourism and the Modern Prison." *Prison Service Journal* 199 (2012): 44–49.

Bebbington, David W. "The Nature of Evangelical Religion." In *Evangelicals: Who They Have Been, Are Now, and Could Be*, ed. Mark A. Noll, David W. Bebbington, and George M. Marsden. William B. Eerdmans Publishing Company, 2019.

Bemis, Bethanee. *Disney Theme Parks and America's National Narratives: Mirror, Mirror, for Us All*. Routledge, 2023.

Blevins, Brooks. *A History of the Ozarks, Volume 1: The Old Ozarks*. University of Illinois Press, 2018.

Blevins, Brooks. *A History of the Ozarks, Volume 3: The Ozarkers*. University of Illinois Press, 2021.

Blevins, Brooks. "Wretched and Innocent: Two Mountain Regions in the National Consciousness." *Journal of Appalachian Studies* 7, no. 2 (2001): 257–71.

Blight, David. *Race and Reunion: The Civil War in American Memory*. Belknap Press, 2001.

Bogue, Allan G. "Frederick Jackson Turner Reconsidered." *The History Teacher* 27, no. 2 (1994): 195–221.

Brucher, Katherine. "Assembly Lines and Contra Dance Lines: The Ford Motor Company Music Department and Leisure Reform." *Journal of the Society for American Music* 10, no. 4 (2016): 470–95.

Carr, Brett. "Kaepernick's Kneel: Performance, Protest, and the National Football League." *Callaloo* 41, no. 3 (2018): 4–17.

Cash, Arthur. "A Memoir of the Toby Shows." *The North American Review* 279, no. 5 (1994): 52–56.

Chandler, Arline. *The Heart of Branson: The Entertaining Families of America's Live Music Show Capital*. The History Press, 2010.

Clark, Larry Dale. "Toby Shows: A Form of American Popular Theatre." PhD diss., University of Illinois, 1963.

Conn, Steven. *The Lies of the Land: Seeing Rural America For What It Is — and Isn't*. University of Chicago Press, 2023.

Coontz, Stephanie. *The Way We Never Were: American Families and the Nostalgia Trap*. Basic Books, 2016.

Cronon, William. "Revisiting the Vanishing Frontier: The Legacy of Frederick Jackson Turner." *The Western Historical Quarterly* 18, no. 2 (1987): 157–76.

Deloria, Philip Joseph. *Playing Indian*. Yale University Press, 1998.

Dowland, Seth. *Family Values and the Rise of the Christian Right*. University of Pennsylvania Press, 2015.

Fellman, Michael. *Inside War: The Guerrilla Conflict in Missouri During the Civil War*. Oxford University Press, 1989.

Filene, Benjamin. *Romancing the Folk: Public Memory & American Roots Music*. University of North Carolina Press, 2000.

Foner, Eric. *Reconstruction: America's Unfinished Revolution, 1863–1877*. Harper & Row, 1988.

Francaviglia, Richard. "History after Disney: The Significance of 'Imagineered' Historical Places." *The Public Historian* 17, no. 4 (1995): 69–74.

Freeman, Lisa. *Antitheatricality and the Body Public*. University of Pennsylvania Press, 2017.

Frizell, Michael Lewis. "A History of the *Shepherd of the Hills* Dramatizations: The Branson Productions." MA thesis, Missouri State University, 1996.

Gilmore, Robert K. *Ozark Baptizings, Hangings, and Other Diversions: Theatrical Folkways of Rural Missouri, 1885–1910*. University of Oklahoma Press, 1984.

Gonczy, Daniel. "The Folk Music Movement of the 1960s: Its Rise and Fall." *Popular Music and Society* 10, no. 1 (1985): 15–31.

Gorsky, Phillip, and Samuel L. Perry. *The Flag and the Cross: White Christian Nationalism and the Threat to American Democracy*. Oxford University Press, 2022.

Gregory, James N. *The Southern Diaspora: How the Great Migrations of Black and White Southerners Transformed America*. University of North Carolina Press, 2005.

Grimm, Heather. "Rank Strangers: Performing the Bluegrass Repertoire in the Contemporary Market." PhD diss., Northwestern University, 2024.

Harkins, Anthony. *Hillbilly: A Cultural History of an American Icon*. Oxford University Press, 2004.

Hemmer, Nicole. *Messengers of the Right: Conservative Media and the Transformation of American Politics*. University of Pennsylvania Press, 2018.

Hendershot, Heather. *Shaking the World for Jesus: Media and Conservative Evangelical Culture*. University of Chicago Press, 2004.

Hernando, Matthew J. *Faces Like Devils: The Bald Knobber Vigilantes in the Ozarks*. University of Missouri Press, 2015.

hooks, bell. *Black Looks: Race and Representation*. South End Press, 1992.

Hoppe, Graham. *Gone Dollywood: Dolly Parton's Mountain Dream*. Ohio University Press, 2018.

Howard, Jessica. "America's Hometown: Performance and Entertainment in Branson, Missouri." PhD diss., New York University, 1997.

Hubbs, Nadine. *Rednecks, Queers, and Country Music*. University of California Press, 2014.

Hughes, Marion. *Three Years in Arkansaw*. M. A. Donahue Co., 1905.

Hunter, Kermit. "The Outdoor Historical Drama." *The North Carolina Historical Review* 30, no. 2 (1953): 218–22.

Ingenthron, Elmo, and Mary Hartman. *Bald Knobbers: Vigilantes on the Ozarks Frontier*. Pelican Publishing Company, 1988.

Johnson, Jake. *Mormons, Musical Theater, and Belonging in America*. University of Illinois Press, 2019.

Jones, Megan Sanborn. "Mormons Think They Should Dance." In *Play, Performance, and Identity: How Institutions Structure Ludic Spaces*, ed. Matt Omasta and Drew Chappell. Routledge, 2015.

Kasson, Joy S. *Buffalo Bill's Wild West: Celebrity, Memory, and Popular History*. Hill and Wang, 2000.

Ketchell, Aaron. *Holy Hills of the Ozarks: Religion and Tourism in Branson, Missouri*. Johns Hopkins University Press, 2007.

Kirshenblatt-Gimblett, Barbara. *Destination Culture: Tourism, Museums, and Heritage*. University of California Press, 1998.

Larsen, Dawn. "The Canvas Cathedral: Toby Shows as Nativistic Social Movements." *Theatre History Studies* 21 (2001): 87–103.

Lassiter, Matthew D. "Inventing Family Values." In *Rightward Bound: Making America Conservative in the 1970s*, ed. Bruce J. Schulman and Julian E. Zelizer. Harvard University Press, 2008.

Lechner, Zachary. *The South of the Mind: American Imaginings of White Southernness, 1960–1980*. University of Georgia Press, 2018.

Ledbetter, Kitty, and Scott Foster Siman. *Broadcasting the Ozarks: Si Siman and Country Music at the Crossroads*. University of Arkansas Press, 2024.

Levin, Josh. *The Queen: The Forgotten Life Behind an American Myth*. Little, Brown and Company, 2019.

Levine, Lawrence. *Highbrow/Lowbrow: The Emergence of Cultural Hierarchy in America*. Harvard University Press, 1988.

Lowndes, Joseph E. *From the New Deal to the New Right: Race and the Southern Origins of Modern Conservatism*. Yale University Press, 2008.

Malone, Bill C. *Country Music USA*. 50th anniversary ed. University of Texas Press, 2018.

Marr, Ron. *The Presley Family Story: The First 74 Years*. Missouri Life, Inc., 2008.

McDowell, Robert. "Bones and the Man: Toward a History of Bones Playing." *Journal of American Culture* 5, no. 1 (1982): 38–43.

McGill, Bob. *Branson's Entertainment Pioneers: A Success Story for Our Times*. White Oak Publishing, 2011.

McGinley, Paige. *Staging the Blues: From Tent Shows to Tourism*. Duke University Press, 2014.

Mickel, Jere C. "The Genesis of Toby: A Folk Hero of the American Theater." *Journal of American Folklore* 80, no. 318 (1967): 334–40.

Miller, Karl Hagstrom. *Segregating Sound: Inventing Folk and Pop Music in the Age of Jim Crow*. Duke University Press, 2010.

Moore, R. Laurence. *Selling God: American Religion in the Marketplace of Culture*. Oxford University Press, 1995.

Moreton, Bethany. *To Serve God and Wal-Mart: The Making of Christian Free Enterprise*. Harvard University Press, 2009.

Morris, Jill Anne. "Disney's Influence on the Modern Theme Park and the Codification of Colorblind Racism in the American Amusement Industry." In *Performance and the Disney Theme Park Experience: The Tourist as Actor*, ed. Jennifer A. Kokai and Tom Robson. Palgrave Macmillan, 2019.

Morris, Patricia, and Tammi Arford. "'Sweat a Little Water, Sweat a Little Blood': A Spectacle of Convict Labor at an American Amusement Park." *Crime Media Culture* (2018): 1–24.

Morrow, Lynn, and Linda Myers-Phinney. *The Shepherd of the Hills Country: Tourism Transforms the Ozarks, 1880s–1930s*. University of Arkansas Press, 1999.

Nelson, Andrew Patrick. "Hollywood Westerns: 1930s to the Present." In *A History of Western American Literature*, ed. Susan Kollin. Cambridge University Press, 2015.

Newman, Joe. *Race and the Assemblies of God Church: The Journey from Azusa Street to the "Miracle of Memphis."* Cambria Press, 2007.

Newton, Margaret. *"Shad": A Biography of Lloyd "Shad" Heller*. Pin Oak Publishing Company, 1982.

Payton, Crystal. *The Story of Silver Dollar City: A Pictorial History of Branson's Famous Ozark Mountain Village Theme Park*. 2nd ed. Lens & Lens Publishing, 2007 [1997].

Pecknold, Diane. *The Selling Sound: The Rise of the Country Music Industry*. Duke University Press, 2007.

Perry, Samuel L., and Andrew L. Whitehead. *Taking Back America for God: Christian Nationalism in the United States*. Oxford University Press, 2020.

Peterson, Richard. *Creating Country Music: Fabricating Authenticity*. University of Chicago Press, 1997.

Phillips-Fein, Kim. *Invisible Hands: The Making of the Conservative Movement from the New Deal to Reagan*. W. W. Norton & Company, 2009.

Pine, B. Joseph, and James H. Gilmore. *The Experience Economy: Updated Edition*. Harvard Business Review Press, 2011 [1999].

Putnam, Robert. *Bowling Alone: The Collapse and Revival of American Community, Revised and Updated*. Simon and Schuster, 2020.

Queenan, Joe. *Red Lobster, White Trash, and the Blue Lagoon: Joe Queenan's America*. Hyperion, 1998.

Randolph, Vance. *The Ozarks: An American Survival of Primitive Society*. University of Arkansas Press, 2017 [1931].

Rayburn, Otto Ernest. *Ozark Country*. University of Arkansas Press, 2021 [1941].

Reagan, Ronald. *An American Life*. Simon & Schuster, 1990.

Rolph, Stephanie R. "Courting Conservatism: White Resistance and the Ideology of Race in the 1960s." In *The Right Side of the Sixties: Reexamining Conservatism's Decade of Transformation*, ed. Laura Jane Gifford and Daniel K. Williams, 21–40. Palgrave Macmillan, 2012.

Rosenfeld, Sam. *The Polarizers: Postwar Architects of Our Partisan Era*. University of Chicago Press, 2017.

Savran, David. "Toward a Historiography of the Popular." *Theatre Survey* 45, no. 2 (2004): 211–17.

Schroeder, Janet. "Choreographing Appalachia as America: The Hazards of Nostalgia on the Concert Stage." *Dance Chronicle* 43, no. 3 (2020): 270–94.

Schulman, Bruce J., and Julian E. Zelizer, eds. *Rightward Bound: Making America Conservative in the 1970s*. Harvard University Press, 2008.

Seabrook, John. *Nobrow: The Culture of Marketing, the Marketing of Culture*. Knopf, 2000.

Slotkin, Richard. *A Great Disorder: National Myth and the Battle for America*. Belknap Press, 2024.

Smith, Brian K. "African Influence in the Music of Mexico's Costa Chica Region." *McNair Scholars Research Journal* 15. California State University Long Beach, June 2011.

Smith, Christian. *American Evangelicalism: Embattled and Thriving*. University of Chicago Press, 1998.

Smith, Erin. "Melodrama, Popular Religion, and Literary Value: The Case of Harold Bell Wright." *American Literary History* 17, no. 2 (2005): 217–43.

Snodgrass, Mary Ellen. "Anita Bryant." In *American Women Speak: An Encyclopedia and Document Collection of Women's Oratory*, vol. 1. Bloomsbury, 2016.

Southern, Eileen. *The Music of Black Americans*. Norton, 1971.

Spencer, Thomas, ed. *The Other Missouri History: Populists, Prostitutes, and Regular Folk*. University of Missouri Press, 2004.

Stevenson, Jill. *Sensational Devotion: Evangelical Performance in Twenty-First-Century America*. Ann Arbor: University of Michigan Press, 2013.

Tagg, Lawrence. *Harold Bell Wright: Storyteller to America*. Westernlore Press, 1986.

Tsing, Anna Lowenhaupt. *The Mushroom at the End of the World: On the Possibility of Life in Capitalist Ruins*. Princeton University Press, 2015.

Turino, Thomas. *Music as Social Life: The Politics of Participation*. University of Chicago Press, 2008.

Upton, Lucile Morris. *Bald Knobbers*. Caxton Publishers, 1939.

Van Cleve, Stewart John. "Beyond the Yellow Brick Road: Queer Localization in the Age of Anita Bryant, 1974–1980." MA thesis, Portland State University, 2013.

Weissman, Dick. *Which Side Are You On? An Inside History of the Folk Music Revival in America*. Continuum, 2006.

Whisnant, David E. *All That Is Native and Fine: The Politics of Culture in an American Region*. University of North Carolina Press, 2009 [1983].

White, Richard. "Frederick Jackson Turner and Buffalo Bill." In *The Frontier in American Culture: An Exhibition at the Newberry Library*, ed. James R. Grossman. University of California Press, 1994.

Williams, Daniel K. *God's Own Party: The Making of the Christian Right*. Oxford University Press, 2010.

Worth, Jennifer. "Real American Entertainment: Performance and Nationalism in Branson, Missouri." PhD diss., City University of New York, 2011.

Wright, Harold Bell. *The Shepherd of the Hills*. A. L. Burt Company, 1907.

Wright, Harold Bell. *To My Sons*. Harper, 1934.

INDEX